MASS MEDIA: A CASEBOOK

Mass Media: A Casebook

Edited by **Richard F. Hixson**
Rutgers – The State University

Thomas Y. Crowell Company
New York   Established 1834

Library of Congress Cataloging in Publication Data

Hixson, Richard, ed.
    Mass media: a casebook.

    1. Mass media. I. Title.
P90.H5   301.16'1   72-10947
ISBN 0-690-52253-3

Copyright © 1973 by Thomas Y. Crowell Company, Inc.

All Rights Reserved

Except for use in a review, the reproduction or utilization of this work in any form or by any electronic, mechanical, or other means, now known or hereafter invented, including photocopying and recording, and in any information storage and retrieval system is forbidden without the written permission of the publisher. Published simultaneously in Canada by Fitzhenry & Whiteside, Ltd., Toronto.

Manufactured in the United States of America

1 2 3 4 5 6 7 8 9 10

To Cynthia

PREFACE

For the first half of this century academic interest in the mass media was confined mainly to student newspaper staffs and schools and departments of journalism whose curricula reflected the needs and requirements of the professional press. In a word, interest was producer-oriented. During the nineteen-fifties and nineteen-sixties, however, interest spread to other academic disciplines, such as psychology, sociology, and English, and the media began to be studied from the viewpoint of the consumer.

Today the mass media are well into a new age—an age of investigation. There are more people paying critical attention to the effects and responsibilities of the media than ever before. Indeed, the size of the media alone, if not their power and influence, is reason enough for a spirit of investigation. Scholars in large numbers have turned their research methods and teaching talents in the direction of the media. Social critics, both amateur and professional, needle the media when they are wayward and praise them when they are brilliant. The Center for the Study of Democratic Institutions maintains that one of the issues central to the well-being of a free society arises from the political, social, and cultural responsibilities of the mass media.

The Ford Foundation, to name but one enterprise interested in media performance, recently invested a large sum of money in journalism education. Schools and departments of journalism and communication are experiencing enrollment increases at a time when their students are studying the media in the broader context of society. But this does not mean that the training of young people for jobs in the media has gone the way of the classics, for today's student of the mass media is an intellectual investigator as well as a job apprentice. It does mean, however, that most curricula, such as the innovative new Department of Human Communication at Rutgers, are emphasizing the historical, philosophical, sociological, and biological environment in which the media function.

It is clear that the media and society at large are interdependent, and this casebook attempts to review the many facets of the media and mass communication as they relate to both producers and consumers of messages.

"The saddest fact of all about our newspapers and our TV programs is that there is nothing new to say about them," Joseph P. Lyford writes in "Media and Messages." Yet Lyford tries anyway, critically and imaginatively, to say something fresh about consumers, effects, technology, and the reporting of issues. His piece serves to identify not only the "media" but also their problems.

No book on the mass media would be complete without the voice of Marshall McLuhan, the one person who has contributed more to the era of investigation, at least in a popular sense, than anyone else. He writes that "our experience with the grammar and syntax of languages can be made available for the direction and control of media old and new." His article, "Myth and Mass Media," is basic McLuhan. It deals generally with language as a mass medium and how myths, old and new, have tortured it. The piece introduces readers to such McLuhanisms as "print is single-leveled" and the concept of "lineal segmentation."

"The mass media have played a key role in making the entertainer too much a hero in American culture," Patrick D. Hazard argues. "And this misemphasis accounts in great measure for the crisis in quality in both American life and mass communication." Hazard suggests ways communicators and educators might help reverse this trend. Although some of his "heroes" may be dated, the "problem" continues to haunt us.

"Why the Mass Media Are That Way," by Theodore Peterson, is a standard historical account. The article is accurate if a bit kind, and I think a reasonably "objective" treatment that is warranted to round out anyone's understanding of the media in relationship to society's other institutions.

Herbert I. Schiller's thesis in "Towards a Democratic Reconstruction of Mass Communications: The Social Use of Technology" is socialistic but rising in popularity among media watchers. Schiller argues that modern communications must be won away from current custodians and placed in the hands of the people. "Technically-advanced America is socially retarded by institutional machinery which preserves outlooks

Preface ix

and practices far beyond their usefulness or applicability," he maintains.

Of real concern in recent years is the media's responsibility toward ethnic minorities, particularly America's large black community. Royal D. Colle's "Negro Image in the Mass Media: A Case Study in Social Change" is concerned with the forces and factors that brought about the change in the black image in television, where it has become most obvious, and in the motion pictures, where Sidney Poitier's films have symbolized a changing attitude of producers and audience. It also offers a brief assessment of implications of the change to blacks and, ultimately, to American society. The article may not reflect the attitudes espoused by the more militant segments of society, but it seems to me an honest historical and sociological treatment.

"Is the Black Press Needed?" by James D. Williams is an essay on newspapers and is far more critical and personal than the selection by Colle. Contemporary students will identify with it because of its "blackness." The answer Wiliams proposes to the question of whether or not the black press is really needed is yes, at least until society is fully integrated. He also assures us that the black press is alive and well.

The next two articles by Andrew Kopkind and J. Anthony Lukas focus attention on three of the godlike characters in modern American media—Henry Luce, Hugh Heffner, and Walt Disney. In "Serving Time," Kopkind writes sardonically of "the largest, most powerful publishing corporation in the world." As a former "Lucemployee," he does it with flare and facts. For instance: "There is no mystery in the way the old Time religion served the development of the Company." Since *Time Inc.* is a household word in America (witness its frequency in college term papers!), it is not out of order to single it out for special comment.

What Disney did, and continues after his death to do, for America's youth, Heffner is doing for the country's aging swingers. In "The 'Alternative Life-Style' of Playboys and Playmates," Lukas queries whether or not the Playboy Life-Style is "an entertainment cartel which goes beyond simply selling fantasies as an escape from life but tries to sell those very fantasies as a way of life[.]"

Otto Friedrich's "A Vivacious Blonde Was Fatally Shot Today or How to Read a Tabloid" develops the notion that "wordmanship—the art of exaggerating without actually lying—is so common in tabloid newspapers that it may be termed tabloid prose, *but it is by no means restricted to tabloids.*" The italics are mine, for, though the old screaming tabloids have passed into history with the death penalty, the clever generalization still applies.

It is with this in mind that "Television and Growing Up: The Impact of Televised Violence," introduction to the multivolume Report of the

Surgeon General's Scientific Advisory Committee on Television and Social Behavior is included.

Next are four case studies of the media in action as they perform under the pressures of time and space. Victor Bernstein and Jesse Gordon offer "The Press and the Bay of Pigs" and conclude that the press did not cover this crisis responsibly. In "The Press and the Assassination," William L. Rivers decides that the press performed generally well but with some notable exceptions in covering the killing of President Kennedy. By the time of the 1968 Democratic National Convention, the press may have been gun-shy, as surveyed by Nathan B. Blumberg in "The 'Orthodox' Media under Fire: Chicago and the Press." Brilliant in its style and insight, Michael J. Arlen's "Television and the Press in Vietnam" takes a provocative look at the nation's biggest news story of the nineteen-sixties.

The Nicholas Johnson selection, "The Media Barons and the Public Interest," also examines the media relative to specific events, and substantiates the need if not the desire for citizens to be aware of who owns the media and why.

The next six articles deal with a handful of other aspects of the mass media—films, the Beatles, the underground press, muckraking, and advertising. They were selected not so much for their catchall nature, but for the originality of the opinions expressed. Stanley Kauffmann, the noted film critic, analyzes the current film generation as "the most cheering circumstance in contemporary American art," but he treads cautiously in terms of its historical staying power. In "Learning from the Beatles," Richard Poirier forces us to take popular culture seriously by making us aware of the communication impact of the rock generation. The entire counter-culture movement, not just the underground press, is discussed movingly by Jesse Kornbluth, a former underground editor. And Louis Filler, the leading historian on muckraking in America, relates the performance of the original era of the media to the expectations of the present one. As the mass media in this country are organized there can be no communication to the people without someone to pay the piper. Who pays the piper and how are concerns of Dallas Smythe in "Five Myths of Consumership." Howard Luck Gossage, who made his living from the business of advertising, takes a friendly bite of the hand that feeds a burgeoning American industry.

Finally, Elie Abel, in "The Press at Bay, 1970," is worried about attacks on the press from certain government officials, but points out that a "cowardly press or one so complacent that it does not see the need for self-improvement in a hurry, will get no better than it deserves." He discusses ways to improve media responsiveness to audience needs, including the creation of community press councils.

By thus revealing these personal biases toward the casebook material, I hope to have stimulated discussion and investigation. The questions at the end of the book are also constructed to facilitate classroom situations and independent study. All social issues, such as the condition of the American mass media, are open-ended and should be pursued thoughtfully and freely.

In twelve years of teaching I have become indebted to scores of individuals, all of whom have influenced my judgments in one way or another. One stands out as the coauthor of all my endeavors, Cynthia, my wife, whose curiosity in matters of the mind has been both a comfort and a challenge.

Richard F. Hixson

Contents

1. **Media and Messages**
   Joseph P. Lyford   1
2. **Myth and Mass Media**
   Marshall McLuhan   16
3. **The Entertainer as Hero: A Problem of the Mass Media**
   Patrick D. Hazard   26
4. **Why the Mass Media Are That Way**
   Theodore Peterson   38
5. **Towards a Democratic Reconstruction of Mass Communications: The Social Use of Technology**
   Herbert I. Schiller   55
6. **Negro Image in the Mass Media: A Case Study in Social Change**
   Royal D. Colle   71
7. **Is the Black Press Needed?**
   James D. Williams   80
8. **Serving Time**
   Andrew Kopkind   93
9. **The 'Alternative Life-Style' of Playboys and Playmates**
   J. Anthony Lukas   104
10. **A Vivacious Blonde Was Fatally Shot Today or How to Read a Tabloid**
    Otto Friedrich   112
11. ***From* Television and Growing Up: The Impact of Televised Violence**
    Surgeon General's Scientific Advisory Committee on Television and Social Behavior   118
12. **The Press and the Bay of Pigs**
    Victor Bernstein and Jesse Gordon   127
13. **The Press and the Assassination**
    William L. Rivers   142

14. **The "Orthodox" Media under Fire: Chicago and the Press**
    Nathan B. Blumberg   151
15. **Television and the Press in Vietnam; or, Yes, I Can Hear You Very Well—Just What Was It You Were Saying?**
    Michael J. Arlen   164
16. **The Media Barons and the Public Interest: An FCC Commissioner's Warning**
    Nicholas Johnson   179
17. **The Film Generation: Celebration and Concern**
    Stanley Kauffmann   196
18. **Learning from the Beatles**
    Richard Poirier   209
19. **This Place of Entertainment Has No Fire Exit: The Underground Press and How It Went**
    Jesse Kornbluth   228
20. **Truth and Consequence: Some Notes on Changing Times and the Muckrakers**
    Louis Filler   237
21. **Five Myths of Consumership**
    Dallas Smythe   250
22. **After Smokey the Bear, What?**
    Howard Luck Gossage   256
23. **The Press at Bay, 1970**
    Elie Abel   264

Bibliography   275

Research and Discussion Topics   279

The Contributors   281

1. Media and Messages
Joseph P. Lyford

It was just ten years ago that Edward R. Murrow delivered a classic blast at the broadcasters. A rereading of the statement leaves the general impression that in television nothing much changes except the quality of the picture tube. The broadcasters are still talking about their special rights under the First Amendment and their sacred responsibility to make as much money as possible; most of the shows are the same old plots dressed up with new titles; and the Federal Communications Commission is still busily supervising the buildup of the mass-media monopolies, mergers, and concentrations of ownership it is supposed to be heading off. At least we can be grateful that there are two commissioners, Nicholas Johnson and Kenneth Cox, who are needling the industry, and we have some highly literate press critics around in *Harper's, The Atlantic Monthly,* and the *Columbia Journalism Review.* But the quality and frequency of the criticism drop off sharply from here. The fact is that with all the talk about the mass media these past years, we still have only the foggiest notion of what they are up to; this is partly because most of the criticism is neither systematic nor continuous and is either vague or centered on isolated cases. Confusion is also generated by the vast quantity of data graciously supplied by the people who run the media and hire researchers who tell us—to use the vernacular of the tobacco industry—that there is no demonstrable link between television and the health of the people who smoke it. Any doubts

Source: *The Center Magazine* 2, no. 5 (September 1969): 53–56, 58–61. Reprinted by permission. The magazine is a publication of the Center for the Study of Democratic Institutions, Santa Barbara, California.

as to the extent to which the broadcasters influence the character of the mass-media discussion should be dispelled by the F.C.C. chairman's recent admission that the Commission does "lean" rather heavily on the broadcasting industry for pertinent data. And the American Newspaper Publishers Association, to prove it isn't asleep at the switch, assured its members at one convention that while it doesn't have an official lobby in Washington, its suggestions about pending legislation affecting the press usually result in desirable modifications.

One of the main difficulties in trying to understand even the most basic facts about the mass media is that communications technology and the people making money out of it are moving so fast that by the time we get a full-fledged debate going on some problem, the problem is obsolete or has dwindled to secondary importance. While the F.C.C. fiddled around with ways of getting UHF receivers on sets to open up competition a little, cable television was already threatening to push UHF aside and American Telephone & Telegraph was getting an unbreakable hold on the satellite program for good. Now Congress has been ruminating about how to save failing newspapers when in fact it ought to be worrying about healthy ones like the *San Francisco Chronicle,* which has grabbed off a rich TV channel, set up a shady [53]* housekeeping deal with the city's only other daily, and gained control of about three-fourths of cable television interests in the San Francisco area.

Another weakness of the discussion about the mass media is the collection of wobbly assumptions on which much of the talk is based. One such assumption is the idea that commercial broadcasters, newspaper publishers, bank presidents, corporation board chairmen, and all the others who control communications properties will respond to vague threats or appeals to their corporate consciences.

If there are going to be any revolutions in the communications business, they will come about because of changes in technology, not conscience.

Since we can't very well get hold of exactly what is happening to the media, it seems more interesting to speculate what is happening to the consumers of the media. We are right back in the thicket of wobbly assumption here, too. Contrary to the widely held belief that TV and newspapers can change or modify our opinions, many respectable people who make a good living counting and analyzing public opinion cite "studies" which show the mass media have no influence whatever on our attitudes—that we are receptive only to those messages which

---

* In the texts of the selections, bracketed numbers indicate the pagination of the original sources. When a page in the original ends with a hyphenated word, we have indicated the original pagination after the entire word.

reënforce our convictions. The ad men who spend all those millions on TV spots obviously don't believe this, but it is quite unsettling to writers and teachers who adhere to the quaint idea that exposure to alleged facts and sales talks determines to some extent how a man feels about Volkswagens or about Richard Nixon after the Checkers extravaganza. Young people hearing an exchange between a journalist and a public-opinion expert are also confused. After two hundred and fifty Berkeley undergraduates listened in shocked silence to Harry Ashmore's description of how Mr. Nixon packaged himself to the Presidency with twenty million dollars' worth of mass-media plugs, they were advised by a Ph.D. in mass-communications research to forget it, that all those carefully contrived TV spots we saw during the Pat Brown-Ronald Reagan California gubernatorial campaign were a waste of money because we had already decided how to vote. There was a further acceleration of confusion some months later when, after pollster Donald Muchmore predicted most people had made up their minds to vote Tom Bradley in as Los Angeles mayor, election day turned out to be Sam Yorty Day. By this time the Ph.D. was safely off campus and unavailable for questions.

It might be good to get things right out on the table and say the mass-media researchers don't know what they are talking about. *Certainly* some of their "scientific studies" have a peculiar ring to them; it is not convincing, for instance, to be told that because several days' propaganda over Cincinnati's TV stations did not increase U.N. popularity in the viewer sample, therefore TV didn't change opinions. What other influences were at work during the test period that might have neutralized the U.N. messages, or simply redirected the viewer's attentions? And how does a researcher calibrate the date of birth, or mutation, or the texture and shape of something as delicate as an opinion? A little delving into the literature of attitude measurement arouses a feeling that some aspects of the business come perilously close to shamanism—any professional body, for instance, that can take a book like *Unobtrusive Measures* in all seriousness needs some looking into.

Suspicious as one might be of the mind-inspectors, it has to be admitted that at least they have some evidence to present, while nobody on the other side has any airtight data proving that a blizzard of anti-smoking commercials has any effect on our thought processes. And there is some support for the idea that we are worrying too much about being exposed to large amounts of information. Reflecting on his experience with mescaline, Aldous Huxley wrote, in *The Doors of Perception,* that he found himself agreeing with the eminent Cambridge philosopher C. D. Broad that "we should do well to consider more seriously than we have hitherto been inclined to do the type of theory which Bergson put forward in connection with memory and sense perception. The suggestion is that the function of the brain and nervous system and sense organs is in the main eliminative and not productive. Each person is at each moment capable of remembering all that has happened to him and of perceiving everything that is happening anywhere in the universe. The function of the brain is to protect us from being overwhelmed and confused by the mass of largely irrelevant and useless knowledge by shutting out most of what we should otherwise perceive and remember at any moment, and leaving only that very small and special selection which is likely to be practically useful."

Huxley implied that the brain and nervous system perform involuntarily the censoring activity which McLuhan advises us all to do very self-consciously to protect our sanity against a bombardment of data. In Huxley's view the whole universe of impressions is funneled through a mental reducing valve, and [54] what comes out at the other end is a "measly trickle of the kind of consciousness which will help us stay alive on the surface of this particular planet." This should be of some comfort to those of us who try hard to keep up with everything that is supposed to be going on. But questions persist. How does Huxley's reducing valve decide what is "likely to be practically useful" at any given time? Does the rejection process change as civilizations are revolutionized by technology? And if, as Huxley says, there are chemical ways of bypassing the reducing valve, may not psychological means for circumventing it or breaking it down be devised?

Huxley's reducing valve will assuredly be tested by the techniques future communicators will develop to get their messages into our heads, come hell or high water. Past technical improvements in film, videotape, and sound will seem rudimentary by comparison. We may discover that the mass media can accomplish by mechanical and psychological means what Huxley felt was possible only by drug-induced changes in the supply of sugar to the brain. We have a very mild scent of what is to come in the vast realism of the film "2001," which has even changed audience seating patterns. Despite the huge screen, many people like to sit in the front rows where they are swaddled in the action, projected into space along with the capsule. The illusion of participation will be enormously expanded by the introduction of such inventions as the living-history film envisioned by Leopold Godowsky, the inventor of Kodachrome, who has predicted that under controlled viewing conditions an audience will be unable to avoid the conviction it is actually confronting the subject of the film. Godowsky's original purpose in developing the film was to use it in interviews with important world leaders, which would become the basis of visual-history archives, but its adaptation to television—and the technical changes TV can make to facilitate transmission of this visual reality—will be a radical step to erase what is left of the boundaries between fantasy and reality.

There can be little doubt that new visual information systems will have the power to subject individual or mass audiences to enormous, unpredictable shock—something film can do now but with much less intensity. We probably need not be as concerned about overt assaults as we are about subliminal or disguised attacks on our equilibrium. Added to the technical perfections of film, tape, and what displaces tape, will be radical new styles of treating subject matter to intensify reality. It seems likely that some of these new methods will be built on *cinema vérité*, which abolishes the artificiality of staging; other methods will use sophisticated abstractions, and still others will use abstraction to hammer home a specific, tangible point. Another change which will enforce the illusion of reality is the magnification of the viewing surface. The enlargement of TV screens to the point where images are bigger than life size will not only increase the persuasive power of the film but it can work the sort of transformations suggested in Robert Snyder's "Small World," a documentary on insects in which the magnification brings the viewer to the edge of extreme revulsion. There is no way of knowing how far the impact of TV can be expanded once it breaks out of its present confines, but it is not difficult to imagine the mind penetration which could be accomplished by a twenty-first-century parallel to Leni Reifenstahl's "Triumph of Will," or by an on-the-spot piece of living history, full size and color, as it unfolds a sequel to Watts or Detroit. One might ask, then, what protections other than Huxley's overworked filter are needed against overt or subtle distortions, or the subliminal effects that can transform opinion into truth. How is one to be defended against the overwhelming crash of reality?

Confronted with these and other riddles, what are the critics of the mass media to do if they want to keep their jobs? They follow the example of the man at the computer who assembles all the sense data and then transforms it into the logical base for all subsequent computations— the very act of faith that propelled early Christians into the Colosseum. The critic leaps over all the riddles in order to get on with the discussion. There is something very reassuring to such people about the current Senate investigation of violence on TV and how it affects children. In the course of such rambling inquiries it is impossible to detect whether any given remark has a bearing on the subject, what the subject precisely is, or whether the remark has any internal validity of its own. In such discussion, nobody should feel inhibited. The politician Senator Pastore, after taking a number of indistinct positions, concludes his investigation with a suggestion that "scientific studies" will provide the answers. At some distance from the hearing room, in California, the scientist Joshua Lederberg replies that this is nonsense, the entire scientific literature on the subject can be read in an afternoon and is shaky and inconclusive to boot. At this point some of those paying attention may remember psychiatrist Bruno [55] Bettelheim's announcement that violence on TV may be good for youngsters because it gives them a look at reality—to which educator Robert Hutchins responds (in the person of his synthetic philosopher Dr. Zuckerkandl) that on television nothing is real because the function of television is to eliminate pain so that we can watch natural disasters and the massacre of subject peoples in our living room without the slightest feeling of discomfort. One escapes from the controversy over TV, violence, and children only by concluding that since all children are destined to be frightened out of their wits a good deal of the time, television might as well be doing the job as the local movie theater or parents who read them *The Pit and the Pendulum* and Grimm's Fairy-Tales.

It is, of course, no more possible to talk about the "effects" of television on children than on any other group. To the child deprived of an alternative the set can become the only source of daylight, and many deprived children, in both Westport and Harlem, adopt TV as a substitute parent at infancy. Children with a great many other resources seem to regard TV as just another piece of furniture. They are more selective than many adults who have had to "learn" television in middle age and they are sometimes better at getting the main, if not the most obvious, point of what they see. Otherwise how does one explain the insistence of a child, watching the funeral of President Eisenhower, on finding out who shot him? The fact that these children show a preference for imaginative commercials over "Gunsmoke" is a tribute to their taste and an indication that they may be growing up with the same contempt for regular television programming their parents have for the newspapers.

If increased familiarity with television does breed boredom and distrust, it might be worthwhile to think some more about the Paul Lazarsfeld-Robert Merton thesis that the mass media reënforce social norms and status symbols. A good many black children who have gone through their teens watching patriotic newscasts and the exploits of honest white policemen seem to have missed the point of all this folklore. One wonders whether television is promoting any norms. There is no question but that a great deal of air time is given to people who are criticizing the Establishment and not all of these critics are apoplectic black ministers. Last June, N.B.C. reporter Nancy Dickerson raked the American Medical Association over the coals in very explicit terms following the President's veto of Dr. John Knowles for a post in the Department of Health, Education, and Welfare, and she seemed to feel quite at ease in doing so. Certainly Senator Hugh Scott did not feel

C.B.S. was enforcing social norms when he attacked the network in 1967 (inaccurately) for featuring more Negro militants than moderates. And one could ask what norms were reënforced by C.B.S.'s coverage of the last Democratic Convention? The norms of politics-as-usual? Of Mayor Daley's Chicago?

When accepted norms have become an object of suspicion even to a white, blue-collar class, television has no choice but to tell us about it. Controversy, action, fury still are what make a top news story on TV or in the papers, and the dissenters have learned how to exploit news media tied to these standards. Sometimes the result of the exploitation has been an oversupply of fake news-drama, but occasionally we have been given some splendid television reporting—on Martin Luther King in Birmingham, Selma, Washington, D.C., and Cicero, and in C.B.S.'s documentaries on migrant farm workers and on hunger in America. Television has as many possibilities as a theater of discontent as it does a forum for complacency. In the very process of illuminating, it affects the course of the history with which it is dealing. The stage, transferred to television, becomes a very different sort of theater, in which the effects of manipulating sound and light, of closeups, intercutting between cameras, selection of personalities, timing, a multiplicity of observation points can invent mythology or history for millions of people. It isn't necessary any longer for us to test and age our heroes, because television can manufacture and peddle them overnight. It has also cut to nothing the time lag between the conception of stereotype, its mass adoption, its elevation to the ultimate, and its quick replacement by something newer. Television's decisions about what is topical and significant have an immediate impact on public and private conversations. So there is always the question as to whether television enforces norms, or is contributing to an impression that whatever is in style today will be gone tomorrow.

It would be an injustice not to acknowledge that television has experimented with the arts many times during the past decade in a very creative way. One of the most exciting of these happenings was N.B.C.'s magnificent taping of the Boston Symphony's last 1967 Tanglewood concert, in which many cameras were so integrated with the music that they could have been part of the orchestra itself. Perhaps there will be an increase in these efforts in the future when audio-visual electronic technology approaches perfection in picture transmission. The possibilities of new experiments with the fine arts are especially exciting. The new technology will make it possible to present painting and graphics with such spectacular reality that viewing fine art will even surpass the museum experience. If television takes advantage of the technical possibilities, for the first time painting and still photography can be brought within reach of mass audiences with the same fidelity as music, long ago liberated from the concert hall by recordings and television staging. Until now the fine arts have had to depend on book and magazine reproduction, which even at its best (in the Skira and Abrams books) loses the critical ten or twenty per cent of the texture and color of the originals, and which have not been able to approximate the originals in size. In addition to truer reproduction, music has had another advantage over the plastic arts, in that the production of musical sounds is a kinetic theatrical event of short duration—all of which has made the musical performance peculiarly suited to television. And music on TV has had such inspiring and lucid translators as Dimitri Mitropoulos and Leonard Bernstein—in contrast to the fine arts, desperately handicapped by the inarticulate verbal confusions of the Robert Motherwells and Elaine de Koonings. With magnification and perfect reproduction, television's projection of painting might significantly promote the integration of the fine arts with modern life, greatly expanding their effect as a means of education and communication. The fine arts will never become popular, regardless of the excellence of transmission, but historically—notably in the Italian Renaissance—they have played an important part in the education of the spirit and the transformation of cultures.

Television's preoccupation with ratings and entertainment shows is not the only reason we have not had more creative, significant reporting on television. Television news producers also have an unhealthy tendency to rate technical excellence ahead of significance of content. They are also convinced that unless something moves it isn't news. Taken together, the obsessions with technique and motion mean that television reporting often misses what Henri Cartier-Bresson calls the "decisive moment" of a story—the single revealing picture which can be studied in its frozen state. Yet the documentary, created from a sequence of still photographs, which does not appeal to movie-minded TV producers, is an inexpensive and more focused way to get at the heart of the subject. An example is the televised photo-essay on Manolete, the bullfighter. Television's "motion sickness" also accounts in part for a reluctance to deal with abstractions or invisible happenings like the technological invasion of the environment.

Television news coverage has also been hampered by internal disagreements over what constitutes "responsible" reporting. The Kerner Commission, as well as members of Congress, has criticized the networks for the way in which they covered the 1967 urban riots, suggesting that television actually contributed to the spread of the disturbance. C.B.S.'s Frank Stanton has said that any agreement or "consortium" between networks designed to suppress live coverage of potentially violent events would not serve the public interest, no matter how worthy the motive for such suppression might be. Yet not long after the 1967 disorder the three major television networks reached an informal understanding, according to *The New York Times,* that they would not give live coverage of the anti-war demonstrations at the Pentagon, the idea apparently being that such coverage might have inflammatory effects. In the wake of this decision, edited film reports on the Pentagon affair gave an extremely distorted picture of what happened and were accompanied (notably in Washington, D.C.) with vituperative commentaries attacking the demonstrators but ignoring the violence of sheriff's deputies and soldiers.

It is certain that the sharp criticism of C.B.S.'s coverage of the Chicago Convention has added to the networks' uncertain state of mind about live coverage of volatile demonstrations, and the networks are proceeding very cautiously. That this should not necessarily be a cause for rejoicing is shown by past cases where the mass media have exercised "restraint" in the national interest. The possibility that the hour-long TV embargo on reporting of the Detroit riot left the field open to dangerous rumor-mongering was conceded by the Kerner Commission.

Caution has been pretty much a life-style for the networks since the beginning. With television right behind automobiles and drugs as the biggest industrial moneymakers, there is little likelihood that the next decade will give the network new courage. But somewhere, usually out of sight, is the talent and imagination to be daring. The N.B.C. White Papers produced under Irving Gitlin, many of them directed by Arthur Zegart, made few compromises in its programs on the exposé of Newburgh, New York's welfare practices (which resulted in a lawsuit against the network), studies of gambling, of state legislatures, and [58] of police corruption in Boston (which also brought N.B.C. into the courts). Also to the credit of C.B.S. were the unvarnished and often unbearable reports on Vietnam which brought that war home in its full reality—reports finally softened as the result of protests by Americans who found it too hard to take. And while on the subject of television's better moments, one has to mention those one-hour UNICEF films of Danny Kaye's and Marian Anderson's visits with children around the world, David Brinkley's look at the Mississippi River, the memorable film of Nikita Khrushchev in retirement, and the documentary on the contrasting boyhoods of James Baldwin and Hubert Humphrey. Recently there have been the two excellent "magazine" shows: "First Tuesday," which has shown us the rituals of life and death in New Guinea, the Nigerian civil war, the massacre of sheep in Skull

Valley by poison gas, and "Sixty Minutes" (Venice, the dying city, and an interview with Marshal Tito). In drama we had Lee J. Cobb in *Death of a Salesman,* the Shakespeare series of plays sponsored by Esso and produced by the B.B.C., and N.B.C.'s grand tour of the Louvre. Children's programs reached a high peak with the imaginative Sunday-night Disney films, the long-awaited cartoon appearances of Charlie Brown, the Christmas productions of "Amahl and the Night Visitors," and—every morning, except Sunday, for years—Captain Kangaroo with puppets, paintings, dancing, animals, and music, from *Carousel* to Beethoven. There were many more good things, but taken all together they weren't enough to make television a very satisfying experience for the young.

If speculation on the future technology of television, if not its quality, is a bit exciting, contemplation of the newspaper business, past, present, and future, is a depressing one. With the usual exceptions, the big daily newspapers are not getting any better, even in those cities where they no longer have to worry about a competitor (which means almost everywhere). The slippage is unmistakable from front to back. Local coverage is mainly the memorializing of pseudo-events, official announcements, and press releases; national and international stories are also slighted and when used are written in the uninformative and purposefully dull prose of the wire services. Many papers which do subscribe to *The New York Times* or the *Washington Post-Los Angeles Times* services ignore their most interesting offerings or gut the pieces unmercifully. Most depressing is the bad writing that we now associate automatically with the sight of newsprint: no section of the newspapers from the columnists and critics to the feature writers is free of the blight. In a talk to Harvard's Nieman Fellows twenty years ago, the late A. J. Liebling declared that newspapers are specially devised for the destruction of style. Liebling echoed Van Wyck Brooks, who claimed that no writing talent can survive more than a year in a city room. A few years later, Professor Theodore Morrison tried again to plead the cause of the reader, with his attack on the "hugger-mugger sentences," the fake emotionalism of journalese, and reporters who cannot come face-to-face with an idea. But such outbursts are valuable only as collectors' items in a country where the newspaper business resolutely refuses to engage in self-criticism and is run by publishers who consider the classified advertisement as the ultimate in paragraph structure.

One prediction that can be made with some assurance about the bulk of existing dailies is that they will continue to resist change even if it means their extinction. Like service on the subways, they become shoddier as the price goes up. At some point, the newspaper will undergo a physical mutation at the hands of the electronics industry, which will put newsboys out of business forever: facsimile editions will unroll from our TV sets, thus making official the fact that newspapers are a tail on the television dog for most people. There is an irony to the fact that while TV news broadcasts adopted the very worst traits of the newspapers, the newspapers tried to compete with the newscasters at their own game—with neither medium able to match the other's peculiar talent for trivialization.

There are all sorts of reasons why per capita newspaper readership in America is declining, and runs well behind readership in many European and Asian countries, but the most important reason is that American newspapers are boring, petulant, distrusted, and run in the main by people who are milking them. Of course television competition for advertising has hurt the papers, but publishers and bad writing and third-rate reporters were killing newspapers long before TV was invented. The trouble with newspapers is that they are managed by the same sort of people who run railroads. For years conservative publishers have put out papers which, by opposing adequate financing of public education, have thereby ensured the decline of the literacy on which newspapers depend. By misreporting or under-reporting the extent and effects of urban and rural poverty and racial discrimination, they have accelerated the deterioration [54] of their cities and the departure of their advertisers and readers to the suburbs. Faced with vast population and economic changes in the cities, the newspapers have failed to adjust. There are exceptions—the *Washington Post* and the *Baltimore Sun,* for instance, are trying to replace their vanishing middle-class circulation by offering systematic coverage of the minority group communities. *The New York Times,* always a fine newspaper, has improved immeasurably in an effort to serve the needs of the world's most tortured city. But most of the urban dailies—and they include some of the traditionally "great" ones—see the ghetto mainly as a source of crime and riot stories.

It may be true that our biggest cities have become just as impossible to report on as they are to govern, and that newspapers, like government, ought to decentralize and assign reporters on a very different basis. The "storefront" reporter, visible in his neighborhood, could be a collector of volunteered information as well as a perennial observer on a new sort of beat. Despite its old reputation for gray impersonality, *The New York Times* has been doing a great deal of prospecting in the city's neighborhoods, on an irregular basis. There is an intimate and very appealing quality to some of its reporting as a result. Oddly enough, the same closeness to subject is frequently achieved in two newspapers thought of as being national rather than local in character—the *Christian Science Monitor* and the *Wall Street Journal*. When they examine a local situation the resulting story is well rounded, colorful, and quite personal in tone. But these are rare examples. A main contention of critics now is that the big dailies and urban TV stations are not in touch with the special problems of their own constituencies, and that they are behaving just like another centralized bureaucracy.

One effect of the urban news factory, heavily weighted with official events, pressure-group propaganda, and "national" stories, has been the raising of the trajectory of people's attention toward remote events, far from their immediate environment. Such material may combat provincialism, but too heavy a diet of it leaves the reader in ignorance about what is taking place next door. And with newspapers and television increasingly directing his attention to "big" issues over which he feels he has no control, his sense of helplessness grows and his inclination to intervene actively in the affairs of his community declines.

The big press and TV news factories are in direct contrast to the underground press, which has built up its circulation primarily by appealing to small and neglected communities, sometimes political, sometimes social. A former *Berkeley Barb* reporter, Stewart Glauberman, compares that newspaper to a sympathetic parent at the breakfast table listening to his son's account of being busted by the cops: what is important is not the facts, it is that in his own home the son is believed and his story will be told to the neighbors as gospel. But one has to look past the established examples of the underground press to find a true community newspaper—the *Barb*, the *Express Times*, and the *East Village Other* are so propagandistic that even their own readers can't afford to trust them. A good example of an insurgent newspaper that tries to serve an unrepresented community is the monthly *Freedom News*, which with volunteer help is flourishing as an antidote to the conservative dailies published in affluent Contra Costa County near San Francisco. *Freedom News* muckrakes, in factual and conversational style, gives the defendant's side of an arrest story, and even has its own columnist on what the Establishment is doing to the natural environment. Another newspaper that has kept its community flavor in spite of its success is the *Village Voice*, whose encouragement of debate, reporting, and criticism has given it a respectably large citywide and national audience. *El Malcriado*, the organ of Cesar Chavez' United Farm Workers Organizing Committee in Delano, California, is something of a disappointment as a community newspaper. Published in Spanish and English, as the union's voice to its own membership, and supposedly as a plea for the attention of the outer community, the paper is a far cry from that classic community journal, *Indian Opinion*, founded in South Africa by Gandhi, whose philosophy deeply influenced Chavez. Of *Indian Opinion*, Gandhi wrote that it was "an open book to whoever wanted to gauge the strength and the weakness of the community, be he a friend, an enemy, or a neutral. The workers had realized at the very outset that secrecy had no place in a movement where one could do no wrong, where there was no scope for duplicity or cunning, and where strength constituted the single guarantee of victory. . . .

"One thing we [the staff] have endeavored to observe most scrupulously: namely, never to depart from the strictest facts, and in dealing with the difficult questions that have arisen . . . we hope that we have used the utmost moderation possible under the circumstances. We should fail in our duty if we wrote anything with a view to hurt. Facts we would always place before our readers, whether they be palatable or not, and it is by placing them constantly [60] before the public in their nakedness that the misunderstanding between the two communities in South Africa can be removed."

Indian Opinion had a far different historic and political role to play than the newspaper of a contemporary American city, but the words Gandhi used to describe the standards and community responsibilities of his journal might serve as a text for modern publishers who consider their newspapers primarily as business properties. The failure of their newspapers to speak directly to their readers and to report about local life in a systematic and credible manner has contributed to the general distrust of the press. If a newspaper does not cultivate familiarity with the problem of that great majority of individuals who are "unimportant," it will not have the capacity to understand them when their actions suddenly become "important"—that is, disruptive, eccentric, or tragic.

The coverage of campus disturbances is a good example of how the press has distorted the nature of those fragile communities and what problems the universities face as they resist suffocation by the larger society. The TV or newspaper reporter casually assigned to a confrontation is no more equipped to understand the bare essentials of violence than he was when dispatched to the rioting in Newark and Detroit. Like a fixed camera, he does not view things in the round, and he is intellectually immobile as well. The fragments he offers his papers as the comprehensive truth will contradict the experience of any reader who has had personal contact with the event; thus the level of distrust is raised again and again. The trend is not likely to be reversed, because newspapers and TV are fascinated with the characteristic rather than the typical, the spectacular rather than the intangible, and the easily categorized rather than the complex. To operate with such criteria means, obviously, that the most important information about almost everything is lost. On very few newspapers are reporters or editors permitted to become students of the society they tell us about. We are being educated by a professional secretariat, and the notion that reporters are supposed to record only "the facts" is, of course, an old notion, but it is not an old-fashioned one.

Only a few months ago, the executive head of the United Press International observed that the purpose of reporting is to "hold a mirror to the world." With such a philosophy, it is not surprising that in all echelons of the mass media there is suspicion of any young journalist who displays a minimum of creative vitality in his writing or in his way of approaching a subject. Such young people can complicate the life of an editor who wants people who can get the gist of anything in an hour, and who can be deployed quickly to trouble spots, like policemen. It is no wonder, then, that the mass media have turned out in force to cover the various wars, declared and undeclared, that are ripping up the world, from Watts to Vietnam, while we are left in ignorance about what is happening across town. Or that hundreds of correspondents every day jam Washington press conferences while the side effects of "scientific progress" that are destroying our air, water, and land have gone largely unreported until recently. And there should be nothing mysterious about the fact that, despite all the newsprint devoted to college riots, Americans understand their educational system no better than they did in 1900.

All of the above observations are questionable, of course, because they are generalizations. Nobody can overlook the diversity of a newspaper press that includes a *New York Times* and a *Daily News* in the same city, or a TV medium which can invent a *Newspaper of the Air* (KQED-TV, the San Francisco educational station) along with the sleek newscasts of its neighboring KRON-TV (owned by the *San Francisco Chronicle*). Also, if pressed, a critic can pick out of the record of the past ten years some examples of change for the better. *Time* and *Newsweek* have both improved their vision as well as their English. *The New Yorker* magazine is giving us all sorts of penetrating insights into life all over the country in the best journalistic prose around. Washington, D.C.'s *Star* and *Post* are getting better all the time. Some individual TV stations are doing a good job of local coverage (KCRA-TV, Sacramento, is a good example). Interesting people like Joan Baez pop up on the "Today" show as well as fusty congressmen. But the hopeful signs are scarce. While the range is great, the overwhelming weight of television is as riddled with blah as it was when Ed Murrow took it to task for its unadulterated commercialism. And a cross-country reading tour of our city newspapers shows them to be at least as trivial, if less plentiful, as they were when the Commission on a Free and Responsible Press issued its criticisms twenty-two years ago. The saddest fact of all about our newspapers and our TV programs is that there is nothing new to say about them. [61]

2. Myth and Mass Media
Marshall McLuhan

When an attempt is made to bring the relatively articulated concept of "myth" into the area of "media"—a concept to which surprisingly little attention has been given in the past—it is necessary to reconsider both "myth" and "media" in order to get at relevant data. For example, English is itself a mass medium, as is any language employed by any society. But the general use of the phrase "mass media" would seem to record an unfavorable valuation of new media, especially since the advent of the telegraph, the telephone, moving pictures, radio, and television. These media have had the same kind of drastic effect on language and culture that print had in Europe in the sixteenth century, or that it is now having in other parts of the world.

It might even be well to avoid so highly charged a phrase as "mass media" until a little more thought can be given to the problem. Languages as human artifacts, collective products of human skill and need, can easily be regarded as "mass media," but many find it difficult to consider the newer media deriving from these languages as new "languages." Writing, in its several modes, can be regarded technologically as the development of new languages. For to translate the audible into the visible by phonetic means is to institute a dynamic process that reshapes every aspect of thought, language, and society. To record the extended operation of such a process in a Gorgon or Cadmus myth is to reduce a complex historical affair to an

2. Myth and Mass Media 17

inclusive timeless image. Can we, perhaps, say that in the case of a single word, myth is present as a single snapshot of a complex process, and that in the case of a narrative myth with its peripety, a complex process is recorded in a single inclusive image? The multilayered montage or "transparency," with its abridgement of logical relationships, is as familiar in the cave painting as in cubism.

Oral cultures are simultaneous in their modes of awareness. Today we come to the oral condition again via the electronic media, which abridge space and time and single-plane relationships, returning us to the confrontation of multiple relationships at the same moment.

If a language contrived and used by many people is a mass medium, any one of our new media is in a sense a new language, a new codification [339] of experience collectively achieved by new work habits and inclusive collective awareness. But when such a new codification has reached the technological stage of communicability and repeatability, has it not, like a spoken tongue, also become a macromyth? How much compression of the elements of a process must occur before one can say that they are certainly in mythic form? Are we inclined to insist that myth be a reduction of collective experience to a visual and classifiable form?

Languages old and new, as macromyths, have that relation to words and word-making that characterizes the fullest scope of myth. The collective skills and experience that constitute both spoken languages and such new languages as movies or radio can also be considered with preliterate myths as static models of the universe. But do they not tend, like languages in general, to be dynamic models of the universe in action? As such, languages old and new would seem to be for participation rather than for contemplation or for reference and classification.

Another way of getting at this aspect of languages as macromyths is to say that the medium is the message. Only incidentally, as it were, is such a medium a specialized means of signifying or of reference. And in the long run, for such media or macromyths as the phonetic alphabet, printing, photography, the movie, the telegraph, the telephone, radio, and television, the social action of these forms is also, in the fullest sense, their message or meaning. A language is, on the one hand, little affected by the use individuals make of it; but, on the other hand, it almost entirely patterns the character of what is thought, felt, or said by those using it. And it can be utterly changed by the intrusion of another language, as speech was changed by writing, and radio by television.

Is, then, what concerns us as "myth" today a photograph or "still" shot of a macromyth in action? As a word uttered is an auditory arrest of mental motion, and the phonetic translation of that sound into visual equivalence is a frozen image of the same, is not myth a means of static abstraction from live process? A kind of mythmaking process is often associated with Holywood and with Madison Avenue advertising agencies. So far as advertisements are concerned, they do, in intention at least, strive to comprise in a single image the total social action or process that is imagined as desirable. That is, an advertisement tries both to inform us about, and also to produce in us by anticipation, all the stages of a metamorphosis, private and [340] social. So that whereas a myth might appear as the record of such extended metamorphosis, an advertisement proceeds by anticipation of change, simultaneously anticipating causes with effects and effects with causes. In myth this fusion and telescoping of phases of process becomes a kind of explanation or mode of intelligibility.

What are the myths by which men have recorded the action of new media on their lives? Is there significance in the fact that the Oedipus myth has so far not been found among the preliterate? Is the action of literacy in the shaping of individualism and nationalism also severe on kinship structures? Is the Gorgon myth an account of the effects of literacy in arresting the modes of knowledge? Certainly the Cadmus myth about letters as the dragon's teeth that sprang up armed men is an image of the dynamics of literacy in creating empires. H. A. Innis in his *Empire and Communications* has given us a full exegesis of the Cadmus myth. But the Gorgon myth is in much greater need of exegesis, since it concerns the role of media in learning and knowing. Today, when by means of a computer it is easy to translate a mere blueprint of an unbuilt plane into a wind-tunnel test flight, we find it natural to take all flat data into the domain of depth interpretation. Electronic culture accepts the simultaneous as a reconquest of auditory space. Since the ear picks up sound from all directions at once, thus creating a spherical field of experience, it is natural that electronically moved information should also assume this spherelike pattern. Since the telegraph, then, the forms of Western culture have been strongly shaped by the spherelike pattern that belongs to a field of awareness in which all the elements are practically simultaneous.

It is this instantaneous character of the information field today, inseparable from electronic media, that confers the formal auditory character on the new culture. That is to say, for example, that the newspaper page, since the introduction of the telegraph, has had a formally auditory character and only incidentally a lineal, literary form. Each item makes its own world, unrelated to any other item save by date line. And the assembly of items constitutes a kind of global image in which there is much overlay and montage but little pictorial space or perspective. For electronically moved information, in being simultaneous, assumes the total-field pattern, as in auditory space. And preliterate societies likewise live largely in the auditory or simultaneous mode with an inclusiveness of awareness that increasingly characterizes our electronic age. The traumatic shock [341] of moving from the segmental, lineal space of literacy into the auditory, unified field of electronic information is quite unlike the reverse process. But today, while we are resuming so many of the preliterate modes of awareness, we can at the same time watch many preliterate cultures beginning their tour through the cultural phases of literacy.

The phonetic alphabet, which permits the translation of the audible into the visible, does so by suppression of meaning in the sounds of the letters. This very abstract technology has made possible a continuous one-way conquest of cultures by the Western world that is far from finished. But it would seem that with the commercial use of the telegraph during more than a century we have become accessible to Eastern art and technology as well as to preliterate and auditory cultures in general. At least, let us be prepared to consider carefully the formally auditory character in the telegraph and in subsequent electronic forms of codifying information. For the formal causes inherent in such media operate on the matter of our senses. The effect of media, like their "message," is really in their form and not in their content. And their formal effect is always subliminal so far as our ideas and concepts are concerned.

It is easy to trace some of the effects of phonetic writing since they are coextensive with the most familiar features of the Western world.

The phonetically written word, itself an abstract image of a spoken word, permits the prolonged analysis of process but does not greatly encourage the application of knowledge to action beyond the verbal sphere. It is not strange, therefore, that the ancient world should have considered applied knowledge under the mode of rhetoric. For writing made it possible to card-catalogue all the individual postures of mind called the "figures" of rhetoric. And these became available to all students as direct means of control over other minds. The oligarchic reign of these figures was swiftly liquidated by printing, a technique that shifted attention from the audience to the mental state of the individual reader

Writing has given the means of segmenting many phases of knowing and doing. Applied knowledge by the lineal segmentation of outward motion comes with print, which is itself the first mechanization of an ancient handicraft. And whereas writing had fostered the classification of the arts and sciences in depth, print gave access to the arts and sciences at high speed and on one plane at a time. While manuscript culture required gloss and commentary to [342] extract the various levels of meaning it held for the awareness, because of the very slow reading necessary, print is itself commentary or explanation. The form of print is single-leveled. And the print-reader is greatly disposed to feel that he is sharing the movements of another mind. Print drove people like Montaigne to explore the medium as a new art form providing an elaborate means of self-investigation in the act of learning, as well as self-portraiture and self-expression.

By contrast, today we live in a postliterate and electronic world, in which we seek images of collective postures of mind, even when studying the individual. In some respects, myth was the means of access to such collective postures in the past. But our new technology gives us many new means of access to group-dynamic patterns. Behind us are five centuries during which we have had unexampled access to aspects of private consciousness by means of the printed page. But now anthropology and archæology give us equal ease of access to group postures and patterns of many cultures, including our own.

Electronic tape permits access to the structure and group dynamics of entire languages. My suggestion that we might regard languages on one hand as mass media and on the other hand as macromyths seems obvious to the point of triteness to the structural linguists to whom I have mentioned these approaches. But it may be useful to point to some of the many nonverbal postures, both individual and public, that accompany changes in the media. That is to say, a new form is usually a cluster of items. For example, in the very first decades of printing at the end of the fifteenth century, people became vividly aware of the camera obscura. The relation of this interest to the new printing process was not noted at the time. Yet printing is itself just such a camera obscura, yielding a private vision of the movements of others. While sitting in the dark, one has in the camera obscura a cinematic presentation of the outside world. And in reading print, the reader acts as a kind of projector of the still shots or printed words, which he can read fast enough to have the feeling of re-creating the movements of another mind. Manuscripts could not be read at a speed sufficient to create the sense of a mind actively engaged in learning and in self-expression. But here, centuries before the movie, is the ultimate magic and myth of the movie in the camera obscura. Perhaps as the camera obscura was the first, the movie is the last phase of print technology. [343]

The movie, which has so little in common with television, may be the last image of the Gutenberg era before it fuses via the telegraph, the telephone, radio, and television, and fades into the new world of auditory space. And as the habits of reading print create intense forms of individualism and nationalism, do not our instantaneous electronic media return us to group dynamics, both in theory and in practice? Is

2. Myth and Mass Media 21

not this shift in media the key to our natural concern with the concept and relevance of myth today?

Printing evoked both individualism and nationalism in the sixteenth century, just as it will do again in India, Africa, China, and Russia. For it demands habits of solitary initiative and attention to exactly repeatable commodities, which are the habits inseparable from industry, and enterprise, production and marketing. Where production precedes literacy, there is no uniform market and no price structure. Industrial production without well-established markets and literacy makes "communism" necessary. Such is the state of our own ignorance of our media that we are surprised to find that radio has very different effects in an oral society than it had in our highly literate culture. In the same way the "nationalism" of an oral world is structured quite differently from the nationalism of a newly literate society. It would appear that to see one's mother tongue dignified with the precise technology of print releases a new vision of unity and power, which remains a subliminal divisive force in the West even today. Unawareness of the effects of our media these past two thousand years and more would seem to be itself an effect of literacy that James Joyce designated as "ab-ced" or absent-mindedness.

The sentiment of spatial and territorial nationalism that accompanies literacy is also reinforced by the printing press, which provides not only the sentiment but also the centralized bureaucratic instruments of uniform control over wide territories.

Perhaps we tend to define myth in too literary a way, as something that can be verbalized, narrated, and written down. If we can regard all media as myths and as the prolific source of many subordinate myths, why cannot we spot the mythic aspect of the current hula-hoop activity? Here is a myth we are living. Many people have puzzled over the fact that children refuse to roll these hoops on roads or walks. A mere thirty years ago a hoop was for rolling. Today children reject the lineal use of the hoop in an external space. They use it in a nuclear mode as a means of generating their own space. Here, then, is a live model or drama of the mythic power of [344] the new media to alter sensibility. For this change in child behavior has nothing to do with ideas or programs.

Such a changed attitude to spatial form and presence is as definitive as the change from the photographic to the television image. In his *Prints and Visual Communication* (London: Routledge and Kegan Paul, 1953), William M. Ivins explains how the long process of capturing the external world in the "network of rationality," by the engraver's line and by ever more subtle syntax, finally reached conclusion in the photograph. The photograph is a total statement of the external object without syntax. This kind of peripety will strike the student of media as characteristic of all media development. But in television the striking fact is that the image is defined by light *through,* not by light *on.* It is this fact that separates television from photography and movie, relating it profoundly to stained glass. The spatial sense generated by television experience is utterly unlike that of the movie. And, of course, the difference has nothing to do with the "content" or the programing. Here, as ever, the medium itself is the ultimate message. The child gets such messages, when they are new, much sooner than the adult. For the adult instinctively retards awareness that will disturb a cherished order of perception or of past experience; the child would seem to have no such stake in the past, at least when he is facing new experience.

It is my point that new spatial orientation such as occurs in the format of the press after the advent of the telegraph, the swift disappearnce of perspective, is also discernible in the new landscapes of Rimbaud in poetry and Cézanne in painting. And in our time Rouault anticipated the mode of the television image by decades. His use of stained glass as a means of defining the image is what I have in mind.

The mythmaking power of a medium that is itself a myth form appears now in the postliterate age as the rejection of the consumer in favor of the producer. The movie now can be seen as the peak of the consumer-oriented society, being in its form the natural means both of providing and of glorifying consumer goods and attitudes. But in the arts of the past century the swing has been away from packaging for the consumer to providing do-it-yourself kits. The spectator or reader must now be cocreator. Our educational establishment naturally lags behind the popular media in this radical change. The young, when exposed to the television image, receive at once a total orientation in spatial matters that makes the lineality of the printed word a remote and alien language. Reading for them will have to be [345] taught as if it were heraldry or some quaint codification of reality. The assumptions about reading and writing that accompanied the monarchy of print and the related rise of industrial forms are no longer valid for, or acceptable to, those being re-formed in their sensibilities in the electronic age. To ask whether this is a good or a bad thing is to express the bias of efficient causality, which is naturally that of the man of the printed word. But it is also a futile gesture of inadequacy to the real situation. The values of the Gutenberg era cannot be salvaged by those who are as unaware of how they came into existence as they are of why they are now in the process of liquidation.

Philosophic agreement is not necessary among those who are agreed that the insistent operation of media-forms on human sensibility and awareness is an observable, intelligible, and controllable situation.

Today, when ordinary consciousness is exposed to the patternmaking of several media at once, we are becoming more attentive to the unique properties of each of the media. We can see both that media are mythic "images" and that they have the power of imposing subliminally, as it were, their own assumptions. They can be viewed at the same time as intelligible explanations of great tracts of time and of the experience of many processes, and they can be used as a means of perpetuating such bias and preference as they codify in their structure.

It is not strange that we should long have been obsessed with the literary and "content" aspect of myth and media. The "form" and "content" dichotomy is as native to the abstract, written, and printed forms of codification as is the "producer" and "consumer" dichotomy.

Unfortunately for the direction and control of education, such a literary bias is quite unable to cope with the new "images" of the postliterate age. As a result of our using literary lenses, the relevant new data have escaped our scrutiny. My book, *The Mechanical Bride: Folklore of Industrial Man*, is a case in point. Turning literary guns on the new iconology of the Madison Avenue world is easy. It is easy to reveal mechanism in a postmechanical era. But I failed at that time to see that we had already passed out of the mechanistic age into the electronic, and that it was this fact that made mechanism both obtrusive and repugnant.

One of the great novelties effected by printing was the creation of a new sense of inner and outer space. We refer to it as the discovery of perspective and the rise of representation in the arts. The space [346] of "perspective" conditioned by an artificially fixed stance for the viewer leads to the enclosing of objects in a pictorial space. Yet so revolutionary and abstract was this new space that poets avoided it in their language for two centuries after painters had accepted it. It is a kind of space very uncongenial to the media of speech and of words. One can gain some idea of the psychic pressures exerted by print in the work of William Blake, who sought new strategies of culture to reintegrate the segmented and fractured human spirit. In fact, the explicit mythmaking of Blake is the greatest monument and antidote to the mythic pressures of the printing press, to "single vision and Newton's sleep." For the matrix of movable type contains the totality of industrialism as well as the means of global conquest, which, by peripety, brought the preliterate world once more into the heart of the industrial metropolis.

The prevalent concept that the mass media exert a baneful influence on the human spirit has strange roots. As Marjorie Nicolson has shown in *Newton Demands the Muse*, it was Newton's *Opticks* that taught poets the correspondence between the inner and outer worlds, between the structure of seeing and the structure of the scene. This notion planted in poets the ambition to gain control over the inner life by a calculus of landscape composition. The idea of verbally constituted landscape, as a lever upon the psychic eye of man, was a dichotomy quite congenial to the culture of the printed word. And whereas external landscape has been abandoned for inner landscape since Rimbaud, Madison Avenue clings to the earlier Romantic concept of consumer control by means of externally arranged scenes. The recent flutter about "subliminal" advertising indicates the delayed shift of attention from outer to inner landscape that occurred in many of the arts in the later nineteenth century. And it is this same shift that today focuses attention on myth in all its modes. For myth is always a montage or transparency comprising several external spaces and times in a single image or situation. Such compression or multilayering is an inescapable mode of the electronic and simultaneous movement of information, whether in popular media or esoteric speculation. It is, therefore, an everyday occurrence for academic entertainment to stress "content," while displaying complete illiteracy with regard to media old and new. For we have now to possess many cultural languages for even the most ordinary daily purposes.

The newspaper will serve as an example of the Babel of myths or [347] languages. When information from every quarter arrived at the same time, the paper became a daily snapshot of the globe, and "perspective" in news became meaningless. Editorials could still try to tie some items together into a chain or sequence with a special point of view or vanishing point. But such views were really capsules for passive readers, while, paradoxically, the unprocessed, uninterpreted, raw news offered far more challenge to the reader to find his own meanings. Today it is easy to see how Edgar Allen Poe, both in his symbolist poems and in his detective stories, had anticipated this new mythic dimension of producer orientation by taking the audience into the creative process itself. Likewise, it is easy to see how the spot news of the telegraph press really acts like the yes-no, black-white dots of the wirephoto in creating an inclusive world image. Yet even now the sponsors of preelectronic media continue to overlay the new myth by injections of earlier myth, creating hybrids of the "horseless carriage" variety in the interests of superior culture.

The same type of confusion exists in education in the concept of "audio-visual aids." It would seem that we must do in education what the poets, painters, and composers have done, namely, to purge our media and test and define their unique powers before attempting Wagnerian concerts. The Gutenberg myth was not a means of modifying the Cadmus myth, any more than the Henry Ford myth modified the horse and buggy. Obliteration occurred, as it will with the movie under the impact of television, unless we choose to restrain the operation of form on form by due study and strategy. We now stand at that point with regard to all myth and media. We can, perhaps we *must,* become the masters of cultural and historical alchemy. And to this end we can, I suggest, find means in the study of media as languages and languages as myths. For our experience with the grammar and syntax of languages can be made available for the direction and control of media old and new. [348]

3. The Entertainer as Hero: A Problem of the Mass Media
Patrick D. Hazard

The American media system, largely to facilitate its function as a marketing agency, has made the entertainer in our culture vastly more visible than he has any right to be. This inevitably means that occupational roles and activities much more crucial to the proper functioning of a free society are less noticeable, even invisible. Teenage idols, television and motion picture stars, sports champions and media-created celebrities crowd out the scientist, educator, legislator and artist from the vision of the great majority of our people. In my judgment, this misemphasis accounts in great measure for the crisis of quality in both American life and mass communication.

That the entertainer is too much a hero in American culture may seem too obvious a matter to document, but it perhaps will be useful to pick up a few coordinates that reveal the depth and breadth of this popular esteem to refresh our memories. When Arthur Godfrey was hospitalized a few years ago, over 200,000 messages of sympathy were sent to him. When Ed Byrnes had a falling out with Warner Brothers over salary and his comb was suspended for five months from "77 Sunset Strip," 90,000 irate viewers besieged the network to bring "Kookie" back. Dick Clark's "American Bandstand" pulled almost 300,000 mail votes in its annual dance contest.

Indeed, the fan club system and its subsidiary communication networks are an institutionalization of the affection many people have for their entertainer heroes. Roughly 25% of the titles on most newsstands

Source: Journalism Quarterly 39, no. 4 (Autumn 1962): 436–44. Reprinted by permission of the author and the publisher.

3. The Entertainer as Hero: A Problem of the Mass Media 27

can be classified in the Fan-Romance magazine category, according to *Newsdealer,* a trade publication.

Combined sales run 33 million a month, almost 400 million copies a year. This total includes *TV Guide,* an enormously successful magazine which itself eschews the fan magazine identification and which indeed has run sound editorials and elder statesman essays on the new medium alongside its personality pieces—both to high consistency readership. The "one shot" magazine specializes in entertainment and do-it-yourself titles. Dick Clark sold 180,000 of his one-dollar one-shot simply by holding it up on the air over "American Bandstand." The Elvis Presley one-shot sold almost a million copies. [436]

But more significant for our purposes—a study of how the entertainer is preempting the attention of the general public to the default of other more serious and necesary purposes—is the way the entertainer dominates general interest media, especially since the rise of television and the emergence of the teenage market have given him greater visibility than ever before.

NBC, CBS and Columbia Pictures have done a confidential study of the familiarity and popularity of 595 performers in 11 categories. The most significant finding that can be released is that no movie star who has not been on TV (except Bing Crosby) scores high in the tenth decile of familiarity while many moderately successful TV stars (e.g., Jack Webb, actually off TV for two years) score higher than standard box office draws, such as Gary Cooper and Cary Grant. Indeed, several television performers were more familiar to the study's split panel of 2,000 than Eisenhower (which may merely mean that golf isn't a telegenic sport).

One way to see the impact of TV on entertainer visibility is to analyze the medium itself. Quite apart from the five-hour daily lien the medium has on the attention of over nine-tenths of American families is the focus of the TV's nonfiction content. In his classic study of popular magazine biographies, Leo Lowenthal found a clearcut shift from heroes of production at the turn of the 20th century to heroes of consumption at the eve of World War II. My investigation of the subjects on "Person to Person," "This Is Your Life" and "The Mike Wallace Interview" affords striking evidence of how the more broadly based television medium has further increased the dominance of the entertainer as the focus of attention. Moreover, the ecology of American mass medium of our culture being what it is, TV's ascendancy as the central mass medium of our culture has caused other media, magazines particularly, to depend increasingly on the entertainer for circulation.

For example, Ralph Edwards' "This Is Your Life" (NBC-TV), has surprised 321 different subjects since it went on the air in the fall of 1952.

One hundred and sixty (50%) were entertainers. Significantly, the summer reruns (presumably the most popular individual shows of the preceding season) had entertainers for subjects 68.9% of the time. "Person to Person," surprisingly—since it was chaired for six of its seven years over CBS-TV by the dean of broadcast commentators, Edward R. Murrow, had an even stronger entertainer bias. Using Lowenthal's categories, politicians or the military were subjects 66 times out of a possible 480 (13%), businessmen appeared 48 times (10%), and entertainers, if one includes journalists, accounted for 368 out of the 480 appearances (76%). On the other hand, four educators appeared in seven years.

It is often difficult to decide at any point in time whether a ubiquitous star belongs to the movies or TV, but by my lights and by the economics of free plugging, the movie star was the most frequent host for the electronic visits of Edward R. Murrow and Charles Collingwood. Eighty-three movie stars took up 17.3% of the quarter-hours. By comparison, 18 businessmen, 8 lawyers, 2 labor leaders, 6 clergymen, 1 architect, 1 designer, 1 philanthropist, and (who are we to bushel our lights?) 1 social scientist were visited. Forty-eight popular singers (10%) swapped notes with 26 (5.5%) serious musicians. There were 26 stage performers, 35 sports figures, 3 dancers, 3 royalty, 2 cartoonists, 1 society bandleader, 1 circus performer, 5 artists, and, last but not lustfully, a minion of Minsky's.

An analysis of a year's subjects on "The Mike Wallace Interview" (March 9, 1959–March 4, 1960) over *WNTA-TV,* the now dark but then offbeat, above-average New York independent station, continues to show TV's overemphasis [437] of the entertainer as hero. Of the 260 programs, 54 (21%) were devoted to politicians or people concerned with the structure of power, 26 (10%) to businessmen, and 180 (69%) to entertainers. This high figure is surprising since *WNTA-TV* had been striving for an intellectual image; perhaps the syndication of these interviews outside the New York market influences the selection of guests. In the 29 weeks that Wallace was on ABC-TV, exclusive of the series sponsored by the Fund for the Republic, 17 (52%) were entertainers, 9 were politicians (30%) and the rest were either from business or unclassifiable.

The Thrust of TV and Teen Culture

When a medium with the reach and advertising impact of television focuses on the entertainer in such a concentrated way, it is a bold medium policy-maker indeed who refuses to yield to the temptation to fight fire with fire. The success of *TV Guide* is partly dependent on the

3. The Entertainer as Hero: A Problem of the Mass Media 29

entertainer covers which in a few cases (Godfrey, Welk, Liberace and the early Presley) "sold" its largely newsstand circulation. The magazines considered competitive with *TV Guide*, the general weeklies, use entertainers to a considerable extent in their editorial and marketing strategies. The Pete Martin "I Call On . . ." features in the *Saturday Evening Post* are often streamered at the top of the outside cover as well as pre-promoted in the advertising fraternity by two-column ads in the daily *New York Times*. In the 51 covers that *Life* ran in 1959, 24 (47%) were entertainer oriented.

Another major magazine category—the woman's service field—is also responding to the thrust of the entertainer on the consciousness of the general public. *McCall's*, for example, a recent success story in this field with accounts for 158,602,092 copies a year, second only to the fan-romance group, has been taking full-page ads in the *New York Times* to publicize its new editorial policies. "Through the pages of *McCall's* pass the most exciting books of our time—making *McCall's* the women's service magazine with the most to read, and the best to read." A footnote explains that a majority have gone from *McCall's* pages to best seller lists. "Read any good books lately?" the copy enjoins. The trouble with this form of literary criticism is that 15 of the 21 books cited are a product of celebrity culture (Fred Astaire, Arlene Francis, Zsa Zsa Gabor, etc.). Of the remainder, four appear to be light humor, and two are autobiographies of Anthony Eden and a photojournalist who has conquered ill health.

In another full-page promotion in the *Times,* the *McCall's* copy reads: "Class of 60: Each member of this distinguished group will have appeared in the pages of *McCall's* in 1960. Each is helping, in 1960, to make *McCall's* first in its class—First Magazine for Women." Eleven out of 20 honorary baccalaureate degrees awarded by this smart finishing school were for entertainers, or entertainment writers: Art Buchwald, Maurice Chevalier, Arlene Francis, Zsa Zsa Gabor, Paul Gallico, Dave Garroway, Jean Kerr, Alexander King, Ogden Nash, Abby Van Buren, Maurice Zolotow. The other members of the class were Anthony Eden, Dr. Fishbein, Dr. Hutchins, Clare Booth Luce, Princess Margaret, Eleanor Roosevelt, Adela Rogers St. John, Ginette Spanier and the Duke of Windsor.

This formula was applied by *Ladies' Home Journal* in its Pat Boone column. Boone's teenage advice book has already sold almost half a million hardbound copies and is out in paper covers. *Good Housekeeping* has found an angle for fitting entertainers into its more austere format by publishing pieces like Richard Gehman's sanctimonious warning about Frank Sinatra's power in the entertainment industry.

The competitive squeeze makes it not surprising then to find a two-column ad in *Look* on behalf of *Reader's Digest* invoking the great bibliophile Jack Paar [438] on behalf of digesting print: "Jack Paar counts on reading to keep his shows vital and entertaining. He says, 'No matter how busy I am, I keep pumping supplies of new material into my reservoir by reading.'"

Even so good a series as "Reading Out Loud" by as enlightened a broadcaster as Westinghouse finds itself using the celebrity to popularize reading in a joint effort with the American Library Association. Its "fifteen of the nation's most prominent people" turn out to be eight stars, two writers, three political figures, one businessman and one TV teacher. The format of the series was to have celebrities read to their children or grandchildren, on the implicit premise that what looks good to these famous people and their families, should look better than it now does to the mass audience.

It may be useful to assess briefly the growing impact of the entertainer on the book industry. The marketability of teenage advice books has already been mentioned although I have yet to recover from Patti Page's philosophical reflections on how to get in tune with God. Once again Jack Paar is instructive: When Marie Torre asked him if he intended to write another book, he replied with characteristic innocence and humility: "I did not intend to. I had no idea how hard it was to fill that many pages. But the first book has turned out to be one of the best sellers of the year, and when you consider that it has neither been reviewed nor even mentioned by any of the New York press, you must admit it is either a good book, or there is a demand for expensive door stops. I was amazed how profitable it turned out to be. I make notes every week now for a second book, 'Son of I Kid You Not.'"

There is indeed some evidence that the Jack Paar show itself may replace *Publisher's Weekly* as the major medium for merchandising books. Paar, Jack Douglas, Cliff Arquette and Hugh Downs have all launched best sellers, or what *Time* deprecatingly calls non-books. Art Linkletter was MC at the convention banquet of the American Booksellers Association in 1960, where he solemnly vowed that in addition to plugging his own memoirs, he was going to stimulate book buying and book reading by mentioning titles at least once a week on his TV shows, "House Party" and "People Are Funny." The two examples he gave at the convention were David Duncan's picture book of *The Kremlin* and *A Pictorial History of Wall Street*. How's that for visualizing the Cold War of ideas?

His publisher, Bernard Geis, specializes in show business books, and when the firm was launched a few years ago, it was a dull night on TV when Groucho Marx wasn't a guest, mystery or otherwise, encouraging reading in the younger generation. Geis thinks the publishing business is too stuffy and that is why Americans are such lazy readers. As the leading impresario of non-books, *Time* interviewed him: "I want to do anything that can be done to get the audience back to books." Then he adds, less piously, "I don't care what kind of book it is."

What this misemphasis amounts to in the long run, of course, is that important sectors of our society—science, business, education and the undramatic institutions that constitute an urban civilization are systematically neglected. I find it significant, for example, that while there are only 58 active and 64 associate members of the Education Writers Association (founded in 1947), there were already over 500 members of the Football Writers Association 11 years after it was founded in 1941.

There are more in the stage and screen section of the Foreign Press Club (150) than there are in our education writers corps. When politics becomes entertainment as in the televised conventions, the press personnel of over 5,000 surpasses the number of delegates. The 1960 Olympic press corps has been estimated at between 1,000 [439] and 1,200; the UN press corps is 405. The National Association of Science Writers has 317 members.

Entertainers and the Public Interest
Ever since P. T. Barnum polished his own tarnished escutcheon by bringing culture to America in the person of Jenny Lind, it has been good public relations in show business to support worthy causes. Indeed, Ralph Edwards has tried recently to counter criticism of programming he produces by pointing to the fringe benefits he provides for his own commonweal. "Edwards," John Crosby writes, "is belligerently defensive about 'This Is Your Life,' which a good many people (including me) find excruciatingly intrusive. 'The show,' he'll tell you, 'has not received—in the eyes of a certain few—credit for what it has accomplished. Its first impact is an emotional one. Most of the things written about the show have never shown what it accomplished. When you can endow an educational foundation of a million dollars, when you can give Medico $150,000 to continue Tom Dooley's great work, when you can raise half-a-million dollars for Hungarian relief in half-an-hour show. We have done things like that dozens of times. This means the show has more than a flimsy format. We believe in our opening statement which says that the show is in the American tradition.'"

The principle involved, it seems to me, is that the entertainer's real responsibility is the quality of his performance and how much of it there is to put up with. His subsidiary roles must be judged individually on their own merits, and are less important intrinsically. His public interest sideshows are less important than the way he interests the public in his main tent. The level of his appeal to the audience is more significant to our society than the appeals he makes on behalf of polio prevention.

Being against disease is a standard ploy of the show business personality. It gets them where most people live (or keep wanting to), and besides it is less demanding than being against sin, the standard crusade. One can sympathize with George Gobel's complaint that the trouble with being a new comedian is that by the time you arrive on the scene they've run out of all the good diseases. And then there's the remark attributed to Sherman Billingsley, who used to greet one of his show business friends with the chilling query, "What's new in muscular dystrophy?" Leave it at this, the entertainer's seriousness about what ails man's body at least gives a sense of grandeur to syndicated gossips like Earl Wilson who flourished in a recent column: "Bob Hope should be pleased to know that 14 leading ophthalmologists from all over the U.S. worked all of a beautiful Sunday not even going out for lunch to apportion the $100,000 for Fight-for-Sight research which he raised by guest-starring on two Arthur Murray shows."

One of the least likely subsidiary roles for the entertainer is as a pillar of formal education. Yet at a recent commencement, Tri-State College of Angola, Indiana, awarded the same Earl Wilson an honorary doctorate, and Springfield College in Massachusetts invented the degree of Doctor of Humanics for Art Linkletter, an ugly neologism for a sinister parody of higher education.

Religion is making similarly questionable compromises with the entertainer ethos. A syndicated TV religious program, "The Christophers," has a format of Father Keller sugarcoating the theological pill with a star and then turning the show over to ordinary people. I watched a program devoted to improving standards of entertainment featuring Ruth Hussey. The theme was that we need joy and fun in our lives; and that we ought to demand from producers "the good wholesome fun God intends us to have." Such as "Monsignor Knows Best," starring Bing Crosby? [440]

Bob Hope hit it just right when he referred to a religious film he was involved in for Father Keller with Bing Crosby and Ben Hogan, as "Faith, Hope, and Hogan." It's hard to tell which is worse, the entertainment itself or the "oh so chummy" plea for better entertainment. At least it avoids the archness of Dr. Ralph Stoody, public relations director for the Methodist Church, in his reflections on "Religion and Madison Avenue": "Centuries before Madison Avenue, U.S.A., even thought of implanting desires for merchandise by singing their virtues over the airways, the church harmonized its appeals, its advantages

3. The Entertainer as Hero: A Problem of the Mass Media 33

and its invitations. The men in the gray flannel suit have obviously borrowed the idea for the singing commercial." And it avoids the intolerable cuteness of a new teenage biography of Jesus, in which Jericho becomes "plush," and the Blessed Virgin Mary "the greatest, the most," and the Magi did not report back to Herod because they were not the type to "blab." Such acquiescence in absurdity makes about as much sense as ordaining "Kookie" to get closer to the teenager. The Rev. Herman W. Gockel, producer of the religious television series, "This Is the Life," is defending Hollywood stars against the charge of low morals and praising them because they appear on his program for pay three to four times below scale. He assures the potential viewer that "The show is not preachy, though. Entertainment is first."

Politics is another public domain where the entertainer is called upon to hypo a glassy-eyed public into some semblance of consciousness. For example, Metropolitan Broadcasting—one of the most provocative of the independent groups—corralled a group of VIP's and celebrities for three-minute spiels to get out and vote. Among them were James A. Farley, Sid Caesar, Al Capp, Cardinal Spellman, Buddy Hackett, Norman Thomas, Milton Caniff, Eleanor Roosevelt and Helen Hayes. Jack Paar, in this as in most things, has his own way. When not fiddling with his visual Gallup Poll, the applauseometer, he is sidling up to candidates and coyly asking on the air of Kennedy, "May I call you John?" Paar was never satisfied with the court jester's role; he aspired to the throne itself.

Fashion marketing also uses an entertainer format. Max Factor Cosmetics, Inc., for example, sponsors "Max Factor's True Skin Beauty Time" which has Barbara Factor dispensing beauty hints accompanied by background music. Rainbow Records (owned by Jack Brown, partnered by writer-producer Jess Oppenheimer) also produced 30,000,000 disks for General Mills to be attached to their "Wheaties" cereal, incorporating eight different disks of children's tunes. This "incognito" label makes its specially designed presses for producing disks from film and various acetate products available to various manufacturers of consumer products, including Times Square type "novelties" such as "the world's smallest long-playing record," a three-and-a-half-inch (size of a record label) disk for Russ Morgan.

The Fuller Brush man, I recently found, leaves four-color brochures that are all but wired for a Jackie Gleason type romance album, with themes such as "my visit to the ski jumps at Aspen, Colorado," one page of brushes followed by one page of vicarious jumping. A foot in the door was bad enough! Contests, too, are big business in advertising. Six hundred thousand "typically average people" tried for prizes in 1960 in contests in the tradition started by Barnum's offer of $200 for the best "Ode to America" for Jenny Lind. This amounts to $50 million in prizes and $500 million in promoting the contests themselves. Stars are also being tapped to give visibility to comprehensive marketing plans. This is standard practice for TV stars, but Kaiser Aluminum once hired Eddie Albert as entertainment consultant for its [441] "planned" city, Hawaii Kai. His first job was to plan the theatres and put closed-circuit educational television in each house and school. "Mr Kaiser builds the cities and I make them fun to live in," was Albert's way of looking at it.

The integration of fun into the marketing system continues also at the level of the salesmen themselves. What Abel Green calls "the free enterprise circuit" really started in the 1930's but grows with each passing year. The Cole Porter "You're the Top!" which opened on Broadway August 16, 1960, happens to be the way Oldsmobile was selling its salesmen on the new (automobile) model. Florence Henderson was the star, Carol Haney the producer, Larry Blyden the director. This example of "the industrial show technique of combining business with pleasure" had a Broadway-size budget of $400–$500,000 for its 10-week stand in New York, Atlanta, Detroit, Dallas and San Francisco. Similarly, Philco assembled its dealers and distributors in 51 cities by holding a closed-circuit open house, after which refreshments (including the Patterson-Johanson fight) were served.

The closed circuit industry also uses TV newscasters such as Frank Blair and Chet Huntley as "lures" for its product demonstrations. This seems to me to raise an important ethical question for newscasters, a problem that was particularly clear in the case of Mike Wallace and Phillip Morris cigarettes. In an article on the president of the firm in *Esquire* (May 1960), it was revealed that the company believed Mike Wallace was a good choice for Phillip Morris because his believability as a reporter and investigator gave an aura of objectivity to his commercials. A related problem of conflicting roles is that presented by Ronald Reagan's "stumping around the country lecturing GE employees on the evils of Social Security, Federal aid for schools and the Tennesse Valley Authority."

Professional Communications Education in the Entertainer's Culture

This survey of typical instances of the entertainer's involvement in roles other than his own leads naturally to some suggestions for a countervailing strategy. It seems to me that at least four areas deserve consideration: 1) the clarification of policy alternatives for media managers;

3. The Entertainer as Hero: A Problem of the Mass Media 35

2) revision of our history of the press to emphasize more sharply the rise of entertainer dominance and particularly the relationships and traditions that obtain between politics and culture, the uses of power and the abuses of leisure; 3) changes in the editorial training sector of communications education based on these new policies and new historical perspective; and 4) changes in the business and marketing phase of communications education to accommodate a more critical climate of belief about the responsibilities of media managers. A few words on these aspects.

1) It seems to me that Edward Stanley and his staff at NBC have worked out a sound interim policy as we (hopefully) dig out from under the burden of the anti-intellectual tradition of entertainer dominance. In his six-program series on cancer in 1959, produced by the network for National Educational Television and the American Cancer Society, he started from the assumption that the threatening aspect of this disease would make almost everyone, and especially those who most need counsel, tune out. To overcome this psychological block, Stanley's staff put scientists and entertainers on a panel together—having used UPA cartoons, Walt Kelly, Ilka Chase and others to arrest the attention of the audience for the series in earlier programs.

In an analogous way, the general public after two full generations of idolizing the entertainers, finds the thought of international peril as threatening as most individuals feel with respect to cancer. Thus when Irving Gitlin engaged [442] movie stars as hosts for projected nighttime documentaries on CBS, or female celebrities as hostesses to wean housewives away from the soap operas when he telecast the daytime documentary "Woman" series, he discovered a legitimate *interim strategy* for brining back the national attention to matters that count.

So long as the editorial control remains firmly in the hands of intellectually responsible people, I see no danger to standards of objectivity and competence (as I do in the case of Mike Wallace and Ronald Reagan—the first providing the illusion of objectivity, and the second the illusion of competence). The long-range goal, of course, is a people not so entertained to death that they can watch a serious presentation on an important matter without having to be wheedled into attention like children.

2) The history of the press needs to be re-examined in terms of the new needs of the 1960's. The crisis in the national purpose is a crisis in moribund idealism. There are traditions of muckracking and respect for excellence that need restatement in our suffocating, bland era in which paid mimeographers are replacing legmen. Such a new history of the American press would bring together communication of every dimension from significant minority statements such

as George Tooker's and Philip Evergood's recent paintings satirizing entertainers, off-Broadway plays about the seamy side of progress such as Jack Gelber's "The Connection" and Edward Albee's "The Zoo Story" to the latest teen fan magazine. Such a history would not be value-free and aloof from the struggle over excellence in America today, but it would attempt to identify and, by describing, amplify mature trends within the media.

For example, there was a most interesting editorial reprinted from the Tulsa *Tribune* in *Editor & Publisher;* with a very shrewd historical sense, Jenkin Lloyd Jones admitted in effect that the entertainer worship that caught on in American media in the 1920's was tolerable in 1930, but no longer was it something to tolerate. Entitled "We grow more thoughtful . . .," the editorial argues: "Who would have thought that the education 'run' would become a big one on our paper. Or that science news—not the gee-whiz-pseudo-science of the old Sunday supplements—but good solid information on the breathtaking rush of the new technology, the new medicine, the new space wonders, should have such high priority with us. . . . No wonder we don't have as much space for the silly gyrations of saloon 'celebrities' and Hollywood exhibitionists as we used to have . . . this editor, and many of his colleagues on other newspapers, have concluded that the thirst for information and the hunger for solutions to the problems of modern living are of far more significance in modern journalism than the scandal-mongering, sensationalism or the purveyance of trivialities. We hope to keep the Tulsa *Tribune* bright. But our biggest ambition is to make it thoughtful."

The next history of the press in America will record, we hope, the rise (and decline) of the entertainment press corps, a group of expendable writers to be replaced by well-paid and literate critics of the popular arts who understand the importance of good education, science, and business reporters and analysts.

3) The communication schools should tool up now for the reporters and critics needed in these new journalistic specialties. It would seem to me that this new cadre of commentators on American civilization would profit if their education were jointly planned by Association for Education in Journalism and American Studies Association members.

4) The business sector of communications education is the part of our common enterprise that I am least familiar with, but I do feel that here, too, there should be more collaboration than there is between specialists in the history [443] and arts of American civilization and specialists in marketing and management. I am not proposing a love feast, because I think in the long run a healthy animosity will keep both parties on their respective professional toes. I think there is bound to be in industrialized America a natural (and possibly useful) tension be-

3. The Entertainer as Hero: A Problem of the Mass Media

tween the speculative and the practical intellectual, between the artist and the salesman. As long as "the smile comes with the territory," there is bound to be a kind of optimism built into our marketing system that in normal times is dangerous enough but in our day may lead to losses we cannot sustain.

For it seems to me that the business community has not honestly faced the historical fact of its responsibility for the prodigality of American culture. In the 19th century, the robber baron strip-mined our natural resources and said "the public be damned." In the 20th century, we have a newer and more subtle form of prodigality. This involves the show business robber baron who knows too much (he may even have an M.B.A. from Harvard) to rationalize his actions by arguing that "business is business." The new assumption is the flashier "show business is show business," and whatever marketing does to the media system and its audiences is therefore justified. The old shibboleth of the public be damned has been replaced by the more flattering demagoguery of "We only give the public what it wants." The result of this new form of prodigality has been the strip-mining of an equally precious artificial resource—leisure. If our culture is to mature (not to beat the Russians, but because it's a damn shame if we don't, considering the breaks history has given us), then our media must mature. I don't think they can as long as our business leaders solve their marketing problems the easy way—by putting the entertainer on a pedestal that casts more rational objects of respect and affection in the shade. [444]

4. Why the Mass Media Are That Way
Theodore Peterson

In the past few years a good many persons have been lining up, like sailors at a shooting gallery, to draw a bead on the various mass media of communication. A. J. Liebling, for one, has published his essays about our "monovocal, monopolistic, monocular press." Newton Minow has spoken about television fare with such vehemence and frequency that he has given the term "wasteland" a currency that T. S. Eliot never did. And Robert Lekachman, in the greatest heresy of all, has charged that our good magazines, our *Harper's* and *Atlantic* and *Nation,* are not good enough, are not the equal of their British counterparts.

Editors, publishers, and broadcasters have learned to live with this criticism, but they have seldom learned to like it. Their reactions have varied from surprised hurt and mild petulance on the one hand to red-faced indignation and savage counterattack on the other.

I cannot agree with those publishers and broadcasters who seem to think that finding fault with the mass media is somehow un-American, like setting out poisoned Ken-L-Ration for Lassie. My aim is not to argue that the American mass media are the best in the world, although I think they are. It is evading the issue to say that our media are the best or even good. The word "good," after all, has many meanings, as G. K. Chesterton reminds us with his remark that a man who shoots his grandmother at five hundred yards may be a good shot but not necessarily a good man. [405]

The truth is that I sometimes agree with what the critics have to say about press performance. But when I do, I often have the uneasy feeling that they are right for the wrong reasons and that one may as well look to Dr. Seuss for richness of character and complexity of plot as to look to them for sensible prescriptions. So what I propose to do is to touch on a major stream of press criticism that I think is bound to be futile, to examine its assumptions and shortcomings, and then to suggest, a little hesitantly, a direction that I think holds greater promise.

The strain of criticism that strikes me as essentially futile blames publishers and broadcasters for all of the shortcomings of the mass media. In its many variations, this line of criticism sees the men who own and operate the media as merely foolish, as irresponsible, or as downright evil. The common denominator of the variations is that the media are bad because the men who own and operate them are in some way bad.

That idea is almost as old as printing itself. In the sixteenth century, even before the newspaper came to England, critics were grumbling about the half-penny chroniclers who scampered off to scribble verses for its precursor, the broadside. When newspapers did appear, the men who ran them came in for some abuse. Samuel Johnson, who had opinions on all subjects worth having opinions about and on a good many that were not, delivered his views on newsmen in 1758: "The compilation of News-papers is often committed to narrow minds, not qualified for the task of delighting or instructing; who are content to fill their pages with whatever matter, without industry to gather, or discernment to select." His observations were mild compared with the American variety, especially those in the period of bitter partisan journalism in the late eighteenth and early nineteenth centuries, when the press deserved all of the criticism it got. James Ward Fenno, an old newspaperman himself, said in 1799:

> The American newspapers are the most base, false, servile, and venal publications, that ever polluted the fountains of society—their editors the most ignorant, mercenary and vulgar automatons that ever were moved by the continually rusting wires of sordid mercantile avarice. [406]

In our own century, by far the great bulk of press criticism, I think, has blamed the owners and operators for the shortcomings of the media. A good deal of it arises from what we might call the conspiratorial theory of press malfunction—the notion that publishers and broadcasters have conspired with big business to promote and to protect their mutual interests, that in exchange for suppressing and distorting media content they share in such handsome rewards as advertising contracts, social position, and political prominence.

Will Irwin set the themes for much of such criticism in a series of articles about newspapers that he wrote for *Collier's* back in 1911. Advertisers had come to realize their power over the press, he said, and in some instances they had been taught it by the newspapers themselves. To attract customers for advertising space, some papers had made concessions to advertisers. In time advertisers came to take these concessions as special privileges—insertion of publicity; biased news accounts; suppression of news harmful to the advertiser, his family, his associates and his business interests; and, in rare instances, a complete change in editorial policy. Irwin was perceptive enough to recognize that many shortcomings of the newspaper arise not from the harmful influence of advertising but from the commercial nature of the press, and he observed that simply because publishers are businessmen, the newspapers they control might be expected to reflect the viewpoint of business.

Irwin was followed by a succession of critics who reiterated his charges, although not always with his perception. In 1912, after he had already clubbed the packing industry with his wooden prose, Upton Sinclair brought out *The Brass Check,* which likened the press to a vast brothel in which truth was the virtue for sale. *The Brass Check* has been almost as durable as its author, who has written a book for each of his eighty-four years, for it went through several editions and was revised in 1936. Sinclair's pitch was that the "Empire of Business" controls journalism by four devices—by direct ownership of the press, by ownership of the owners, by advertising subsidy, and by direct bribery.

The "empire of business" idea was a favorite one in the Depression of the 1930's, when businessmen were low in popular esteem, and critic after critic described how knights of that empire worked [407] hand in hand with the press to thwart the common good. Harold L. Ickes contended that publishers made up America's House of Lords, a body enriching and enhancing the power of the economic royalists whose ideology had a well-filled purse as its core. George Seldes saw the lords of the press as polluting the fountain of truth by suppressing news or distorting it and plotting evil behind closed doors at meetings of the American Newspaper Publishers Association. Ferdinand Lundberg wrote scathingly of Imperial Hearst, and other writers did portraits of other publishers in acid.

Today critics seldom speak of "lords of the press," a term that sounds a little dated, but they sometimes do number media owners among "the power elite." And quite a few critics evidently do assume that Sinclair and Seldes and Ickes were right in blaming the owners and operators for a good share of what is wrong with the media.

Their line of thought, let me confess, is rather appealing. For one thing, there is enough truth in it to make it seem valid. The media *are* big business, and their outlook *does* tend to be that of big business generally. For another thing, the way to improvement is then comparatively easy: Somehow, through punishment or persuasion, we must make the media owners pure of heart; then the press will be as great as publishers say it is during National Newspaper Week, and television will become man's greatest achievement since the pyramids. Charles Dickens had a similar explanation for the ills of nineteenth-century England, and his solution was equally simple: Let evil-doers be shown their errors, and they will join their nobler fellows in a merry dance of brotherhood around the Christmas tree.

Criticism that does little more than blame the men who own and operate the mass media is bound to be futile, I think, for it rests on debatable if not downright erroneous assumptions.

One is that most owners and operators lack a sense of social responsibility. Now, some publishers do show a deeper concern over what paper costs than over what they print on it, and some broadcasters do regard the public airwaves as their personal, exploitable property. Even so, I am prepared to argue that most publishers and broadcasters have a greater sense of public responsibility than a good many critics give them credit for having—one as high as that of most leaders in business and government, and perhaps higher. At times [408] their standards of performance may not be the ones that most intellectuals would set if they were running the media, but the eggs that make one man's souffle make the next man's omelet.

A second assumption is that the nature of the communications system is determined primarily by the men who now own and operate the media. They of course do have a good deal to say about what the mass media pump out. But in one sense what they choose to include and omit, as I will try to show, is not entirely of their own doing.

Let me make it abundantly clear that I am not suggesting that publishers and broadcasters are sacrosanct, like Harvard, J. Edgar Hoover, and the Marines. I am not defending the shortcomings of the media for which they can be held accountable. What I am saying is this: Criticism that concentrates on them and their motives at best can explain only a small part of reality and at worst can obscure a genuine understanding of why the mass media are what they are.

Jay Jensen, in an article in the *Journalism Quarterly,* argued that genuine criticism of the press must begin with an understanding of the mass media as an institutional order.* His approach enables us to see the mass media from an entirely different perspective. It changes our

---

* Jay W. Jensen, "A Method and a Perspective for Criticism of the Mass Media," *Journalism Quarterly* 37 (Spring 1960), 261–66.

focus from the transitory, short-term effects of the media to the relationships of the communication system to society in their most fundamental form. It enables us to see that the communication system performs certain objective functions quite irrespective of the intents and interests of the men who operate it.

For criticism to be valid and fruitful, Jensen said, it must meet three requirements. First, it must be objective. It must be conducted without bias or censure arising from ideological presuppositions. Second, it must take into account the influence of social, political, and cultural forces in the historical development of the media. And finally, it must put the media into the context of their environment; it must take note of the demands, values, aspirations, and life interests of the society in which the media operate.

Criticism meeting those three tests can come about, he said, if we will look at the mass media from an institutional perspective. Man [409] has devised various institutions to help solve different aspects of the problem of human existence. Each institution is a complex pattern of values and behavior designed to meet some persistent and pressing social need. The family exists to sustain life, the church to give it meaning and direction. An institutional order is simply a larger and more complex pattern of values and behavior, for it is made up of several institutions by which man attacks the over-all problem of existence. In that functional sense, then, the mass media are an institutional order. They are a way of dealing with one phase of existence—the necessity for social communication. So wrote Jensen.

In a sense, human societies arose from and are maintained by communication. What makes man unique among all creatures is his capacity for creating symbols. Throughout history, in all societies, mankind has had certain fundamental means of communicating—gesture, imitation, what Sapir calls social suggestion, language. Using them, both primitive man and civilized man have surrounded themselves with a web of symbols.

Man, in fact, seems to have some inner compulsion to create symbols. They give him his image of himself and locate him in the vast stream of time. As Kenneth Boulding reminds us, a dog has no idea that there were dogs before him and that there will be dogs after him. But man, through his symbolic creations, has a sense of the past that stretches centuries behind him and a concept of the future. Symbols are man's chief means of communicating with his fellow man, the carrier of the social process. Through them, he can express his fears, his hopes, his plans, his ideas of the world he lives in, and through them he achieves the consensus that is necessary if he is to get along with his fellow man. They are the means whereby man copes with his environment and gives meaning to his existence.

4. Why the Mass Media Are That Way 43

Man's propensity for creating symbols has given human beings a whole new environment. For man, alone of all creatures, reacts not just to his physical surroundings but to a pseudo-environment, a symbolic environment, and it may be more important than the actual one in governing what he thinks and does. Only with comparative rarity does man deal with physical reality at first hand; for the far greater part, he deals with ideas about reality. In short, he interposes a symbolic system between himself and his purely physical universe. [410] This is not to say, of course, that he moves in a world of utter fantasy. The symbols he has developed are his attempts to organize his sensations and experiences into some meaningful form, to bring some order and meaning to his existence, and thus to deal with his environment. And indeed through the use of symbols man can alter and shape his environment.

What one sees from the institutional perspective is that the mass media are but one aspect of human communication in general. Like the semaphore and tribal drum, they are technical extensions of this primary social process that I have been talking about. As purveyors of symbols, the mass media help society to function. They are carriers of the values, the beliefs, the distinctive tone of the society in which they operate. As Walter Lippmann observed some forty years ago, they interpose a sort of pseudo-environment between man and physical reality. But if they are a force for stability, they are also a force for change. And because they are technical extensions, they can transmit their messages across vast sweeps of space and time.

What one further sees from this institutional perspective is that the mass media are not really autonomous but are adjuncts of other orders. Looking back through history, one sees how various dominant institutions, unwittingly or by conscious design, have used the media to maintain and strengthen their power. So it was when the church used the printing press to reinforce and extend its influence. So it was when the Crown held the press of England in thrall. So it is today in Soviet Russia, where the mass media are an adjunct of the political order, or in the United States, where they are an adjunct of the industrial.

What one sees still further, however, is that the media are a force for disrupting the status quo as well as for perpetuating it. Under the bejeweled but firm hand of Queen Elizabeth I, the press was a means of consolidating the power of the crown and of achieving the nationalism that echoes so gloriously through the chronicle plays of Shakespeare. Yet in the hands of dissidents the press became a powerful weapon for wresting the scepter from the monarch and reducing his presence on the throne to the largely ceremonial. Or consider another instance. When printing came along, its immediate effect seems to have been to disseminate and perpetuate the very [411] superstitions that scientists were trying to combat. In the November 1962 issue of *The Ameri-*

can Behavioral Scientist, Livio C. Stecchini summarized the effects in this way:

> In the sixteenth century books of geography consolidated the outmoded conceptions, just when navigators and discoverers were revealing completely new worlds. The press was greatly responsible for the general wave of opposition to the Copernican doctrine. Copernicus' book *De revolutionibus orbium coelestium,* published in 1543 A.D., was not reprinted for twenty-three years, while in the interval there appeared a cataract of popular works on astrology. Not until the beginning of the seventeenth century did the non-academic public, reading in vernacular, become sufficiently enlightened to make it possible for Galileo to impose his views by appealing especially to them. The surprising epidemic of witch trials which began in the sixteenth century can be blamed partly on enterprising publishers who discovered that there was an excellent market for books on magic and witchcraft.

Yet true as all of that may be, few persons would dispute the subsequent influence of the press on the dissemination and advancement of learning.

If we look at the press from an institutional perspective, we should be especially concerned, I think, with the forces that have helped to make our mass communications system what it is. From here on, I would like to talk about two environments in which our communications system grew up. Both of those environments, as I will try to show, have played a tremendous part in determining the nature of our communications system. On the one hand, the mass media have been conditioned by an environment that exists largely in the minds of men. They have been profoundly influenced, that is, by the way we have answered such fundamental questions as the nature of man, the ideal relationship of man to the state, and the nature of truth and knowledge. On the other hand, the media have been shaped by such powerful social and economic forces as the rise of democracy, urbanization, and the industrial and technological revolution.

The classical libertarian theory of the press derived from the ideas of the Enlightenment, and among its several assumptions are these: That man is a creature of reason who wants to know the truth and will be guided by it, that he can find truth by applying his reason, [412] that he is born with certain inalienable natural rights, that he forms governments of his own volition to protect those rights, and that hence the best government is that which governs least.

In brief, the libertarian theory of the press came to be something like this: The press must have only the most minimum of restraints imposed

4. Why the Mass Media Are That Way   45

upon it because man can find truth only if there is free trade in information and ideas. No one need worry about the wide arena of freedom, though, for the natural working of things provides certain built-in correctives and safeguards. If some parts of the press lie and distort, if some parts abuse their freedom, other parts will find it expedient or profitable to expose them. And, after all, man puts all information and ideas to the powerful test of reason. He may find some truth amidst falsehood, some falsehood amidst truth, but over the long pull truth will prevail.

The government should keep its hands off the press for several reasons. For one thing, free expression is a natural right, one the state must preserve and protect. For another, the state has traditionally been a foe of liberty and is always likely to use the press for its own selfish purposes. For yet another thing, the state by intervening would surely upset the delicate dialectic by which truth emerges. The press, then, is best left in private hands, to make its own way in the market-place, free from the pressures of any one group or interest. In short, freedom under libertarian theory consists simply of the absence of restraint; to put it another way, a negative freedom is an effective freedom.

As that theory evolved, certain social functions came to be ascribed to the press. The press, for instance, is charged with enlightening the public and providing it with some entertainment. It is charged with servicing the political system by carrying the information and discussions that the electorate needs for its decisions. It is charged with protecting individual rights by sounding the alarm whenever they are threatened or infringed. It is charged with servicing the economic system, largely through advertising, and with earning its own financial support.

In the twentieth century especially, many of the assumptions of traditional theory have been seriously challenged if not indeed actually undermined, and some of us have found signs that a new theory of the press, a social responsibility theory of the press, has [413] begun to emerge. But social responsibility theory is still largely theory, and our traditional ideas still guide a good deal of thinking about the press and still influence its workings in many ways. Let me give just one rather detailed example.

One tenet of Anglo-American theory is that the government should stay out of the communications business. My purpose is not to debate whether or not that idea is a good one. My point is that the idea has profoundly affected the nature of our communications system, although someone from another society may find it as quaint as we find the Yurok salmon fisherman's belief that he must not eat in his boat. From his parochial viewpoint, the Yurok has good reason for that bit of dietary abstinence: eating on the water violates his tribe's belief that various channels of nature must be kept apart. From our parochial viewpoint, so ingrained are the laissez faire doctrines of Adam Smith and the experiences of men who fought for press freedom in the past, we think we have good reason for keeping the government's hands off communications; for control necessarily follows support, we reason, and the government can weight the scales on which truth is measured. In each case, a sacrosanct belief has affected life's crucial affairs—getting enough to eat in one, communicating with our fellows in the other.

Let me give just one illustration of how our faith in laissez faire has affected our communications system. Broadcasting depends upon the use of a limited number of channels, and other countries have handled the ownership of radio and TV facilities in various ways. The assumption is that the airwaves belong to the people. There is nothing in the nature of the medium demanding that it be left to private entrepreneurs, or, if it is, that its programs be surrounded by and punctuated with pleas to buy this product or that.

But broadcasting costs money, and someone has to pick up the tab. In our society the financing, described crudely, goes something like this: Broadcasters pay for programing and all of the equipment for transmitting it, but they are more than reimbursed by advertisers. Presumably the advertisers are not out of pocket, though, for they are reimbursed by listeners and viewers, who also must invest in receiving equipment. So ultimately the consumer bears the cost of broadcasting, but his money is channeled through private rather than governmental hands. True, the government regulates [414] broadcasting, but the Federal Communications Commission has severe legal and practical limitations on its powers.

So strong is the conviction that communications must be kept in private hands that the federal government was reluctant to assign frequencies for educational and other non-commercial broadcasting. When it did, it acted in accord with the negative tradition of our press theory. It simply granted schools and communities permission to operate stations, but it made no provision for getting them on the air or keeping them there. Many stations got their money from state funds, a form of government support that was only partially taboo, since the cause was "education."

Once a year the Yurok suspends his tribal taboos, and in 1962 Congress waived one by authorizing the expenditure of $32,000,000 to encourage the growth of educational TV. Even though that sum was only about 60 per cent of what Procter & Gamble spent on network TV in 1961, Congress hesitated for months before actually appropriating just a small part of it.

4. Why the Mass Media Are That Way 47

Although critics have found fault with our system of broadcasting, attack is not my aim here. My object is simply to show how an idea, central to public thinking about the press, has contributed to the nature of the system.

It is not just ideas, however, that have given us the sort of communications system we have. Social, economic, and political forces shaped the media too, and a combination of ideas and these other things made the media what they are.

In a way, it is not surprising that the mass media should be described as an adjunct of the industrial order. The rise of journalism paralleled the rise of capitalism, and printing itself was one of the earliest forms of mass production. Many early printers in England and America were primarily businessmen. Indeed, the fight for press freedom in England arose not just from political causes and the philosophical principles of free inquiry; it also came about from the trade demands of London printers and stationers who wanted to pursue wealth without state interference.

Today our communication system is characterized by bigness, fewness, and costliness. Small units have grown into huge ones. The *Reader's Digest,* for instance, began publication in a Greenwich [415] Village basement in 1921 with a capital of $5,000 and a list of 1,500 charter subscribers. Today it publishes more than forty editions around the world, and its domestic edition alone reaches slightly more than one in four of U.S. adults. As the media have grown, there has been need for fewer of them. Three networks serve the great majority of TV stations, and two major wire services supply the great bulk of international, national, and regional news to the nation's dailies. As the media have grown, they also have become costly. A century ago one could start a metropolitan daily like *The New York Times* for $50,000 to $75,000. Today one can spend more than a million getting a daily going in a medium-sized town such as Jackson, Mississippi, and then have it fail.

In all of those things, the media are not much different from other businesses and industries. Bigness, fewness, and costliness are characteristics of much of our economic order. The electronics industry is dominated by a few huge complexes, and the automotive industry has its short list of giants. Most cities have a few large department stores, and it would be about as quixotic to establish a new one as to run a Republican in an Alabama election.

What happened is that the media were moulded by forces that conditioned American industry generally and that tremendously affected other social, economic, and political institutions. These forces wrought a powerful revolution that affected virtually every aspect of American life, especially after the Civil War, although their foundations were laid long before that.

Those forces, closely interrelated, were the rise of democracy, the spread of popular education, the industrial and technological revolution, urbanization, and, in this century, the redistribution of income.

In the nineteenth century, the electorate broadened as restrictions on voting gradually broke down, although it was not until 1920 that women got the right to vote. Meanwhile, qualifications on the right to hold office were giving way; no longer did a candidate need to own property or meet religious tests before he could hold office. One result of all this was that the common man, for the first time in history, achieved effective political power. Another was that he was called upon, at least in theory, to make innumerable decisions that once had been made for him, decisions that required information, [416] decisions that countless special pleaders were anxious to help him make.

A concomitant of universal suffrage was the spread of free popular education. By 1850, in principle if not in practice, the issue of a common-school education for all children at public expense was settled in the North and in parts of the South. In the half-century after 1860, the number of high schools increased a hundredfold, from 100 to 10,000, and a growing proportion of children entered their classrooms. After the Civil War, assisted by the land-grant movement, colleges began a period of expansion that has made the bachelor's degree a commonplace. All of this gave the media a vast audience equipped at least with the rudimentary tools of literacy and at best with far-ranging intellectual interests.

Between the end of the Civil War and the start of the new century, industrialization and mechanization hit America with all the force of revolution. So pervasive were the changes they brought about that a man of George Washington's time would probably have been more at home in the Holy Land of Jesus Christ than in the America of Teddy Roosevelt. A web of shiny rails held the nation together, and factories sprouted up where once corn had grown. Inventor after inventor came up with machines and gadgets to do the tasks that man once had performed by hand. Steam power replaced water power; electricity and the internal-combustion engine replaced steam. In the sixty years after 1850, the average manufacturing plant increased its capital more than thirty-nine times, its number of wage earners nearly seven times, the value of its output more than nineteen times.

Beneath much of that change, of course, lay a system of mass production and mass distribution. The system depended upon standardization and mass consumption; so long as consumers would accept goods

4. Why the Mass Media Are That Way 49

tailored to averages instead of to individual preferences, they were treated to a profusion of products at relatively low cost. Mass production changed the conception of markets from areas to people. The typical manufacturer no longer produced only for his own locality; he sought out buyers wherever they lived. Now, all of the characteristics of mass production—greater use of product, standardization, and so on—had implications for the mass media, as I plan to show. [417]

But one is so important that I wish to mention it now—the development of advertising. For one thing, mass production and mass distribution needed some kind of inexpensive mass salesmanship. For another thing, the media and appeals that worked when markets were regional or local did not suffice when markets became widely-scattered consumers. For still another thing, manufacturers had no great need of advertising when their production was barely above subsistence level. But as assembly lines turned out a seemingly endless flow of products of seemingly endless variety, as consumption became essential to keeping the stream of goods flowing, manufacturers had to make consumers conscious of dimly-sensed needs and desires, had to channel human drives to exploit the psychic values of their wares, had to make the consumer want to consume. For yet another thing, as unlabelled merchandise gave way to the brand-name product, the manufacturer saw the financial advantage inherent in his name and trademark. If he could convince the consumer that his product was more desirable than all others, he could charge a premium for it. Advertising grew, and as it did the media clutched at it for financial support.

Along with the industrial and technological revolution came the crowding of Americans together in cities. Farm workers put down the plow to tend the machines of the factory. Boat after boat brought immigrants seeking new opportunities—some 11½ million of them in the thirty years before 1900—and although many of them huddled together on the coast, many others ventured inland, some no doubt encouraged by the special rail fares that let them journey from New York to Chicago for as little as a dollar. All in all, the nation's population just about doubled between 1870 and 1900, and the city became home for an increasing proportion of it. Gathered in one place, people were natural markets for the media. And the immigrant, in many ways, had an influence on the media. The foreign-language newspaper, for instance, provided a link with the homeland and with others from it, helped adjustment to a strange land but also encouraged reading of regular American dailies. The early movies, low in price and heavy on pantomime, were an ideal medium for the foreign-born struggling with a new tongue and wanting escape from the drudgery of the factory.

In our own century, we have seen a redistribution of income so [418] apparent that it probably is unnecessary to document it. It is true, of course, that despite all of our talk about the affluent society, poverty stubbornly exists and that many Americans still live in actual want. It is also true that disparities of income still exist, although not on the grand scale of 1900 when Andrew Carnegie's personal tax-free income of $20,000,000 was at least 20,000 times that of the average workingman. The middle-class American is considerably better off financially than he was in 1900, and that point is important to the mass media, not only because he has money for TV sets, transistor radios, and newspaper and magazine subscriptions but also because he has money for the advertisers' washing machines, hi-fi sets, and automobiles.

My little excursion into history has turned up little that is unfamiliar, I am sure. I have dwelt on the past at such length because critics have looked back to it surprisingly little when they have tried to explain why the media are what they are. My pitch is that the communications industries, like other industries, were affected by the social and economic forces I have just outlined; they changed, in short, from personal craft industries to impersonal mass-production industries, and today they share many of the characteristics of other mass-production enterprises.

First, the mass media usually carve out little markets of their own, much as manufacturers and retailers do. The publisher of a confessions magazine no more expects every literate American to curl up with his tales of sin and redemption than an overall manufacturer expects every American to wear his blue jeans. Each has a pretty clear idea of who is a good prospect for what he turns out, and he fashions his product accordingly.

Usually the market of a medium coincides with that of its advertisers. A newspaper typically concentrates its circulation in the trade area served by local retailers, for instance, and a magazine like *Farm Journal* aims at people who buy the tractors and chemical fertilizers extolled on its advertising pages. Even TV programers do not necessarily expect the people who guffaw at the Beverly Hillbillies to sit entranced by Meet the Press.

Media that do not carry advertising quite often pick out specialized markets, too. The book clubs neatly illustrate the point. [419] Sired by that middle-aged grandfather, the Book-of-the-Month Club, their tribe has multiplied to include clubs for antique collectors, gardeners, cooks, farmers, educators, salesmen, executives, Civil War buffs and other amateur historians, Irishmen, outdoorsmen, drama and art lovers, science fans, yachtsmen, writers, Catholics, Jews, Lutherans and other Protestants, young children, teenagers, and grapplers of prose in its original French and Spanish.

4. Why the Mass Media Are That Way 51

A second consequence is what we might rather grandiosely call a democratization of content. In simple words, the mass media as a whole turned from a class audience to a mass audience and adjusted their content accordingly. Newspapers began their transition from sober organs for the mercantile class to lively sources of news for quite literally the man on the street in the early nineteenth century. Magazines began their change about a half-century later. Movies, radio, and television, born into a world of cities and technology, went after a mass market from the start.

As I have already said, the media seek out their own little publics. But in speaking to those publics, the media tend to address themselves to some center point, to some common denominator of taste, interest, and capability. In the nature of things a publisher or broadcaster must conduct his business pretty much as any other manufacturer must. A magazine publisher and a refrigerator maker, say, both want maximum saturation of their chosen markets. The media need audiences to exist, and to get and hold them they must please the majority of their chosen market. They can no more tailor their product to the specifications of a single individual or tiny group than can the dressmakers in New York's garment district. Overall, then, they tend to reflect the concerns, values, beliefs, and tastes of the great majority, and therein lies their essential conservatism.

Third, the mass media have become standardized in content and in technique. Newspapers across the land are pretty much alike in size, format, and overall appearance; in the ways in which they get their news; in the ways in which they write it, headline it, and present it; even in the relative play they give to national and international events. Magazines depend upon a pattern of content that carries over from issue to issue, and the big ones play a relatively small scale of major themes. Television programs are remarkable more for their basic sameness than their variety; the past season offered [420] more than a dozen series in which Western badmen found death on the dusty streets of frontier towns, for instance, and depending on how one counted them, between twenty-three and thirty situation comedy series. And TV programs themselves, as any viewer knows, are developed in familiar, standardized ways. This standardization seems an almost inevitable result as the media increased their reach, their speed, and their efficiency by adopting such techniques of mass production as division of labor and mechanization, but consumer convenience and expectation also have probably played some part.

Fourth, as content became democratized, as technological advances enabled speedy output, there has been an increased use of the media. Today the typical American spends more time looking at and listening to the mass media than at anything else except his work or sleeping, and the typical youngster leaving high school has spent more time in front of a TV set than in the classroom. Newspapers, magazines, radio, and television all penetrate deep into the population.

Fifth, the media have become more efficient, just as many other mass-production enterprises have. The telegraph, wireless, train, and plane have enabled the media not only to take the entire world for their beat but to cover it with astonishing swiftness. Until the middle of the last century, England was still two or three weeks away, and at home news was slow in traveling from one part of the country to another.

When Andrew Jackson successfully defended New Orleans in the War of 1812–14, New Yorkers did not read about the outcome until a month afterwards. And as they learned from their papers five days later, the battle itself had been fought two weeks after the peace treaty was signed in London. But when the Korean War broke out in June, 1950, Jack James's United Press dispatch reached Washington almost at once—several minutes before the State Department's own cable, in fact.

New means of communication and improvements in the old ones have made possible vast audiences for the media. High-speed presses and mechanical typesetting allowed newspapers and magazines to seek their large circulations, and the electronic media have put a speaker into instantaneous touch with millions of persons. We often forget how very recent some of these changes are. In my own childhood, [421] in 1919, when President Woodrow Wilson wanted to sell the Treaty of Versailles to the nation, he spent twenty-seven days traveling more than 8,000 miles in seventeen states to deliver forty formal speeches and many more informal talks, only one of them with benefit of public address system. In December, 1962, when three TV networks carried "Conversation with the President," John F. Kennedy was in instantaneous touch with an estimated 21,960,000 American homes, according to A. C. Nielsen figures.

Finally, the mass media, like other industries, have used the assembly-line technique of division of labor. Once even the publisher of a metropolitan daily could operate as James Gordon Bennett did in 1835, when he gathered his own news, wrote it up, handled business affairs, and waited on customers at a desk made of two barrels with a plank across them. By the 1870's those days were largely gone, and by the 1890's the large-city dailies had staffs about as specialized as they are today. All of the other media, too, have come to depend upon a variety of specialists to put together the finished product. As they have, the individual employee has lost most of whatever chance for self-expression he ever had. He became one of a team turning out mass-produced

4. Why the Mass Media Are That Way 53

images, and too large an investment rides on his efforts for him to produce with anything but the market in mind.

Those, then, are the forces that have joined to give us the sort of communication system we have, and in large measure they are responsible for the many strengths we too often take for granted. They have contributed to the development of a communication system that reaches virtually the entire population and that in the aggregate makes available an astonishing amount of entertainment and an astonishing array of information, viewpoint, and interpretation on a wide array of subjects with incredible swiftness and superb technical skill. They have contributed to the important part that the media have played in bringing about our high material standard of living.

But in large measure those forces also are responsible for the faults that have sent many a critic reaching for his thesaurus of epithets. They have contributed to the superficiality, the sameness, the blandness, and the blindness that characterize a good deal of media content. They have contributed to the bigness, fewness, and costliness that some critics see as jeopardizing the free trade in information [422] and ideas, putting control of a powerful social instrument into the hands of the few and converting the personal right of press freedom into a property right.

All of what I have said, I immodestly think, has some implications for those who are serious in their criticism of the mass media.

First, those who examine the press should try to achieve objectivity in two meanings of the term. On the one hand, as they set out to discover what the mass media are and why they are what they are, they should leave their ideological baggage behind, much as a good cultural anthropologist does. They should look deep into the past for clues to present understanding. They should examine the interrelationships of the media with other parts of society. On the other hand, they should explore the objective social functions that the media perform, quite apart from those ascribed by normative press theory. As Jensen suggested, the media have a reality of their own. Although they are man-made creations, they have developed certain objective functions distinct from the tasks assigned them by their operators and by society. Desirable or not, those functions exist, and it is the duty of the serious critic to understand them.

Second, critics should put up for serious examination our traditional theory of the press, which in many ways seems out of joint with the times. That theory may have been adequate in the eighteenth and nineteenth centuries, when both the world and the communication system were far less complex than today, but one might ask if it is in accord with contemporary thought and reality. Some such examination has already begun; and as publishers and broadcasters themselves have discarded parts of traditional theory as outmoded, there are indications that a new theory of social responsibility is emerging. As a part of this intellectual overhaul, which should begin with the questioning of basic assumptions, I hope we could also re-examine some of the notions that have long surrounded traditional theory. For instance, are we right in the notion that although the media have a responsibility to enlighten the public, the public has no special responsibility to be enlightened? Are the media right in their notion that in enlightening the public, the demands of the market are the best test of how well the job is being done? Are we right in the notion that bigness is necessarily badness? Does a multiplicity of communications units necessarily mean a multiplicity [423] of viewpoints? Are small media operators necessarily more socially responsible than large ones? Does control necessarily follow financial support?

In conclusion, let me say that I am not proposing that we grant the media absolution for all their sins, venal or otherwise. Some, I know, will read my message that way. In looking at the press from an institutional perspective, some will conclude that publishers and broadcasters are swept inexorably along by powerful, impersonal social and cultural forces and that there is nothing that they or we can do about it. That conclusion implies a degree of predestinarianism I am quite unwilling to accept. Man with brain and hand has given the media the milieus in which they operate, and man if he will can change them. [424]

5. Towards a Democratic Reconstruction of Mass Communications: The Social Use of Technology

Herbert I. Schiller

Radio and television broadcasting in the United States is largely a private activity that has grown into a powerful industry with far-reaching, though mostly unacknowledged, social consequences. Government control of broadcasting has been limited and, what there is of it, ineffectually implemented. The regulated more often than not impose their will on the regulators.

Operating in a market economy and measuring performance by incoming revenue, broadcasting's internal dynamics, like those of other industrial sectors, move inevitably toward economic concentration. Stations and channels derive their profitability, and therefore their value, from the size of their potential audiences. Time rates are calculated on a listener/viewer per program ratio, and metropolitan signals heard by large numbers are easily the most attractive to prospective advertisers.

Control has tightened in broadcast communications as the economics of radio-television have fostered giantism and concentration. A clutch of corporations (common carriers, manufacturers of electrical equipment, and a few network broadcasting companies) interlock and attempt to arbitrate among themselves, not always with complete success, the domestic communications scene. Meanwhile, as American power has thrust outward in recent years, the authority of this national communications complex has moved into the international and spatial arenas as well.

Source: Herbert I. Schiller, *Mass Communications and American Empire* (New York: A. M. Kelley, 1969), pp. 147–64. Reprinted by permission of the author.

Mass communications are now a pillar of the emergent imperial society. Messages "made in America" radiate across the globe and [147] serve as the ganglia of national power and expansionism. The ideological images of "have-not" states are increasingly in the custody of American informational media. National authority over attitude creation and opinion formation in the developing world has weakened and is being relinquished to powerful external forces. The facilities and hardware of international information control are being grasped by a highly centralized communications complex, resident in the United States and largely unaccountable to its own population.

The speed of innovation in electronics technology and the already-deployed strength of American communications have produced a spirit of confidence among the leaders of the United States' informational system. Dr. Charyk, the president of Comsat, for example, told a congressional committee in 1966 that he believes "we stand on the threshold of a communications revolution. [The establishment of Comsat and Intelsat] has set in motion technical, political, and economic forces whose ultimate global impact will be profound. Sometimes we hear that satellites afford simply another supplementary or complementary means of communication. But particularly when one talks of international communications and when one looks at the new capabilities which satellites bring into being, there is little doubt in my mind that we are at the dawn of a new age."[1]

If this is so, and it may well be that it is, is there a predictable character to this "new age"? Will it be directed from some imperial center, which unilaterally and arbitrarily decides the course of international events? Inside the "center," are we moving irresistibly toward "knowledge conglomerates," integrated private informational structures which unify the learning and educational process from infancy to the grave, efficiently discarding troublesome messages? Or, is the prospect opening before us a more hopeful one of multiplying opportunities to utilize the new technology for international cooperation, human improvement and individual enrichment? Indeed, *for whom* is this a new age?

The Utopians once enjoyed elaborating designs for social improvement, but they lacked the means for implementing their models. Today the situation is reversed. Utopias are out of fashion just at the time when they are literally attainable. Never before in history have [148] the basic educational and cultural needs of humanity been so widely appreciated.

---

[1] *National Communications Satellite Programs,* Hearings Before the Committee on Aeronautical and Space Sciences, United States Senate, 89th Congress, 2nd Session, January 25 & 26, 1966, Washington, 1966, p. 51.

5. Towards a Democratic Reconstruction of Mass Communications

But while the resources to satisfy these requirements are physically available, they are directed to other ends. The engineering means exist, but the will and the enabling social structure are absent. The resources and the technology, known and available, are capable of monumental physical transformations. The modern obstacles, no less imposing because they are social rather than material, are the institutions which govern human affairs.

Today the fundamental questions concerning communications do not involve process or discovery. Social issues such as ownership, control, financial support, national sovereignty and the character of the programming constitute the unsettled agenda. No longer, as in the past, is there a universal problem of providing every adult and every child with the technical means of receiving information. For poor nations this remains a great concern, but not for the American community. In the United States, the question is *what* message to receive, not *how* to receive it.

Technically-advanced America is socially retarded by institutional machinery which preserves outlooks and practices far beyond their usefulness or applicability. Paradoxically, the most modern sector of the economy, electronic communications, often serves as the chief conservator of outmoded behavior patterns. Yet the mass media's compulsion to reinforce the status quo is understandable. The radio-TV establishments, in their character and structures, are microcosms of the larger social organism. They could hardly not be committed to its survival. If monolithic corporate enterprises command the informational apparatus, this is in keeping with the distribution of power in the economy at large. If the "tube" presents an unending parade of violence and triviality, are these not apt reflections of the wider social environment?

It is possible that institutions eventually may be eroded by changing technology, but this presumes a considerable historical process. Also, the erosion may be uneven, and certain, perhaps vital, institutions remain untouched, while others are altered. Those left intact may still command the overall direction of existence. For the moment, which may endure far beyond an individual's life-span, institutions preside over technology. Operating in this narrower time dimension, can we realistically expect a beneficent social orientation, an appropriate outlook for mankind, simply because the rapidly [149] changing technology of communications make available the possibility of universal coverage, multiplication of services and strikingly effective impact? Are we justified in expecting technology to "wash out" our institutional problems and lift us, almost against our will, onto a higher plateau of existence?

It is a comforting notion, but also, I believe, a very misleading one. We will either direct our technology or it will be used to direct us. In communications the second course has been evident for some time.

Now that startling innovations are feasible in the technology of information distribution there is a pause while the technologists reveal the opportunities that their creativity has provided. There is with us, for a moment, the vision of what could be. The routine is broken. The acceptance of unsatisfactory living patterns and popular acquiescence in the shocking underperformance in humanizing the social process are temporarily interrupted. We are given a glimpse of a different social balance in which the prevailing priorities are somehow or other made inoperative. We are left briefly to imagine that a higher standard in the quality of life is attainable because it is physically realizable.

Buckminster Fuller has argued eloquently for years that the world can be engineered into abundance. Even if he is right, and I believe that he is, the institutional structure disregards his blueprints and brushes off his plea for "anticipatory design." The fact of the matter is that the efficient use of global resources, the goal to which Fuller has dedicated his enormous talent, as well as the utilization of communications in the service of man, will not be achieved as an effortless by-product of advanced engineering processes. The road to the social use of technology runs through the rugged terrain of interest groups, privileged classes, national power, and self-satisfied decision-makers. Prodding, opposing, and perhaps even storming and overturning these ancient but enduring governing coalitions are the means by which the humanistic use of the new technology may be secured. It is willful escapism to believe that technology, by itself, will soon force its way out of the restrictive social web that now surrounds it. The generalized insecurity overhanging industrially omnipotent and economically affluent America is strong evidence of how badly the campaigns to liberate technology have gone in recent years.

The utilization of the new communications technology for human needs requires a thorough reordering of the social process which regulates the informational system at all levels of personal and national existence. The dilemma is, however, that the controlling crust of the industrial state calls on the communications media to resist the social reorganization that must precede the technological reformation.

The development of modern electronic communications illustrates the ability of the prevailing institutional framework to shelter itself from technological subversion. Radio and television have been controlled continuously by the industrial concerns that organized their discovery and development. Television came into the market as the research product of electrical equipment and radio manufacturing corporations

5. Towards a Democratic Reconstruction of Mass Communications 59

and then, incidentally, as a new medium of communications. Corporate interests determined the timing of the product's introduction, the pace of its technological growth, the speed with which it was delivered to the public, the character of its financing and the content of its programming. Consequently, society's cultural process, its deepest concern, has remained largely removed from general consideration and public decision-making. Television, the most educative force in existence, has been left almost entirely to private considerations and the vagaries of the marketplace. The cost of overlooking the generalized social need when treating a vital matter of community well-being is now only beginning to be appreciated. John Platt's point that what we teach [or do not teach] today may well affect our survival, is a helpful reminder:

> "Evidently the time is approaching," he writes, "when our whole society will begin to be self-conscious about what it may become, when we will begin to choose it deliberately instead of accidentally. We now realize that the society we can and will become is shaped by what we teach, by the kind of human nature we are producing day by day in our children. This means that there is a problem of choice in our teaching, a collective problem far larger than any single wise educator can solve for us. The old and yet remarkably new discovery of the plasticity of human nature means that all of us—natural and social scientists, psychologists and teachers, historians and writers, students of economics and politics, government and university leaders, philosophers and citizens—all of us will be deciding and need to be deciding what kind of human nature and what kind of personal and [151] social relationships we want to teach our children to have so that they will be able to make a better society in turn for themselves."[2]

How and where do we introduce into the teaching process social decision-making when the most effective instrumentation of learning has been available only marginally for public utilization and collective responsibility? One TV trade journal boasts that "the average kid has watched four thousand hours of television before his first day of school."[3] And Federal Communications Commissioner Nicholas Johnson notes that this "instruction" from [the child's] home set is "twice as many hours . . . as he will receive in class during the entire four-year span of his college tenure."[4]

---

[2] John R. Platt, *The Step to Man*, John Wiley and Sons, Inc., New York, 1966, p. 163.

[3] "The Preteen Market," Caroline Meyer, *Television Magazine*, July 1967, Vol. XXIV, No. 7, p. 37.

[4] Nicholas Johnson, "The Public Interest and Public Broadcasting: Looking at Communications as a Whole," September 11, 1967.

The technology of modern communications must be won away from its current custodians. It should be generally apparent, although it is not, that the aims and practices of the commercial market are not always in step with the social requirements of the human commonwealth. Moreover, in an advanced industrial society, the problem goes beyond the commercial influence in the mass media. Shifting the responsibility from private goods-sellers to public (governmental) authorities, can no longer, if it ever could, be considered a foolproof alternative which guarantees a socially-minded guardian for the sensitive informational apparatus.

The interdependencies in an essentially privately-run modern nation have produced a governing coalition that occupies public as well as private office. Now, in America, governmental control of the communications media could produce a more sophisticated expertise in audience control than the commercial sublimators ever have managed to construct. It is important to be straightforward about such a possibility, especially at this time. The American public, having tolerated for twenty years the impoverishment of "educational television," and accepted what one former FCC Chairman termed an "electronic Appalachia," now indicates a growing dissatisfaction with [152] the state of affairs of commercial television. The development of space communications technology and the spreading, if still limited, disenchantment with commercial programming, have produced a growing sentiment for a broader public broadcasting authority. A government-supported broadcasting corporation has received congressional authorization. The most obvious defects of unlimited commercialism can be mitigated by this public enterprise, but the prospect is not an unqualified cause for celebration.

It can hardly be disputed that the recent trend in public discussion initiated by the Ford Foundation's proposal for a non-profit public broadcasting corporation has been beneficial. At the very least, it has given the public an opportunity to be acquainted with the monopolistic communications system that presently functions in the United States. It has also restated some forgotten truths. The foremost of these is that the messages a system transmits are inseparably tied to the character of that system's structure and control. The question the Ford Foundation people made central had not been asked for years. It was, Communications for what? Put in self-critical terms, the question becomes, What does it avail a community to possess an instrumentation of miraculous capability if it is placed in the service of mediocrity or irrelevancy or subjugation?

Can a governmentally-financed noncommercial system begin to provide the critical substance that private, advertiser-supported television

5. Towards a Democratic Reconstruction of Mass Communications

has rarely offered? The original Ford Foundation plan foresaw informational services which would include the coverage of significant congressional hearings and debates, news interpretations, interviews and discussions with national and international leaders, and political campaigns; cultural programs which would feature the best in the universe of national and international arts and humanities; and a level of instructional service going far beyond anything currently broadcast.

Are these realistic expectations, given the present distribution of income and decision-making in the United States? Furthermore, do these intentions, exciting as they are in comparison with present arrangements, go far enough? Is it possible to create an autonomous structure that will take up the serious and challenging tasks of national education and revitalize the (sadly sagging) democratic spirit in the population? Desperate as we are to answer these questions affirmatively we do ourselves no service by ignoring the realities [153] of contemporary American life. More than a board of honest men, overseeing a public television establishment, will be necessary to reverse the strong anti-democratic tide that has been running in the country for a generation. We are no longer at the point where some modest meliorative changes in our informational fare will suffice. Unfortunately, it is past the time where a little less hucksterism in the programming and a few more hours each week of public service broadcasting will make any substantial difference—either in the popular outlook or in widening the public comprehension of the enormous social problems that have gone unconsidered for so long.

The information process in the United States continues to rest firmly in the grip of tenacious stand-patters. These cannot and will not begin to do the job of meaningfully explaining to their viewers and listeners the revolutionary changes appearing in domestic and international life. It is also doubtful that the creation of a public broadcasting corporation, superior as it unquestionably will be to the present system, will represent the scope of change, either in outlook or allegiance, that the current social situation demands. The chief opposition to a governmentally-financed public broadcast system, incidentally, has come from those sections of Congress and the community which fear that the system will be "captured" by advocates of extreme social change. Sadly, the probabilities are all the other way. It is difficult to imagine a public corporation, with its directors appointed by the President and its money raised through annual congressional authorization, independently criticizing, for any length of time, establishment sentiments. Such an expectation would be tantamount to imagining the Voice of America transmitting as its dominant message to Southeast Asia the arguments of the United States peace movement against the American engagement in Vietnam. Yet the state of the contemporary world, and the domestic situation in particular, require an informational apparatus in the United States totally different from what we have grown up with and with which we now feel some, but not enough, irritation.

In many areas of current scientific work, systematic research is producing results that are consciously sought and sometimes even hypothesized well before the inquiry is undertaken. Nature is coming under the deliberate control of the scientific community. This process is least advanced in the social sphere. In the realm of human affairs, a minimal effort is still applied to designing the future. If the reasons [154] for the lag are fairly well known, the consequences are none the less potentially catastrophic. Traditionally, social change has followed one sort or another of social crisis. Slavery, war, mass unemployment have sometimes provoked large scale resistance from their victims. Struggles arising from popular dissatisfaction have on occasion produced reforms throughout the entire social sphere. Change induced in this fashion may not be sufficient to prevent the recurrence of the initial crisis. It always comes after some manifestation of social breakdown. It generally is accompanied by strife and violence. Crisis, therefore, is a very primitive mechanism for creating new social conditions. It is incongruous next to the ordered efforts characteristic of the scientific sphere.

Is there a way for the social sector to emulate its scientific component? Can anticipation and design replace crisis and conflict as the instruments of social change? This, in essence, is the function and the role, if they were to be taken up, of mass communications in the United States today. Radio-television broadcasting, coming into practically every American home, can alert and instruct the disinterested, the ignorant, the misinformed and the apathetic. Communications, subtle yet forceful and entertaining while educational, are the principal hope we have of substituting thoughtful human preventive action for social breakdown and violent, visceral human response. The sense of inevitability need no longer be inevitable.

But to provide invigorating and enlightening communications, the mass media must *lead,* not follow. Commercial broadcasting cannot do this. Public broadcasting, though theoretically capable of such efforts, will probably find its support threatenend if it moves resolutely in this direction. What then remains? The answer may have to be found outside the usual terms of reference. The potential exists, I believe, in some forces stirring in the national community itself. An informational apparatus that provides substance, insight and an unshakable integrity in offering social direction, can develop only alongside of and assisted by the most dynamic elements in the community. Mass communications, if they are to do what has to be done to illuminate the march of events

5. Towards a Democratic Reconstruction of Mass Communications 63

and compel individual awareness and participation in the social process, must be associated intimately with the popular, though unheard-from, agents of social change in the commonwealth.

Linking the mass media with what Gunnar Myrdal calls the [155] "underclass" and other unaffiliated underdogs is not suggested out of sentimentality. The Establishment is top dog and its outlook, its methodologies, and its behavior have demonstrated their total incapability of extricating us from onrushing disasters, much less of perceiving incipient crises in advance.

Are there centers of dynamism in the American community with which the mass media, set free of their current ties, might identify and, in doing so, lead the way to popular acceptance of social change? Where, in short, is there skepticism in the community toward the prevailing social and political processes? In fact, a few sources of potential change are readily ascertainable.

Some elements in the *public sector* of the economy reveal sharp antagonisms to the status quo. Teachers, social and health workers, and municipal employees in essential services are foci of discontent and dissatisfaction. For the moment their complaints are mostly economic. However, their relatively pinched positions in the affluent society make it likely that their personal demands will be broadened into national policy reassessments. Better conditions for the working force in the expanding public services demand a review of the fundamental (and neglected) issue of public versus private priorities.

The *universities,* too, are beginning to simmer with awareness and a criticism that arises from perceived incongruities. The devotion of staff and facilities to war-related research; the dependence of university funds on the continuing state of war emergency; and, the training, not the education, of students for employment in impersonal bureaucracies, are matters of deep concern to increasing numbers of faculty and students. The most orthodox and insulated campuses are experiencing currents of dissent, still relatively weak, but significant by the fact of their existence.

The most explosive element in contemporary American society is the developing *black social movement.* Emerging from the city ghettoes and the rural slums, thousands of young, articulate militants are questioning the fundamental assumptions of American life that have gone unchallenged for three hundred years. The black rebellion cannot be contained, and each new outbreak produces new layers of involvement. It reveals also unexpected weaknesses and fissures in the governing coalition.

These are the present forceful and forward groupings. Unresolved crises, domestic and international, *already in the making,* are likely [156] to produce additional elements whose allegiance to the now-dominant structure will peel off as the pressures intensify.

Avoidance of social catastrophe necessitates that these emergent forces have the informational apparatus at their disposal. Yet the very suggestion sounds naive and puerile. It is not fortuitous that the governing complex is most concentrated in the communications sector. The mass media, as they now operate, can only be regarded as the strongest support of the ruling estate. Expectations that the communications process will reflect in a significant way the purposes and the outlook of the "other America" have little reasonable foundation.

Though it is important to be clear on the basic structure and orientation of privately-directed mass communications, it is useful also to recognize that the mechanism of information control is far from monolithic. Besides, the system is not averse to engaging in tactical maneuvers that could prove disarming to unwary challengers. Concessions are conceivable. "Tokenism," the techniques of coopting a tiny stratum of a dispossessed group into the privileged orders, the device that has worked effectively in the past in splintering "out group" solidarity, is potentially applicable in broadcast communications. Even now there are signs of its presence. For example, there may be one show during the week's 140 hours of programming that presents imagery of realistic conflict. Or there may be the single character in an army of performers who utters an honest line of dialogue.

Beyond these very limited actions to mollify dissidents or to create an appearance of objectivity, there is the wider option of minority broadcasting. This is the market economy's contribution to diverse interests in the community. An entire station (or channel) may be devoted to the views and sentiments of a particular social stratum. Though this may be edifying to the group concerned, most often its consequence is the further separation of that segment from the largest social unit. FCC Commissioner Johnson explains it this way:

> . . . although a splintered market will assure minorities that their interests and problems will be aired it will not assure that anyone outside of their group will hear . . . a communications system which caters very well to minority views may be, to that extent, *less* capable of getting those views across to the public.[5] [157]

At this time, there is little cause to believe that student activists, black power leaders, public sector spokesmen and university faculty critics are going to be seduced with the exclusive use of individual channels for the dissemination of their hopes, fears and findings. Still it is not

---
[5] *Ibid.*

unimaginable, but rather likely, that representatives of these groupings will increasingly find themselves before the public eye. The test of significant impact, however, is always the breadth of exposure, the degree of dilution and the extent of continuity. Tokenism and minority broadcasting are insufficient by any yardstick to create the degree of environmental and attitudinal change that we are proposing.

Therefore the basic problem remains. The forces of enlightment must find means to confront the *general* public with the issues of the times, the options that exist, and the considered consequences of one or another courses of action. Students, blacks, teachers and scientists are not special people, but the matters that distress them go far beyond their personal interests (though these of course are involved). It may seem curious that this should be so, but it is demonstrable that their individual concerns affect the *general* welfare in the fullest measure.

The university's role, for example, which the students are beginning to examine and find wanting, is not a parochial question, limited to the campus enclave. The quality and character of the total educational process are at issue. The aspirations of 20 million blacks cannot be evaluated as a minority matter that is of import to only 10 per cent of the population. The black-white relationship is as critical to the well-being of the national psyche as any other element in the social order. The work of the country's social and natural scientists and how it may be most beneficially applied for the community's security and prosperity are not the province of a handful of administrators. More than anything else, it is the substance for general public debate and decision, for, sooner or later, the entire population is to be affected.

It is because the dynamic centers of the society are altering the foundations of social existence that they are in conflict with the power structure, which is itself built on these threatened supports. There is an urgent need for these developing forces to instruct and inform national and local publics of what they are about. Their work is for the most part constructive, their goals, generally [158] desirable. Yet failing to explain and to explore their aims and actions with the popular majority, their efforts may be futile and their objectives will be distorted by their adversaries. They will be swamped by a numerically overwhelming coalition, manipulated by the traditional governors.

Where then is a breakthrough possible? If the informational channels are denied, how may the messages of the creative undergroups penetrate the larger community? It is in this respect that the technologists have a contribution to make. The new communications technology will not of itself overcome the structural order and overturn the levers of control that now limit creative change and prevent adaptation to contemporary needs. It can, however, be of enormous assistance if grasped by the social groups most insistent on restructuring the decision-making process. If the groups that are pressing for rationalization of existence in the industrial state and a reconstitution of the social order can claim *massive access* to the new communications, hitherto an impossibility, hope remains that the disasters that a mindless yet powerful economy is provoking may be survived.

The changing character of communications technology could be a saving factor in an otherwise totally negative situation. One of the original arguments which supported the present system of concentrated space communications ownership and control—costliness—is being refuted by a technological flood of communications innovation. Though space satellites are not going to be sold soon at five and dime counters, they are quickly becoming accessible to a wide range of purses and purposes. As a result of massive outlays on space research and hardware, launching expenditures and particularly the costs of the broadcasting "birds" themselves are declining dramatically. The opportunities are expanding for specialized single-purpose satellites.

On the ground, cable television opens the door to a far wider group of program initiators, permitting many more signals into each home set. UHF broadcasting has been extended and additional channels are also being made available in this range of the spectrum. Finally, home video recorders and cameras now are being retailed to a general public. Amateurs have the opportunity to develop skills in the production of material. Set owners with home recorders will be enabled to tape programs and build up libraries of shows they have found compelling and well worth repeating. [159]

Some of these developments may very well move along the familiar road of commercial pre-emption, individual fadism, mass market programming and a system of monopolistic control. But, and this is of critical import, it no longer is technically necessary for communications control to be arbitrarily concentrated. New options, at least for the time being, are open.

The American Telephone and Telegraph Company exercises almost total domination over the country's telephonic communications. Its control of the ground lines and repeater facilities makes the national broadcasting networks dependent on this one corporation for interconnection, vital to national programming. Now, Comsat, already an exclusive and chosen instrument in the international field, seeks to impose its domain over domestic space communications as well. Its argument is efficiency. It claims that a multi-purpose system, under (its own) unified control, will be less wasteful than several individual purpose satellites, each owned and directed by different entities.

There can be no assurance at this early date that individual purpose

5. Towards a Democratic Reconstruction of Mass Communications 67

satellites, individually controlled, will insure the accessibility of hitherto excluded groupings to the newest mode of communications. Indeed it is difficult to imagine the arrangements that would make available a satellite system to social dissidents. The technological barrier still seems formidable. There is, on the contrary, a very good prospect that a multipurpose system, under the thumb of one, powerful private corporation, will almost automatically maintain social communications in their present unrepresentative and concentrated form. The need at this point is to keep open the technological options for diverse use, even at the sacrifice of some efficiency. Indeed, the concept of efficiency may be in itself a reflection of traditionalism, and the "wastefulness" of alternate systems may be in reality the most promising method of assuring an industrial society some measure of informational liberty.

Turning the new communications technology to democratic advantage will require above all else continuous aggressive popular pressure on several fronts simultaneously. Individuals outside the established production centers can experiment (as some are already doing) with cameras and TV recorders now coming into their possession. Their efforts, perhaps eventually supported by local, regional or even national social groups, may provide the basis for altogether new [160] sources of communications techniques and programming. Selective taping of the occasional and exceptional program emanating from the commercial system will contribute to libraries of value and substance which can be made available repeatedly for organizational and individual use. Most important of all, requests for new channels and reassignment of stations held by owners indifferent to social needs should become a common and insistent demand of the social "out groups." These demands can be expressed locally as community actions.

The federal and state governments, through their regulatory machinery and the Federal Communications Commission in particular, must be held accountable for the social maximization of the nation's radio spectrum resource. Campaigns to improve mental health and eliminate physical disease generally rely on local initiatives for their support. Similar efforts can be expended in monitoring communications channels and insisting on their utilization for the community's psychic well-being.

Whereas radio and television stations are ranked now according to their market importance—how much they are worth depending on the size and sales potential of their audiences—new criteria can be evolved and applied. In Britain, for instance, the Independent Television Authority has the responsibility for shifting franchises of the most valuable properties if it believes other owners will provide more socially constructive programming. It has done so even at the cost of near-confiscation of heavy private investments. In the United States, commercial licenses have never been revoked on the grounds they have failed to serve the public interest—a case that probably could be made against practically any commercial station now broadcasting. Community pressure can change these rules.

Political action has generally been understood in the United States as the support of one or another candidate for office. This has produced, on occasion, changes in personnel with no corresponding changes in the structure of decision-making. The time may now have arrived for political action which takes up seriously the question of changing underlying structures. Modern political action might find a good starting point in revamping the ownership and control of the informational media at all levels of organization.

It should be evident too that transfers of control can not be regarded as merely one-time actions. No single shift can offer the [161] assurance of perpetual informational flexibility and freedom. Underlying this principle of accessibility to the mass media is the premise that an alert community remains vigilant in respect to its informational needs and retains the vigor and the will to continuously assert itself. The continuing utilization of the broadcasting media for human enlightenment requires the closest attention and participation of all the forces that are engaged in the ongoing process of humanization.

On the international plane, informational needs are enormous, absolutely and qualitatively. There are a billion illiterates in the world. Their education depends on the instructional power of radio and television mobilized for this purpose. Though we are still very far from undertaking such a heroic task, it would be a relatively routine effort insofar as the existing methodologies and educational resources are available. The missing element at this point is the will to act which expresses itself in lamentably inadequate educational budgets. By way of contrast, the Pentagon spends *annually* about one billion dollars for its communications system, a large part of which is designed to alert the military once "trouble" has erupted in the "have not" world.

Much more than money and facilities, however, are required if the mass media are going to assist us to achieve humanity. In his book, *The Wretched of the Earth*, Frantz Fanon wrote: "The news which interests the Third World does not deal with King Baudoin's marriage nor the scandals of the Italian ruling class. What we want to hear about are the experiments carried out by the Argentinians and the Burmese in their efforts to overcome illiteracy or dictatorial tendencies of their leaders."[6]

Will this information come from the international space communica-

---

[6] F. Fanon, *The Wretched of the Earth*, Grove Press, Inc., New York, 1965, p. 162.

5. Towards a Democratic Reconstruction of Mass Communications 69

tions system now being organized under Washington-Comsat's direction? We return, in conclusion, to our point of departure. The world's desperate communications needs, first for literacy and education but also for meaningful information, are deeply dependent on and influenced by the communications structure and system that operate in the United States. American power, expressed industrially, militarily and culturally, has become the most potent force on earth. Its impact [162] transcends all national boundaries. Directly by economic control, indirectly by trade and a foreign emulation effect, communications have become a decisive element in the extension of United States world power. Consequently, the link between America's domestic cultural condition and the world's informational-educational requirements can hardly be overstated. The fetters that bind American talent and limit its national engagement are essentially the same as those which are hobbling the social utilization of global communications. Antiquated and narrow perspectives and structures at home and abroad are choking human potential.

More than this, the technological advances that are reducing the world to thimble size, if not assimilated by anticipatory and unselfish behavior on the highest order of international cooperation, can only evoke mean and regressive national responses. This may already be occurring. How otherwise can weak nations defend themselves against globe-girdling satellites that will soon possess the capability of broadcasting messages directly into living rooms throughout the world? What protection is available to developing states against skyborne programming, commercial or nationalistic, that may transmit images and ethics that are incompatible with developmental designs and priorities?

The prospect for a genuinely international space communications system, which operates to satisfy global educational and cultural aspirations, is heavily dependent on the degree to which American domestic space communications are utilized for the social benefit of its own population. The absence of an American model which concerns itself with meaningful programming for its domestic audience deprives the developing nations of an advanced system upon which to draw for support and against which to evaluate their own creative work. Also, a structure of mass communications in the United States that is revised to take into account social needs may spur the changes in the international space communications system that are necessary to provide a similar orientation.

The efforts of our local dynamic centers to assert an increasing influence on the communications media have an international as well as a domestic urgency. Failure to reshape domestic communications to a form which makes room for human development and environmental adaptability can only deepen the disorders already wracking American society. The continuation of the present policy of national [163] hegemony and commercial monopoly in space communications will accelerate in the international community the disintegrative forces of nationalism and competitive chaos. Paradoxically, a viable international order may be attainable only if the efforts of America's present social under-groups to achieve domestic societal restructuring are successful. [164]

6. Negro Image in the Mass Media: A Case Study in Social Change
Royal D. Colle

While the real world has made but faltering progress toward integrating the Negro into the mainstream of American life, the fantasy world—that exhibited primarily by the mass media—is portraying him as a full-fledged member of society. This represents a significant change in the Negro image in the mass media, for where once only white cowboys rode the range, now spurs, six-shooters and ten-gallon hats adorn Negroes as well. In place of servant, dance and "crap-shooting" roles, Negroes now are seen throughout the United States and much of the rest of the world as espionage agents, psychologists, judges, nurses and just plain people.

This article is concerned with the forces and factors which brought about the change in the Negro image in television, where it has become most obvious, and in the motion pictures, where Sidney Poitier's films have symbolized a changing attitude of producers and audience. It also offers a brief assessment of implications of the change to Negroes and, ultimately, to American society.

Negro Image in Early Films

Typical of the way motion picture pioneers made the Negro the butt of humor was the Sambo and Rastus characterization ("How Rastus Got His Turkey," "Rastus Dreams of Zululand" and "Coontown Suffragettes") which lampooned Negroes mercilessly. Others accentuated the Negro's

Source: *Journalism Quarterly* 45, no. 1 (Spring 1968): 55–60. Reprinted by permission of the author and *Journalism Quarterly*.

inferior position in a white society. One which did not—a 1910 film showing Jack Johnson (Negro) knocking out ex-champion Jim Jeffries (white)—ran into official bans because it was so "disturbing" to white audiences *and to Negroes as well.*[1]

Three of the major landmarks in the development of the motion pictures portrayed the Negro in negative stereotypical fashion. One, D. W. Griffith's creative masterpiece "Birth of a Nation," capitalized on new film techniques to depict a passionate story of the Civil War in which the "good" Negro was docile, loyal and happy and the "bad" Negro was an arrogant, revengeful, conniving power-seeker. The emotion it aroused spilled over into the [55] streets as it met injunctions, censorship and picketing, as well as enthusiastic audiences willing to pay $2 for tickets, making it one of the most controversial and most famous films ever made. It also generated interest in others to make anti-Negro films and ride the crest of Griffith's popularity. While it has been withdrawn from public showings, it turned up as recently as 1955 during the Little Rock school integration turmoil.[2]

A second landmark was the coming of "talkies." The motion picture which signalled this new era was "The Jazz Singer," a film in which Al Jolson—made up with burnt cork—performed as a minstrel singer. This, while irritating by itself, was probably not so damaging as the chain of events it set off, for the coming of sound helped rekindle the stereotype of the Negro as "a happy, laughing, dancing imbecile, with permanently rolling eyes and a wide-spread empty grin" epitomized by Step'n Fetchit.[3]

David O. Selznick's epic production "Gone With the Wind," widely regarded as one of the all-time motion picture triumphs, pictured Negroes as "liars, would-be rapists, mammies and devoted field hands."[4] Besides being a major box-office success (so much that it has not been released to television), it precipitated an upsurge in the use of color in motion pictures, thus making it another landmark.

There were motion pictures made in which Negroes were treated more favorably, but through 1944, a survey by Reddick of the 100 motion pictures which had Negro themes or Negro characters "of more than

[1] C. D. Reddick, "Educational Programs for the Improvement of Race Relations: Motion Pictures, Radio, the Press and Libraries," *Journal of Negro Education,* 13:369 (Summer 1944).

[2] Robert Landry, "The Menace of the Naive Artist," In Nathan C. Belth and Morton Puner, eds., *Prejudice and the Lively Arts* (New York: Anti-Defamation League, 1963), p. 9.

[3] Peter Noble, *The Negro in Films* (London: Skelton Robinson, 1949) pp. 49–50.

[4] Reddick, *op. cit.,* p. 376.

passing significance" showed 75% would have to be classified as anti-Negro, 13% as neutral and 12% as definitely pro-Negro.[5]

Broadcasting and the Negro Image

Radio, the other major entertainment medium in the days before World War II, had a somewhat better record in its depiction of Negroes. "Amos 'n' Andy" was an anathema to some Negro groups, but was vastly popular with others. The Negro press criticized the "Radio Reader's Digest" for regularly presenting the Negro as a chicken thief or coward, but, except for comedy and the tendency to make heroes and heroines white Protestant Americans, radio gave Negroes the fairest treatment of any of the mass media.

Reactions against unfavorable presentations of Negroes became prominent in the late 1930s and particularly in the 1940s when an effort was made to rally all Americans behind the war effort. The NAACP, the Negro press, prominent show business people, talent and writer groups and the Federal Government joined in the effort to eliminate the disparaging Negro image.

And change did take place. But attending it was an unintended consequence. For in the late 1940s and throughout the 1950s, one of the chief concerns that arose among Negroes and their white supporters was the *absence* of the Negro in the mass media. The Negro was less stereotyped but more invisible.

This relative invisibility was documented by a "racial" analysis of television programming on the three major networks in 1962 by Dr. Lawrence Plotkin. Plotkin discovered that Negroes appeared on the screen about once every two and a half hours and that half of those were for less than three minutes. Furthermore, in half of the appearances, they played traditional Negro roles, most often as singer, dancer or musician. Programs designed especially for women and children systematically excluded the presence of the Negro on the American scene.[6] [56]

The situation was dramatically illustrated a year later when knots of Negro children peered at television screens through the windows of a Harlem hotel looking for Negroes. A major civil rights organization had promised them a silver dollar for each Negro—other than baseball players—they could spot. Over a stretch of six Saturday afternoons, the organization paid out only $15.

A number of conditions in the broadcasting industry conspired to

[5] *Ibid.,* pp. 368–69.

[6] *The Frequency of Appearance of Negroes on Television,* The Committee on Integration, New York Society for Ethnical Culture, 1964.

restrict appearances of Negroes on television. Habit was one culprit noted by an executive producer for the United States Steel Hour. Producers, writers and casting people were thinking "white"—or not thinking "black." Many felt, for example, that it was unrealistic to have Negroes in Westerns, yet historically it would be quite accurate to have Negroes ride the ranges.[7]

Also, fear of losing customers in the South caused advertisers to avoid having Negroes in the programs they sponsored and discouraged a sagging film industry from alienating potential theater audiences. The problem was forcefully illustrated in 1955 when the Philco Playhouse, in the last program of its series, did "A Man Is Ten Feet Tall," with Sidney Poitier becoming the first Negro to have a major role in a television drama. Newspaper editorials, petitions, name calling, threats from consumers never to buy a Philco product, and cancellation of distributorships by Philco franchise holders stood out as a reminder to other advertisers who might tread into this delicate area. In fact, when the "Nat King Cole Show" was launched by NBC several years later—it was the first television series to have a Negro as the star performer—advertising support could not be found, and the show was cancelled before the season was half over. [57]

To remind advertisers and broadcasters of the consequences of too liberal an attitude, an organization called Monitor South was created in 1961. Its architects planned to encourage economic sanctions against sponsors of network programs which were "distasteful to Southerners."[8]

The Image Changes

But by the mid-1960s, changes were conspicuous to even the casual observer. Magazines, motion pictures, advertisements and television programs integrated their content without a display of self-consciousness. For example, during a "preview" night of television network programs for the 1966–67 season a Negro performer could be seen in all but one half hour of prime time. Also, thumb through a recent Sears Roebuck catalog or a *New York Times Magazine* or fashion supplement and see the persons of different races or unidentifiable races modeling clothes. Though some call it "tokenism," it still represents a significant change in previous patterns of use of Negroes and other minority groups.

The converging and intertwining of a number of factors rather than

---

[7] See Philip Durham and Everett Jones, *The Negro Cowboys* (New York: Dodd, Mead, 1965).

[8] *Broadcasting*, April 10, 1965.

6. Negro Image in the Mass Media: A Case Study in Social Change 75

any single one seems to have been responsible for the breaking down of racial barriers in the mass media. These include:

Widespread public espousal by key organizations in the mass media of a non-discriminatory policy. Throughout the 1950s and 1960s, industry organizations such as SAG, AFTRA, WGA, AAAA, NAB, MPAA and the television networks established, strengthened or reaffirmed codes, policies or contracts which showed their liberal stance in regard to race relations. Action, however, lagged behind policy.

Persuasive actions became more forceful. In 1962, the New York State Commission for Human Rights, in cooperation with the television networks, assigned George Norford from the ranks of NBC to arouse an awareness of the dual problems of employment opportunities and racial image in personal [57] conferences with high level executives and every producer of every program appearing on the networks. At the same time, Mayor Robert Wagner's Committee on Job Advancement approached some 500 New York City based advertisers and advertising agencies urging them to integrate their advertising. Meanwhile, the NAACP confronted the motion picture and television people on the West Coast with the ultimatum that if there was not more favorable treatment of the Negro, vigorous action would be taken. One target would be advertisers whose television programs and commercials failed to portray the Negro fairly or which treated him as the "invisible man."[9]

The motion picture industry was threatened with protest demonstrations at studios, distribution centers and major theaters. There was reason for concern: published and unpublished surveys indicated that as high as 63% of the Negro population, representing $12 billion of purchasing power, might support boycott efforts.[10] Undoubtedly there was awareness of both sides that oil dealers, bakeries, restaurants, governments and a number of other kinds of enterprises had previously buckled under the weight of Negro action groups.[11]

Stronger, more articulate minority group organizations had developed. That major industries could be tackled by civil rights groups in itself was testimony to the fact that the latter had gained in strength and confidence, a confidence fed by landmark victories in school integration and voting rights battles.

Legal action was started. The United Church of Christ petitioned the FCC in 1964 to deny license renewals to two Mississippi stations which

[9] *Broadcasting,* July 1, 1963.

[10] *Broadcasting,* November 18, 1963; *A Study of the Negro Market,* unpublished report of The Center for Research in Marketing, Peekskill, New York, 1962.

[11] Hannah Lees, "The Not-Buying Power of Philadelphia's Negroes," *The Reporter,* May 11, 1961.

were accused of unfair presentation of Negroes and Negro affairs in a county where 45% of the population was Negro. Ultimately all of the stations had their licenses renewed but the warning was clear: they had to serve all members of their communities. Earlier a U.S. Circuit Court of Appeals in another broadcasting case had indicated that it expected the FCC to look into racial discrimination in programs, and more recently the FCC required a public hearing over the license renewal of WXUR, Media, Pennsylvania, which was accused by several community organizations as being "a forum for anti-Semitic, anti-Negro and anti-Roman Catholic programs."[12]

Other forms of legal action have also threatened, such as the NAACP's promise to petition the California State Fair Employment Commission if its complaints against unfair treatment of Negroes were not heeded.

Marketing considerations were changing. For more than 40 years, the motion picture industry had relied on the overseas market for about half of its income, and in some cases foreign screens provided the profit margin for a film. With the spread of television abroad, a similar pattern has developed. However, because of various import and quota restrictions along with increased world competition, U. S. producers have had a more difficult time selling theatrical and television film in the traditionally receptive outlets.

On the other hand, opportunities for distribution in the developing nations have been slowly opening up but it is a market which is sensitive to how colored persons are portrayed.[13] It behooves a producer of films and television programs to assess carefully the economic [58] *advantages* of casting Negroes in dignified roles. For example, motion picture producer Darryl Zanuck suggests that the wide publicity given America's racial problems has engendered an avid curiosity about the American Negro. This is one of the reasons he has dared involve the races romantically—risking the loss of the Southern market to gain the foreign market.

To this must be added the fact Negroes comprise nearly one third of the motion picture audience in this country. Four years ago a major studio hired a Negro press contact as a permanent part of its publicity staff.

Industry training programs started providing more talent. In 1964, the

---

[12] See *Broadcasting*, April 20, 1964, and Aug. 30, 1965, on the court decision; *The New York Times*, Oct. 15, 1967, for WXUR.

[13] In 1963, Kenya and West Africa banned the "Amos 'n' Andy" television series after CBS Films announced that it had been sold in those two countries. Three years later, CBS withdrew the program from its catalog, announcing that it was outdated. *The New York Times*, Feb. 20, 1966.

6. Negro Image in the Mass Media: A Case Study in Social Change 77

Broadcast Skills Bank idea was pioneered by Westinghouse Broadcasting president Donald H. McGannon. Its intent was to promote training and scholarship opportunities, to serve as a clearing house for job opportunities, and not incidentally, to let Negro young people know that Negroes were succeeding in radio and television in other than top star or variety roles. Similar programs have been started in the motion picture industry. Now, more and more talent and backup people are being trained by the industries themselves.

The structure of the industries changed. In the motion picture world, the Paramount case broke the concentration of power characteristic of the 1930s and 1940s and gave way in mid-century to a bevy of independent producers willing to experiment with low-budget productions, new talent and different themes. While no really startling opportunities have opened up for Negro talent—except for Sidney Poitier—the looser structure undoubtedly will allow changes more readily in the future. For example, Godfrey Cambridge and Jim Brown are playing non-racial film roles and may crowd Poitier out of the distinction of being "the only one who made it."

In broadcasting, the system of advertising began changing in the late 1950s, moving away from a *"sponsorship"* system in which one party has strong control over talent and scripts, to a situation where a number of companies share commercial support. This gives networks and program people committed to more liberal policies regarding minority groups, firmer control over production elements in their shows.

Pioneers served as examples. A few producers in motion pictures and television helped break down the previous patterns by casting Negroes in parts that might as easily have been assigned to whites. Herbert Brodkin, Stanley Kramer and Robert Cohn cast Negroes in respectable roles in their productions not entirely because of hyperactive social consciences but because it added realism to their stories.

The social climate changed. Mid-century America witnessed more concrete examples of Negro-white interaction in schools, on the job, in public life, in housing, in the military and in other social, economic and political contexts—although the amount of real progress may have been amplified by the repetitiveness and persuasiveness of news reports in the mass media.

Thus, desegregation and integration in the 1960s, born of protests, legislation and other social processes, probably created a social climate in which the professed liberalism of advertising, film and broadcasting people could more safely be expressed in providing a more frequent and more flattering image of Negroes in the mass media.[14]

---

[14] Cf: Robin M. Williams, *Strangers Next Door* (Englewood Cliffs, N.J.: Prentice-Hall, 1964), pp. 138–42.

Implications of the New Image

What is most important about this change is its ultimate impact on Negro Americans. For years, the Negro has been confronted at almost every turn with an image exposing him as backward, lazy and inferior to whites. He saw it in the mass media, school textbooks, in employment, housing and through "all the great fine mesh of capillaries in the white man's vast and all-enveloping [59] system."[15] The late Gordon Allport among others contended that this has had a telling impact on the personalities of Negroes. What we now must wonder is whether this new image so widely and publicly displayed will contribute to a new, more favorable self-image, or merely serve as a narcotizing force, allowing its audience the vicarious pleasure of seeing others who "made it."

The *potential* of motion pictures and television in motivating people to see *alternatives* to the world in which they exist has been suggested by Pool, Lerner, Schramm, McClelland and others in their studies of developing nations.[16] Similarly, a study by the author made in an upstate New York Negro subcommunity[17] indicates that the new Negro images in the mass media serve as symbols of what Negroes might accomplish. Furthermore, a majority of the respondents in this same study indicated that they make an effort to point out to their children or friends occasions when Negroes are being shown favorably. It was clear from their testimony that Negroes were well aware of this new image and that for many it was meaningful to them in terms of developing self-respect.

The inevitable problem may be that the new Negro image in film and television may inaccurately reflect the actual alternatives open to Negroes. It is not enough that our popular media change images and build self-respect and motivation. These psychological states must be coupled with opportunity in their real worlds—otherwise they may generate frustration and aggression.[18] Therefore, another dimension of the problem is the meaning of these changes to white America. And here we can only speculate that the new image may further stimulate whites in the notion that Negroes belong in the mainstream of American life.

---

[15] Harold Isaacs, *The New World of Negro Americans* (New York: John Day, 1963), p. 57.

[16] Lucian W. Pye, ed., *Communications and Political Development* (Princeton, N.J.: Princeton University Press, 1963).

[17] Royal D. Colle, *The Negro Image and the Mass Media*. Unpublished Ph.D. dissertation, Cornell University, 1967.

[18] Cf: Daniel Lerner, "Toward a Communication Theory of Modernization," in Pye, *op. cit.*, pp. 249–50.

6. Negro Image in the Mass Media: A Case Study in Social Change 79

An indication that this may well be the most important outcome of the whole struggle was given by the description by British journalist Beverly Nichols of his impressions seeing a Negro on a Boston television station:

> As the picture came on the screen I saw to my astonishment, that the newscaster was a Negro. Why I should have been so astonished I do not know, presumably because I had never seen a colored man in such a role before. But the psychological impact was immediate and almost salutary . . . .
>
> *The unfamiliar is always frightening.* And here he was, in my room, in a million rooms, speaking to me. This strikes me as a supremely sensible method of integration. One of the prime causes of what we call the "color" problem is sheer unfamiliarity; the very fact that a very large number of British people have never had a colored man in their homes makes them scared of the idea, and the fact that they are scared sets up countless unhappy reactions. Well, if they got used to the idea of having Terry Carter in their homes (I was so impressed by him that I rang up Boston to find out his name), they wouldn't be scared any more. It's simple ideas like these, ideas that spring from people with a heart, that changes the lives of nations. [60]

7. Is the Black Press Needed?
James D. Williams

Separated in time by nearly a century and a half, John Russwurm and the Kerner Commission were closely aligned in thought when both concluded in language that differed but whose meaning was essentially the same, that the white press treats black Americans rather shabbily. Russwurm found his proof in the anti-black bias of the *New York Sun*—so pronounced that the editor refused to publish a letter refuting a racist attack until the black man paid for the space and the text of the letter had been edited. Somewhat embittered, Russwurm began publication of the Nation's first black newspaper, *Freedom's Journal,* in 1827.

With little modification, the credo that Russwurm set forth in the initial issue of his newspaper contains valid reasons for the existence of black newspapers today.

"We wish to plead our own cause. Too long have others spoken for us. Too long has the public been deceived by misrepresentation in things which concern us dearly, though in the estimation of some mere trifles. . . . We intend to lay our case before the public with a view to arrest the progress of prejudice and to shield ourselves against its consequent evils."

Russwurm was saying in effect that the white press could not be trusted to represent the best interests of black people. So little changed in the intervening years that in 1968 the Kerner Commission could report:

Source: Civil Rights Digest 3, no. 1 (Winter 1970): 8, 10–15. Reprinted by permission of the publisher.

"Most Negroes distrust what they refer to as the 'white press.' As one interviewer reported: 'The average black person couldn't give less of a damn about what the media say. The intelligent black person is resentful at what he considers to be a totally false portrayal of what goes on in the ghetto. Most black people see the newspapers as mouthpieces of the power structure.' "

The depth of this distrust of the white press is only dimly perceived by the white community, even those enlightened members who are sympathetic to the aspirations of minority groups. Stories about blacks appear with some regularity in the daily press—more now than pre-Kerner Commission; editorials sometimes support measures that will advance civil rights; black brides from the black elite have been pictured on some society pages from time to time; and these are judged by non-blacks to be evidence that the white press does care about the black community, and perhaps the antagonism of blacks is somewhat paranoid.

Based on their own experiences, however, blacks feel their suspicion of and cynicism about the white press are completely justified. Given the opportunity to air their views, as they were last May in Nashville during a two-day consultation on Mass Media and Race Relations sponsored by the Metropolitan Human Relations Commission of Nashville-Davidson County, Tennessee, two daily newspapers, and the Community Relations Service, blacks literally rip the white press from page one to the back. They can cite instance after instance where they believe the white press has mistreated them and each instance has increased their bitterness. As the official and pessimistic overview of the consultation stated:

"If the views expressed . . . are an accurate reflection of black community sentiment, then Nashville is confronted with a serious racial problem. Sadly, there is every reason to believe that the views expressed were indeed an accurate reflection of black community sentiment."

The real tragedy of the Nashville session was that, with very few changes, the scenario would be applicable to the white press in almost any city in the country. Spokesmen for the press attempted to explain their sincere efforts to improve news coverage of the black community but the rage and frustration felt by the black participants were so great that the efforts were brushed aside. Out of what was said the sponsors compiled a list of general conclusions that can best be characterized as a blueprint of a failure in communications and a warning that the Kerner Commission did not understate the case when it spoke of distrust of the white press.

1. There is a gaping crevice of mistrust that stands between the

black community and the white community in Nashville. The black people see the "press on the other side."

2. The black community sees Nashville's newspapers, television stations, and radio stations as all part [8] and parcel of the same "press" that looks not, sees not, and cares not for the community conditions that adversely affect Negroes.

3. The black community feels excluded from the press. It is, in the mind of the black community, a white press which does not honestly or adequately cover news about the black community, or cover news about black people in the same way it covers news about the white community.

4. The black community feels the press goes out of its way to find stories of interest about the white community, but accepts stories about the black man only infrequently and then when crisis threatens.

5. The black community feels that the "attitude of the white press" is intentionally discriminatory against Negroes.

6. The black community feels that this discrimination involves not only news coverage, but also the employment of black people in media jobs of importance and prominence.

7. The black community feels that stories concerning violence and rioting are overplayed by the press in order to sell papers or attract attention to a specific television or radio station.

8. The black community does not understand, and in fact has no sympathy for, internal media problems which limit the amount of local news that can be presented in any given newspaper or on any television or radio news show. The feeling is that there is no effort by any of the media to give to the black community a fair shake in what time and space there is available for local news.

Editors of the white press may well argue that the indictment alleging such massive failures, as represented by the foregoing conclusions, is too harsh; that as professionals they recognize past deficiencies and are undertaking every possible reasonable effort to insure the equitable treatment of blacks. That defense, though it is often made, as it was in Nashville, cannot overcome the reality that blacks see the daily press negatively. In any discussion of race and media, this is the important factor—not what the white press says it is, but what blacks think it is.

It would be a mistake for the white press to believe, if only briefly, that all that is required to overcome this attitude is the hiring of a few black reporters, the end of the use of racial designations in news stories, and finding space for a few more stories about black people. Much more needs to be done, but the purpose here is not to describe those methods but to demonstrate, through an examination of the shortcomings of the white press, why a black press* exists.

The attitude that has been described is held not only by black laymen, who may be unaware that publishing a newspaper is a complicated business, but by blacks who have spent lifetimes in the journalism profession and are no strangers to its problems. How many of them feel was summed up by veteran black newsman Simeon Booker, Washington bureau chief for Johnson Publications, in his book, *Black Man's America*.

"Of all the creative fields that are characterized as liberal and understanding, journalism ranks in lowest esteem; it has done little for the Negro, not only in the hiring of qualified personnel but in interpreting his plight. As a lifelong journalist, I am critical of my profession, which I love and feel is important in the maintenance of a free society. It has done much, along with the movies, to establish the image of the unworthy Negro."

To balance the scales, to fill the void left by the white press, to provide an image of more than the "unworthy" Negro, the black press was created. Told on every hand that they were inferior, blacks were forced to develop their own institutions in which they could function with dignity and a sense of themselves as individuals, and the black press was one of these institutions.

From their inception until today, black newspapers have been written primarily for black people, and it is in this context that they must be viewed if their peculiar relationship to the black community and civil rights is to be understood at all. Many of the critical appraisals that have appeared on the black press have ignored this peculiarity and made the mistake of attempting to judge the competence of these papers on the basis of how closely they resembled the white press. Black papers have emerged on the short end of such comparisons, not because they were inferior, but because they were being judged by someone else's standards and not on the more sensible basis of whether they did or did not fill a relevant role within the framework in which they operated.

If black papers were carbon copies of white papers, they would be worthless. They are purchased by their [10] readers for the specific

---

* The definition of "black press," as used in this article, is restricted to include only newspapers. A number of black magazines are being published—among them *Ebony, Jet, Sepia*—but their role is somewhat different than that filled by the newspapers and they require separate treatment.

reason that they are not white papers; that what they purport to do is to report events of concern to black people from a black viewpoint.

This approach carries with it the implication that news can be different when reported in the white and black press, and while this observation tends to fly in the face of the "objectivity" which the daily press says it maintains, the experience of blacks has been such that the implication has the strong ring of truth about it. The "objectivity" of the white press, from where blacks stand, has been more myth than fact.

The Kerner Commission gave substance to this when it reported: "The media report and write from the standpoint of a white man's world . . . the white press . . . repeatedly, if unconsciously, reflects the biases, the paternalism, the indifferences of white America."

Thus, reports of police violence against black people are generally ignored by the white press, but taken seriously by the black press. A St. Louis newspaper dismisses as a "teapot tempest" allegations that a major Federal contractor has not performed well in the area of equal employment opportunity, while the black community regards this as a catastrophe. A Baltimore paper covers an Urban League affair and concludes the most interesting item is that a number of blacks rode up to the hotel in Cadillacs. In the Fall, 1969, issue of the *Columbia Journalism Review,* Frank Ferretti, a New York Timesman, in writing on New York's thoroughly reported black anti-Semitism scare growing out of the Ocean Hill-Brownsville school dispute of 1968, concludes that "there was, with the predictable exception of Harlem's *Amsterdam News,* no real effort made to present the black man's side of the conflict."

In reading accounts of the same news events in the black press and the white press, it is sometimes difficult to believe that the same events are being reported on. Illustrative of this is an incident of several years ago that began at a public swimming pool in a park in the center of a white low-income neighborhood in Baltimore. A number of black families lived on the periphery and their children had traditionally bypassed the pool for another in a black neighborhood several miles away. Under the sheltering wings of a youth leader, black youngsters began to use the pool to the dismay of whites. Tempers boiled over on Labor Day when several thousand whites gathered in the park and acted in such a hostile manner that police had to take the black children out of the public facility in a paddy wagon.

When the caravan reached the black neighborhood a number of people, concerned about the children, were on the streets. They had heard a rumor that a mob planned to march on the area and were interested in what the police would do. They found out quickly. In a few minutes the police appeared with dogs and chased everyone off the street.

The only paper to give any attention to this was the black newspaper, the *Afro-American*. Other coverage centered on what had occurred in the park—a confrontation. The *Afro* editors felt that the attitude of the police, as expressed by their use of dogs to force peaceful citizens into their homes while no such efforts were made to disperse the mob in the park, was important; that if the entire story was to be told, the attitude of the police when they dealt with black people had to be reported.

What the *Afro* did was nothing more than it and other black newspapers do as a matter of routine—report the black man's views without apology or self-consciousness. That this perspective has legitimacy—that is, it has not been conjured up out of thin air as part of some black mystique—is clearly evident in the misreading of the inner feelings of black people that has characterized so much of black-white relations in this country.

More than any other formal institution, with the exception of the church, the black press is immersed in the life of black people. Through its closeness to the black community, the manner in which it is wrapped up in the totality of black life in terms of the people who make it function and its interests, it cannot escape a black perspective.

Black reporters employed by white newspapers have lately come to the realization that they too can hardly disassociate themselves from a black perspective. They are the sum of a thousand different experiences unknown to whites and to have lived through this is to have had perceptions and insights colored in a very special way. Many of these reporters have progressed past the point of pretending that their blackness makes no difference in reporting news—a bow here to the tin god of "objectivity"—to aggressively asserting that their blackness does make a difference.

The position of the black journalist in the field of white media was stated bluntly in a full page advertisement that appeared in two black New York newspapers in February of this year following the subpoenaing of a black reporter for the *New York Times* by a grand jury investigating the Black Panther Party. The [11] ad began—"Message to the Black Community from Black Journalists"—and declared: "We will not be used as spies, informants or undercover agents by anybody. We will protect our confidential sources, using every means at our disposal. We strongly object to attempts by law enforcement agencies to exploit our blackness."

Having thus assured the black community that they were conscious of their close and sensitive relationship to this community and they would not allow this relationship to be used by outside agencies, the journalists declared:

"The black journalist is different—he is black. Many will, in all probability, cover the black community for the rest of their careers. . . . He will assign himself to cover the black community out of a sense of responsibility to bring about a greater understanding and clarity of the dynamics and nuances of the black revolution. This is frequently the black reporter's reaction to the lack of real understanding in too many of the media's stories about black people. For one thing, when the black reporter leaves the office to cover a black story, he goes home. Home is the black community. . . . We are not spokesmen for the black community. As black journalists we are attempting to interpret, with as great an understanding and truth as possible, the nation's social revolutions."

The 15 Largest Black Newspapers

Name		Circulation
Amsterdam News (New York City)		82,123
Philadelphia Tribune		
Tuesday	38,571	
Friday	36,284	
Total		74,855
Michigan Chronicle (Detroit)		72,776
Baltimore Afro-American		
Tuesday	31,832	
Friday	33,022	
Total		64,854
St. Louis Mirror		51,500
Pittsburgh Courier		48,798
Los Angeles Sentinel		41,482
Berkeley Post		40,000
Chicago Defender (Weekly)		36,458
Birmingham Times		36,000
Chicago Defender (Daily)		33,320
Atlanta World (Daily)		30,100
Los Angeles Herald Dispatch		29,500
Norfolk Journal and Guide		29,213
Cleveland Call Post		29,183

(The information above was taken from the *Editor and Publisher Year Book*, 1969. While the several newspaper chains operate a series of newspapers so that total circulation would be higher than that shown here, the figures cited are only for individual papers. *Muhammad Speaks*, with an estimated circulation of 400,000, was not included in the E&P listing.)

The advertisement was signed by reporters for the *New York Times, Associated Press, New York Daily News, New York Post, St. Louis Post Dispatch, Philadelphia Bulletin, Buffalo Evening News, Life, Look, Time, Fortune*, a number of radio and television stations, several black newspapers, and author-photographer Gordon Parks.

Whether they work for black newspapers or white newspapers, black reporters are almost universally conscious of the special relationship between them and the black community. Reporters who work for the [12] black press, however, are better able to discharge their responsibilities to this community since they are working for organs that have a basic commitment to the community.

The black press began life as a protest organ against the mistreatment of its people and it has maintained this characteristic, to the consternation of some critics who charge that its strident tones often pass over into the area of "rabble-rousing." One of the reasons, however, that it does possess credibility with its black readership is this willingness to speak out on issues that it deems important. Among the many ironies of American history is that the black press, condemned and reviled in one decade for its "radicalism," has found that radicalism vindicated in succeeding generations. In espousing the causes of civil rights, the black press has continually been ahead of what the country was willing to do at that time—end lynching, secure the right to vote for all people, open public accommodations to all, integrate education, and a host of other causes.

When slavery ended with the Emancipation Proclamation, the black press turned its attention to securing the civil rights of blacks in the face of indifference and hostility. At best, most of these papers were marginal operations, unable to command the financial resources available to their white counterparts. That they were able to survive at all has to be regarded as a tribute to the tenacity and determination of their editors—many of whom were ministers and therefore able to exercise some degree of independence from white society.

Circulation of these papers in the 19th century was limited since their appeal was directed to the small but influential group of educated and informed blacks. The situation changed after 1905 when Robert S. Abbott established the *Chicago Defender* and aimed it at a much wider audience by using the techniques of yellow journalism. He introduced sensationalism to the black press, and having thus captured the attention of a mass audience, he was able to operate from a base of strength in pushing for civil rights. The formula worked so well that Abbott and the *Defender*, in the period following World War I, are generally given a great deal of credit for inspiring the flood of blacks to leave the South for the more hospitable climate of the North.

By 1940 some 200 black newspapers were being published, and a survey of 144 of them in the period 1942–44 showed a circulation of 1,613,255. Most of them were published in urban areas where they could find concentrated circulation, but wherever they were, they hammered away at civil rights issues, sometimes as the only voice raised in public outcry. Typical of their concern were the publicity and editorial support they gave to a threat by A. Philip Randolph to stage a March on Washington, in the midst of World War II, on behalf of jobs for blacks. To prevent this, President Roosevelt signed his fair employment practices order.

One of the most articulate and effective of the black editors of that period was the late Carl Murphy who built the Baltimore *Afro-American Newspaper* into the major black institution in that city and established sister papers in Washington, D.C., Richmond, Philadelphia, and Newark. The *Afro* engaged in a running series of civil rights battles campaigning for black policemen, better schools, black elected officials and judges, better housing, open public accommodations, and many other issues. The *Afro* was not unique in its activities, and its record rather accurately reflects the same type of issues that engaged the attention of other black newspapers.

The period immediately after World War II saw the black press in a most favored position vis-à-vis the black community. Its credibility was at an all-time high and it enjoyed a virtual monopoly in the coverage of black news and in providing employment for aspiring black journalists.

On the matter of revenue, the position was not so favorable. The white press derived the principal share of its revenue from advertising, rather than circulation, but the reverse was true for the black press. Large advertisers refused to use the black press for their messages, and while their refusals were often couched in diplomatic double talk about duplication of effort, it was evident that many of them felt they could not offend customers by advertising in militant media or they held the black market in low esteem.

Black newspapers, as a consequence, had to take advertisers where they could be found, and this included hair straighteners, skin bleachers, and fortune tellers. Critics could point to these and cite them as an ambivalence on the part of the black press—preaching racial uplift on the one hand and catering to dubious tastes on the other. In their defense, the papers needed revenue to survive and it was more important that they continue to serve the information needs of their readership than it was for them to turn away advertisers to satisfy an outsider's sense of right and wrong. [13]

Operating in such an almost complete monopolistic situation, black newspapers in the midfifties were scarcely prepared for the implications of the movement that began in Montgomery, Alabama, with a bus boycott and quickly spread to other cities throughout the South in the form of protest demonstrations, sit-ins, sleep-ins, and wade-ins.

Suddenly, the white press began to take note of black people. At times it appeared that the further away black people happened to be from the home base of the white press, the more attention they received, but at the very least, they were no longer ignored. This development brought the black press to a problem—if the Nation were to achieve the type of integration envisioned in such cries as "black and white together," there would be no need for a black press. Since there were to be no separate societies, no separate press would be needed.

One of the major newspaper chains thought this possibility so real that it offered cash prizes to its employees for the best essays on why there was a continuing need for the black press. As events later proved, worries over the possible demise of the black press were somewhat premature.

Integration as a complete and total fact has not been achieved and reflecting this the white press still presents an almost all-white picture in terms of personnel and coverage.

In the Spring, 1969, issue of *Journalism Quarterly,* Dr. Edward J. Trayes, assistant professor of journalism at Temple University, reported on a survey covering 32 of 48 major newspapers published in 16 of the 20 largest U.S. cities. Of the 4,095 news executives, deskmen, reporters, and photographers employed on these newspapers, 108 or 2.6 percent were black. Out of 532 news executives—assistant city editor through editor—only one was black.

The argument is not being made that only blacks can cover news in the black community, but certainly unless they are employed in increasing numbers the white press will continue to suffer from a lack of personnel capable of correctly interpreting a community whose very complexity is enough to drown a non-member.

Given time, the numerous recruitment and training programs undertaken by private foundations, schools of journalism, and the media themselves will result in more black journalists on more papers in positions of increased importance. This hopefully will improve the nature of coverage given to black affairs, but the white press will still be concerned with its primary readership, the white audience. This focus means that it can devote only limited coverage to a community that is becoming more and more aware of its own identity and more and more aware of its own informational needs.

Attention must also be paid to the already noted distrust of the white press which makes coverage by the white press of black affairs somewhat difficult, even when black reporters do the covering. Instances in which blacks refuse to talk to representatives of the white press are no longer uncommon, and while this development is regrettable, it has to be seen as what it is—a roadblock in the path of meaningful communication.

These reasons argue persuasively that blacks will continue to look to black newspapers as a primary source of news about themselves. Hoyt Fuller, managing editor of the *Negro Digest,* put this view in these words in the *Ball and Chain Review,* a monthly publication of black media workers in the San Francisco Bay area:

"I do think that the black community is turning inward and is no longer interested in having its activities interpreted for it by the white press. It is no longer interested in having anything interpreted for it by the white press, and this is why blacks will turn more and more toward their own newspapers."

This "put-down" of the white press is disturbing and quite understandably should arouse the hackles of the many white journalists who believe that the press has been made the scapegoat for the faults of the total society and that such an attitude contains the destructive seed of separatism. The point here is not to argue whether such an attitude should exist—and in truth this seems rather moot since it does exist—but to explore the role the black press can and should play today and tomorrow in advancing the cause of civil rights and one society.

The black press is in an unparalleled position to inform and influence its readers. Almost without exception it has the confidence of the public it serves. Its readers know that what appears in the pages of the black press is aimed at them. They know the men and women who produce it are part of them, have gone through similar experiences, and are not likely to desert them when hard decisions have to be made.

The black papers are not all paragons of virtue. They have their faults and their weaknesses. An alarming number of them are still designed primarily for the [14] middle-class black, with too little attention paid to those who have not yet made it up the ladder. They tend to accept at face value the efficacy of old formulas, without taking full account of shifting priorities and techniques devised to answer new problems. They sometimes expend their resources on insignificant news events at the expense of those events that should be explored in greater detail. Their coverage, because of the thinness of staff, is sometimes spotty.

They have, by and large, not done well in attracting new recruits and they have lost key personnel to other media because of more attractive financial arrangements. Of all the new programs designed to attract black youth into communications, apparently only one—sponsored by the Ford Foundation and operated by the *Richmond Afro-American* and the Virginia Council on Human Relations—has been designed to attract young people into black journalism. Only one predominantly black school, Lincoln University in Missouri, offers a degree in journalism.

These are faults, however, that the black press can correct. The increased revenues it is receiving from advertisers, as more and more merchants discover the effectiveness of their messages in a black newspaper, should enable them to attract and retain capable journalists. Then, too, there is the freedom they can offer a journalist to express himself in a meaningful way. There is also the very real possibility that the wave of black awareness that is rolling through various communities will persuade young people that they can serve their "brothers and sisters" by speaking through the black press.

The black press badly needs to reevaluate itself in terms of relevance to today's problems, but even at this point, with its faults, it is the one institution with the potential of reaching and influencing people at all levels—the militants, the moderates, and the quietly resigned. It has no master except the people it serves, and from this vantage point it can work in the best interest of its community, it can report on blacks as three dimensional people, it can champion the cause of civil rights, and it can be a leader.

The black press cannot accomplish all that it should completely on its own. Schools of journalism, which have virtually ignored the black press, should pay more attention to this medium as part of their regular curriculums, and they should be interested in exploring methods by which they can utilize their knowledge to help the black press strengthen itself. More efforts should be undertaken to recruit new blood for the black press through foundation-backed intern programs and fellowships.

While the black press serves primarily a black readership, it can also serve the total community. At a time when frustration is a common commodity, it can point to those areas where positive achievements have been made within the framework of a democratic society, while never ceasing its demands for the correction of those ills still existing. It can and should argue against racism in any form, against a drift toward two societies. Its voice is accepted among its readers with a degree of receptivity that outside agencies cannot match—no matter how deep their commitment.

Any program that seeks to end this drift, no matter who the sponsor may be, should take this into account. In too many instances, the black press has represented a second thought, a low priority method of communication, and well-intentioned programs with a civil rights or human relations focus have suffered as a result. This could be due to the ignorance of many whites about the existence of a black press, but the sorry state of interracial communications indicates that such ignorance is no longer tolerable. With more than 160 of these papers being published every week (there are two dailies, the *Chicago Defender* and the *Atlanta Daily World*) they are too important to be ignored in any effort that seeks to bridge the gap between the races. These papers can help blacks understand their relationship to a total integrated community and at the same time they can help whites understand the perspective of blacks.

Looking to the future of the black press, the words Gunnar Myrdal wrote in 1944 are still valid:

"No feasible widening of the reporting of Negro activities in the white press will substitute for the Negro press. What happens to the Negroes will continue to have relatively low 'news value' to the white people and even the most well-meaning editor will have to stop far short of what Negroes demand if he wants to satisfy his white public. Whether or not this forecast of an increased circulation for Negro newspapers comes true, the Negro press is of tremendous importance."

In a fully integrated society, the black press would shrink and eventually vanish, much in the manner of the foreign language press. Pending that, however, it is alive and well. [15]

8. Serving Time
Andrew Kopkind

I used to work for *Time;* or was it sell? A Lucemployee is always a salesman first, and then a journalist of whatever degree. For most of three years, I was listed on the masthead as a correspondent in the San Francisco and Los Angeles bureaus, where I was assigned coverage of anything that could conceivably find its way into the magazine (except, of course, politics, which was left to wiser heads). I once investigated the left-foot braking trend—that is, the use of the left foot to apply the brakes on cars without a clutch. The trend was soon aborted. Shortly thereafter, I accompanied Conrad Hilton halfway around the world on a sentimental *chevauchée,* from one Hilton hotel to another. That ended abruptly when Pope John's untimely death canceled the gala opening of the Rome Hilton. On other occasions, I was sent to Fairbanks in late December by a superior who seemed to be made nervous by my presence in his bureau; to Aspen to ski-along with the Kennedys; to Tijuana to follow El Cordobés into the bullring; to Portland to watch open-heart surgery; to Baja California to observe the copulation of whales. Some of all that activity (and a lot of Business Section reporting, which I have repressed) eventually became bits and pieces of articles. But it occurred to me, long after I left *Time* for the distinctly drearier world of liberal political journalism, that reporting had been my secondary function. First of all, I was a drummer for the largest, most powerful publishing corporation in the world.

Time's business is to promote Time Inc. as a corporate empire. Like

Source: *New York Review of Books,* September 12, 1968, pp. 23–28. Copyright © 1968 The New York Review. Reprinted by permission.

all imperial systems, it is ultimately self-justifying; worlds must be conquered because they are there. Along the way, one or another rationalization can be made: it makes money for stockholders, employs talented journalists, imparts useful information to a mass audience, invigorates the economy through advertising, and helps US policy in Vietnam. All that may be true, but the basic urge is to its own expansion. The metastasis is the message.

For shorter or longer periods, *Time*'s writers and reporters can believe that their jobs are largely separate from the machinery of the imperial corporation. They do their journalistic thing and the business types do theirs. Except for a few annoying extra-reportorial chores (I can recall two: finding scuba equipment for Clare Boothe Luce, and checking out a graduate school for an executive's son), correspondents are generally left to their whales and what-not. In their minds they perceive a gulf fixed between them and the corporate side. But at last it is only in their minds. They are company men [23] as surely as any ad salesman. They function not as independent journalists but as operatives of an institution which is not primarily journalistic. Interests which have nothing to do with news reporting form the context in which the reporters must work, and the institutional values flow accordingly. Careerism, status, non-involvement, flippancy, a patronizing tone: it's all built into the system. Whatever it once may have been, working for *Time* is not now like working for *Le Monde* or *The National Review* or the *Arkansas Gazette*. A *Time* reporter might as well be a junior executive at Hunt Foods or Unilever: all corporate conglomerates are essentially the same.

John Kobler's thin, chatty—altogether *Timey*—biography of Henry Luce[1] lists some of the effects of *Time*'s "corporate journalism," but it hardly discusses the implications. Luce's life—at least in the telling of it—has a certain one-dimensionality, a uniform gruffness that leads biographers to proclaim honesty, integrity, and foresight and then find themselves stumped for a second chapter. (Luce's co-founder of Time Inc., Briton Hadden, was much more interesting, but he died of a sore throat at an early age.) In any case, Luce is only the beginning of the story of *Time*.

In that beginning, Luce had a dream (fantasy?) of "corporate journalism." There were two inspirations—Calvinism and capitalism—and two aspects: the corporate process in which reporters, writers, and editors work assembly-line fashion; and the corporate adventure to assemble power on a national (and now international) scale.

---

[1] *Luce: His Time, Life and Fortune*, Doubleday, 312 pp.

8. Serving Time   95

There is no mystery in the way the old Time religion served the development of the Company. Luce imparted the strict missionary values he learned from his parents in Tengchow to the corporate child of his own creation. Professor Tawney could have had no better case study. Kobler reports that Luce used to turn on to acid, but it seems hardly necessary (anyway it was Clare's idea); he was on a permanent Presbyterian high. From time to time on that trip he would see John Calvin, Adam Smith, and George Washington walking together through the gates of Paradise. *Time* reflected that hallucination. The company's financial success was final proof of its moral validity.

Like its two sources, the two streams of corporate journalism fed each other. *Time*'s internal organization was uniquely suited to its external development. Like Alfred Sloan's General Motors, Luce's Time Inc. built its power on a base of decentralized divisions. The company was able to expand in depth and extent with equal facility. What was most important was the role of the individual: isolated, dependent, and fragmented. *Time* journalists are kept out of the general community of journalism by the peculiar anonymity of their work. At the same time, they become profoundly dependent on the Company for visible and invisible means of support. Finally, their work within *Time* is so utterly fragmented that, after a while, they seem to lose integrity even out of the office. The ultimate alienation (metaphorically) takes place on Saturday evenings, as the major front-of-the-book sections of *Time* are closing: writers, editors, and researchers are served an elegant Restaurant Associates dinner, cafeteria-style from steam tables, in a barren meeting room on one of *Time*-Edit's floors in the Rockefeller Center building. Then each person takes his or her tray back to his or her little cubicle, a modular-plan office which can be reshaped or eliminated entirely overnight (and often is). The meal is usually eaten in silence and isolation, and when it is over, the diner places the tray outside the sliding door on the clickety-clackety floor. At some indeterminate time during the next few hours, an underpaid Puerto Rican pads by with a cart and removes the tray. Very clean; very efficient.

In group journalism, an individual reporter or writer is reduced to an unnecessary and insufficient production component. Even the collectivity is unimportant; only the process counts. The local bureaus and the various news departments in New York are not communes of journalists, but units of journalistic production. No one individual or unit ever sees a piece of work—the article—through from beginning to end. The correspondent reports it, the researcher checks it, the writer writes it, the senior editor changes it, and the top editor disposes of it both ideologically and mechanically. The lines cannot be crossed. If a correspondent in a bureau wrote the perfect "finished" *Time* story, all fit to size and complete in every detail, he would be reprimanded. His job was to write the perfect unfinished research file, containing ten times as much information as "New York" needed to know.

Like the state of grace, *Time* is inevitable. It appears each week regardless of the works of men, who nonetheless feel themselves prisoners, under a crushing imperative to act as if what they did really made a difference. The basic Calvinist contradiction—the necessity of work against its unimportance—drives most *Time* staffers to distraction, or bars, or other jobs. In recent years, the more contemporary among *Time*'s managers have tried to devise various methods to support their workers' individuality. There are intra-office congratulations, occasional plugs in the Publisher's Letter, and once in a great while, a direct quotation from a correspondent's file in an actual printed story. But most *Time* writers have to read their names in six-point type on the masthead each week just to be sure that they are still alive.

Except for an occasional appearance on "Meet the Press," or a freelance article in a "non-competing" publication, *Time* journalists have no opportunity to earn a reputation outside the company. The *New York Times*'s David Halberstam became a national celebrity as a reporter in Vietnam; *Time*'s Charles Mohr (who had more experience, a bigger salary, and a larger circulation) was virtually unknown until he quit the magazine and told all (to Halberstam, naturally, who wrote it all up). If reputation is a writer's capital, *Time* staffers can never invest. On the contrary: they are forever in debt to *Time* itself; which supports them in a manner to which they quickly become accustomed, and from which it is extremely hard to descend.

Time's institutional importance may lend a reporter a certain anonymous status on the scene ("there's the man from *Time*") but he cannot claim the fame as his own; it belongs to the company. Inside *Time*, office politics offers its opportunities for advancement, but only vertically in Rockefeller Center, not laterally to other publications. (Once staked out exclusively for gentile Ivy Leaguers according to Luce's preferences, *Time* is now meritocratic enough to allow a midwestern newspaper reporter almost as much chance as an Eastern preppy.) *Time* is liberal with its salaries and positively radical with its expense allowances, which serve as indices of a reporter's success in covering his field. Traditionally, new correspondents are called in by their bureau chief after the first month's expense record is lodged, and told that they must entertain and travel more freely if their value is to be appreciated in New York. "You have Air Travel cards. Use them!" a news service memo once urged in a directive to correspondents, who thereupon winged off in all directions. There are minor restrictions, but for the most part Time staffers are free to spend almost anything for any purpose and "put it down as a lunch." The phrase is almost a corporate philosophy. Many young journalists who come to work for Time reckon that they will stay for lunch and then leave after a few years, just at the moment that their souls begin to slip away to corporate ownership. Some do eat and run; but it is harder than they think. The process of assimilation into Time style (corporate and literary) begins quickly, and before very long they are both selling and sold.

What we disliked most about Time was not its politics or its style or its support of this or that idea, but its manipulation of us. All the rest we had come to accept, and we knew it was no better on other magazines or papers. (The New York Times too has terrible politics, worse style, and it supports bad ideas.) But what dominated our lives was the Time process; it was the topic of every four-martini lunch. The atmosphere of extreme alienation helped produce many of the effects which readers of Time can easily spot: the phony crisis, the false narrative integrity of a story, the flip cynicism, the hollow know-it-all airs, the adolescent sexual leers. In any case, the formulization of Time stories[2] became almost a ritual response to our situation; the obsessive puns and excessive jokes were a pathological symptom.

The simple mechanism of alienation was universal un-responsibility. Correspondents believed that nothing they wrote would ever be printed in any recognizable form, and any facts they might supply (or invent) would be checked and corrected by researchers at some point along the way. Writers had no connection at all with the realities of the stories they wrote; they just supplied the structure (Otto Friedrich, of Newsweek and The Saturday Evening Post, once described it all in a Harper's article called "There are 00 Trees in Russia." In the classic newsmagazine tradition, writers never need know facts at all; they leave blanks for researchers to fill in). No one was accountable for anything. Dissimulation to sources became the only possible defense; to an interviewee, devastated by a brutal attack in Time, a correspondent will always say: "I wrote it better."

If Time style is at least partly a function of the reporting and writing process, Time's content is largely determined by its corporate role. Bureaus are more than news-gathering depots; they are missions to

---

[2] The basic structure of the Time formula is the extrapolation from insignificant detail to cosmic truth. It has its origin in an (apocryphal) Life photo caption: Under a one-column cut of Hitler eating from a bowl with a spoon: "ADOLF HITLER EATS cornflakes for breakfast, wants to conquer world."

centers of power. Bureau chiefs naturally have ambassadorial status. Kobler reports that Luce told a correspondent on his way to Berlin in 1940, "When you get there, remember you're second only to the American ambassador." Abroad, Time editors travel in semi-state formality, commanding interviews with native potentates and, occasionally, granting interviews themselves to important figures. Time Inc. for many years had a roving ambassador-without-portfolio, John Scott, whose job was to travel abroad for periods of time and then make speeches about world affairs to businessmen's dinners in the US (he had other jobs, too, but they remained shadowy).

In domestic bureaus, Time reporters have a less stately but more critical role. They minister to the interests of the local business and political leaders, or at least those with whom Time Inc. must do business or politics. In Los Angeles, for instance, the bureau chief is given a large subsidy for a fancy house in which he [25] can entertain Southern California fat cats in a style they will appreciate. Every so often, one of them is encouraged in his appreciation by a favorable story. The highest tribute is a cover story (followed by the presentation of the original cover portrait to the subject), and the cats all scramble for that honor. Over the last several years, the L.A. bureau has done covers on Mrs. Norman Chandler (Los Angeles Times, University of California, culture patron), Charles "Tex" Thornton (Litton Industries, ex-whiz kid at Ford), William Pereira (architecture and planning), Courtlandt Gross (Lockheed), Norton Simon (Hunt Foods), Tom Jones (Northrop Corporation), Conrad Hilton. Each of the articles may contain one or two uncomplimentary facts or comments (Mr. X picks his nose at dinner parties) but by and large they eulogize the subject and all his works. Over the years, coverboys and girls represent those interests with which Time Inc. will associate itself. On the simplest level, the subjects help provide advertising for many of Time's publications. But beyond that, they are tied into the same elite establishments as Time, and mutual back-scratching is the rule of that club. Along with Time's cover on Mrs. Chandler ("Buffy"), for example, Time Inc. made an enormous gift to the L.A. Music Center, which was her personal promotion.

My own realization of Time's public relations function came by way of the first assignment I had in Los Angeles. As a young "trainee" in the bureau, I was asked to check on a minor development in the business dealings of Edward Carter, the head of a huge department store chain (as well as a chairman of the Board of Regents of the University of California). I phoned Carter's office, assuming an assistant would give me the required information. But Carter himself answered and immediately offered to come to see me. He was in my office in a flash. I remember wondering why he had been so incredibly eager and accommodating; when he left, an older reporter told me that Carter would do just about anything for a cover story in Time. (He hasn't made it yet.) The pay-offs for *Time*'s favors are by no means direct (nor always forthcoming). *Time* will cut an important political figure as often as promote him, and it is difficult (perhaps irrelevant) to determine the reason. Hatchet jobs may spring from the whims of an editor as well as from his ideology, or *Time*'s corporate interests. In a way, it makes good sense to build a certain arbitrariness into the magazine. Back-of-the-book cover stories (culture, science, education) are generally throw-aways as far as the business of *Time* is concerned, but there are occasional benefits there too. The most enjoyable work I ever did for *Time* was a cover file on Andrew Wyeth, but I see now that that story began a long and profitable association of *Time* with Wyeth. (Besides, *Time*'s original reasons for choosing Wyeth were philistine—and wrong.)

In the long run, it is perfectly clear which side *Time* is on—not because of its particular stories but because of the meaning of the magazine as an institutional package. Stories are just one item in the box. They give the offering a certain appeal, but overall they are of minor significance. Insofar as *Time* promotes a view of what's important about the world, the advertising copy is far heavier than the news. Readers can easily challenge a particular piece of reportage; advertising works much more subtly. Over the weeks and years, it is the ads which tell readers what to think, how to dress, what to buy, and what to value in life. Much more than the articles, the ads transmit a sense of social class and a basic political consciousness. The preponderance of insurance, airline, securities, Scotch whisky, and communications media advertising (not to exclude those toney double-page "institutional" ads featuring abstract designs and scribbled quotations by Lucretius, Lao-Tse, and Alfred North Whitehead) makes the point. Further, the whole feel of *Time* (and the other Time Inc. publications, in their various ways), its design, its audience, its marketing methods, and its trans-verbal tones give it a cultural position—and by extension, a political one—which mere articles could never establish.

Journalists promote the package; the package promotes the corporation. From an event in journalistic history which changed everyone's conception of news presentation, *Time* became an event in marketing history. Surely Henry Luce had not dreamed of that eventuality, even if somewhere down below the possibilities were embedded in corporate Calvinism. But *Time* is largely a product of what has happened to America in the last half-century: specifically, how corporations have developed an organizational position so controlling that the whole system can be called "corporatism." Time's movement is nicely illustrative of that process. Since Luce's death, *Time* has became more "liberal" while burrowing deeper into the corporate ethic. Reactionary social policy does not promote the image of the new establishment, which is more interested in co-optation than repression, more concerned with creating new markets than restricting consumption. The recent [26] change in *Time*'s managing editorship—from the middle-brow midwestern conservative Otto Fuerbringer to the sophisticated Viennese cosmopolite Henry Anatole Grunwald—reflects the corporation's new conception of itself.

In the early sixties, we received a teletype memo in the Los Angeles bureau announcing the establishment of a "Research and Development" office for Time Inc. The idea struck us as pretentious and amusing; *Time* seemed to be imitating the technological corporations of Southern California about which we had been writing. As things turned out, it was not at all that funny. *Time*'s managers (in particular, Luce's successor, a brilliant, Kennedyesque, former *Fortune* editor named Hedley Donovan) began to understand the dynamic of empire: rationalize or die. One way of looking at things, which was Donovan's way, was that *Time* was in the "education business," and education theory was in a highly volatile state. McLuhan was just peeking up from underground, a generation of new educationists was coming into its own, and John Kennedy was preparing to spend billions of dollars on schools.

At the same time, Donovan was worried that Time Inc. itself was irrationally and inefficiently managed. Too many decisions were left to chance encounters at Piping Rock, and the cleverest people in each magazine did not have the bureaucratic space to analyze their own problems objectively. Donovan's solution was to set up "R and D" outside the traditional flow-chart of Time Inc., a super-department apart from the publications and business divisions. Its first job, in 1963, was to study the future of mass magazines, and in due course there appeared a report which was, among other things, sharply critical of *Life*. The burden of the criticism was that in trying to compete with television (basically, for advertising revenue), *Life* had become impossibly confused and unprofitable to boot. The report recommended a change of format and personnel, both of which were quickly effected. There were a few other studies (videotape, closed circuit television), but the major effort was a research project undertaken by Charles Silberman, a *Fortune* writer (author of *Crisis in Black and White*), on the future of the education industry. Silberman assembled a high-powered staff (Jerome Bruner was a consultant) and came up with a secret report that explored the implications of the new educational technology. Various intellectual and managerial arguments raged on the issues Silberman raised, but in the end the burden of his conclusions was accepted. The most important tangible result was Time Inc.'s deal with General Electric to form the General Learning Corporation, to develop, produce, and promote "teaching machines" and programs.

The debate on the issues along the way would make a fascinating study in itself. Donovan worried about the shortage of talent for new projects; Andrew Heiskell (whose contacts with G.E. as head of Urban America led to the final deal) was worried about financing; James Linen was worried about profit. Some executives were troubled by the Lucean myth that Time Inc. was not out to make money but to further the public interest (they obviously had *not* read Professor Tawney), but Donovan assured his colleagues that if making money was not *Time*'s objective, it was both a means for reaching that objective and a measure of success. In the fullness of time, expansion provided its own rationale, and the objections were discarded.

As it happened, the experience with G.E. was disappointing. According to some Time Inc. cynics, G.E. thought it was "buying *Time*'s Washington bureau for its $18.5 million, in order to sniff out where the contracts were at the Pentagon and the Office of Education." Time Inc. was presumed to be an innocent led astray by the G.E. heavies. Francis Keppel, the former Commissioner of Education who became head of General Learning, was said to be confused as to the direction his corporation should take. In fact, the problem was mostly managerial. G.E. certainly wanted its inside track, but so did Time Inc. In those years—as a consequence of John Kennedy's Keynesianism—corporation planners began to see that they might eventually make as much money out of domestic "welfare" contracts with government agencies as the defense industries had done with the Pentagon. The idea was to substitute corporate planning for socialist planning. By doing their own R and D, defense companies had been able to "make policy" and thus calculate their needs far into the future. Now non-military corporations—both Time and G.E.—wanted the same kind of advantage. By developing and producing teaching "systems" (the theory went), General Learning could in effect make educational policy, and be able to plan ahead for financing, materials, marketing, and personnel. Its (temporary) failure was in poor management and an inaccurate estimate of the readiness of American education to accept a wholesale imposition of the new systems. (Also, the theory is incomplete, as G.L.C. now knows.)

Only slightly put off by General Learning's inadequacies, Time Inc. has continued to advance its frontiers. R and D has been renamed and re-fashioned "Corporate Development." Time Inc. has embarked on a series of mergers with other publishing outfits; the latest acquisition is Little, Brown (a deal to buy the Newark *Evening News* was canceled at the last minute, but Time is said to be in the market for other newspapers). The basic impetus is to branch out horizontally into all the reaches of the "communications" industry, ready to take advantage of whatever McLuhanesque developments may appear. Like RCA, which owns the Random House complex, Time Inc. needs to prepare for the coming age of electronic publishing.

Already, Time's own Book Division, which was started in 1961, is a $60 million business. Time owns 300,000 shares of MGM stock, and has interests in prestige publishing houses in Europe (Robert Lafont in France, Rowohlt in Germany). In the US, Time has its legal quota of television outlets and a string of radio stations; it controls, or has an interest in, television in Venezuela, Argentina, Brazil, New Zealand, Germany, and Hong Kong. In Italy and Argentina it publishes a magazine called *Panorama* with local companies; in Japan it puts out *President*. In the US it has interests in pulp and paper mills, a marketing company and printing firm, and the New York Graphic Society. And of course it publishes those magazines. It all comes to $500 million a year, give or take a few million, and makes Time Inc. [27] the 174th largest industrial corporation in the US.

Time's sheer wealth and power would be intimidating enough, like some imposing Alp. But the implications of rapidly expanding corporate journalism are much more dreadful. For the society (and now that Time is international, for many societies), it can produce mass ideological manipulation, create worthless demand, and impose a whole range of values which are important to the interests of the corporation but destructive of the individual. Time has tried its hand at all that, and in some instances (China lobbying; anti-communism; the "business ethic") its success is impressive. If it seems now that the mass media are much more vulnerable than people used to think they would be, it is still true that it takes a great deal of energy to overcome their effect. Resistance is difficult to organize; *Time* can be uncommonly subtle. Its treatment of the hippies, for example, amounted to a puff-piece on one level. But in a deeper sense, the tone of the article and, more important, what surrounded it in the magazine had the effect of isolating, patronizing, and ultimately discrediting the hippie phenomenon as a kind of amusing piece of social pathology (which nonetheless held lessons for all us straight, healthy people).

Corporate journalism's effect is much more clearly seen on the consciousness of its employee/victims. I know that *Time* worked its power on me, as it does on all its journalists, and I am sure that none of us can escape a lasting taint. The best example of the mechanics of corruption in my own *Time* experience concerns a situation in California in

1964, just before I left the magazine. That fall, I was commuting between the Los Angeles and San Francisco bureaus. In Berkeley, almost within sniping range from *Time*'s offices in a San Francisco skyscraper, the students had begun the first demonstrations in the Free Speech Movement. That story was being covered by another reporter in the bureau. My feeling was that he had no basic understanding of the movement; but although I remember "supporting" the students from instinct, I did not try to take the assignment of covering their actions. I probably rationalized by saying that I had other work in progress, or that the bureau colleague got to Berkeley first, or that reporting a riot is too messy. But if I had cared enough, all those excuses would have melted away.

I think I did not care because *Time* wouldn't let me. (A few months later, when I was part of a different institution, I found that I cared about the FSM enormously, so I concluded that the trouble had been with my situation, not my constitution.) At lunch or cocktails in San Francisco, I defended the student movement, but in all those months I never even crossed the bridge to Berkeley to see it for myself, either in my role as a reporter or simply as a person. I knew that I could have no real effect on *Time*'s attitude toward student revolution, even if my research "file" had been brilliant, and I guessed that any report I did would have too many half-conscious "qualifications" thrown in to appease hostile editors and convince them of the legitimacy of my political judgment. The contradiction between how I knew I would respond to the FSM and what I knew I could accomplish was too pressing; without knowing why, I fled from the dissonance, back to stories which presented no such problems, and a social life which offered no conflicts of conscience.

In a very general way, that must be how most people react to conflicts in the wider society. The big "system" turns people off the way *Time*'s smaller system did. It is too painfully dissonant to confront issues without the power to effect solutions, even partially; it is difficult to admit discord with the neighbors or the boss. *Time* (and the big system) supports those who like insurance companies, airlines, Nelson Rockefeller, and the American Empire; it makes life difficult for those who dig black revolution, hippies, and the Viet Cong. There is nothing surprising in that, but before I went to work selling *Time* I never knew why it was so. [28]

9. The 'Alternative Life-Style' of Playboys and Playmates
J. Anthony Lukas

The Big Black Bunny soared high above the frozen stubble land of northern Kansas. Snug in his orange shag compartment, Hugh Hefner confidently surveyed his holdings and plumped down $280 for Marvin Gardens. His secretary, Bobbie Arnstein, rolled next, won second prize in a beauty contest and collected $10. Then it was my turn, and with monopolies coalescing all around me, I needed to deal. Hefner and his girl friend, Barbi Benton, sitting side by side on the facing banquette, had most of the attractive properties, but I was wary of dealing with either of them. Early in the game Barbi had lured me into a bad bargain, giving her the pale blue Oriental-Vermont-Connecticut monopoly on which she was already building a Levittown of little green houses. Then Hefner had persuaded me to take his Water Works (which along with my Electric Company would give me 10 times the roll of the dice if anybody ever landed on one, which they never did) in exchange for my Short Line Railroad (which along with the three other railroads he soon assembled gave him $200 every time somebody landed on one, which they always did). But now Hefner had Tennessee Avenue, which I needed to go with my New York and St. James. For five minutes we haggled over our chicken bones until finally he induced me to part with Virginia Avenue and $700. Only as the Big Black Bunny made its final approach to Chicago's O'Hare Field did I realize that I'd made my third mistake. Hefner's properties now sported not green row houses but phalanxes of big red hotels which marched up the board like the coast-

Source: *New York Times Magazine*, June 11, 1972, pp. 13–15, 72–74. Copyright © 1972 by J. Anthony Lukas. Reprinted by permission.

9. The 'Alternative Life-Style' of Playboys and Playmates   105

line of Miami Beach. And I was rounding Go, heading right for them. As the plane came to a halt in front of its hangar, the issue was still in doubt—there were those who felt that Hefner's resources were overextended and his cash supply dangerously low—but from the sunshine yellow of Ventnor Avenue to the deep purple of St. Charles Place, the Hefner Empire looked well entrenched. And so it is with Hefner's terrestrial empire. In recent years Playboy has erupted from a thriving but narrowly based magazine-club operation into a manifold "leisure time" industry which sprawls voluptuously across the game board of American life. Hefner and his colleagues have made some bad moves—two illconceived television shows, two abortive magazines, Playboy Tours that led nowhere—and some of their other ventures look shaky. But with a combination of cool calculation and brash audacity they have now accumulated a dazzling hand in anybody's game: *Playboy* Magazine (circulation more than 6.5 million) and its three projected foreign language editions (French, German, and Italian); a new American magazine, *Oui;* 17 Playboy Clubs (15 in this country, one in Montreal and one in London); three British gambling casinos and another on a Caribbean cruise ship; resort hotels in Lake Geneva, Wis., Miami Beach, Great Gorge, N.J., and Jamaica; one in-city hotel, Chicago's Playboy Towers; two movie theaters, one in New York and one in Chicago; a film division which, in collaboration with other companies, has already produced one movie ("Macbeth"), is producing another ("The Naked Ape") and has plans for at least three more; a book division now publishing 20 hardcover and dozens of softcover books a year; [13] a book club, a line of greeting cards; a music publishing and record company; a Chicago model agency; a Los Angeles limousine service, and dozens of products—from cufflinks to beer mugs—marketed with the Playboy rabbit trademark. All this and a few odds and ends, wrapped up in Playboy Enterprises, Inc., and selling—the last time I looked—at 21¼ on the New York Stock Exchange.

While extensive and diverse, the Playboy Empire should not be compared with conglomerates like Italy's I.F.I. or Japan's Mitsubishi, which dump a potpourri of industries into one cauldron. Playboy officials emphasize that their realm is a "congeneric," an organic grouping of parts which complement each other (as in Monopoly, where the key to success is the grouping of color-coordinated properties). Robert Preuss, a soft-spoken but tough-minded accountant who was Hefner's college roommate and is now Playboy's executive vice president and secondin-command, says, "Don't confuse us with the guys who go out and buy a sewing-machine company one week and a sparkplug firm the next. Everything we do comes out of the Playboy idea, the Playboy outlook."

There is even something called the Playboy environment, an idea that has been floating around the company's Chicago headquarters for years now. A few years ago one executive envisioned it thus: "A man gets up in his Playboy trailer, brushes his teeth with Playboy toothpaste, puts on his Playboy suit. . . ." When I threw that at Bob Preuss, he grimaced. "Yes, we've been talking about a Playboy Environment, but it's not trailers and toothpaste. Let me give you an idea what it might be, though. A man gets up in his Playboy townhouse at Lake Geneva, calls a Playboy limousine to take him to the airport, where he gets into a Playboy chartered plane, flies to New York, takes a Playboy limousine to a Playboy hotel in midtown Manhattan, changes into his Playboy suit, takes a Playboy ferry to a Playboy convention center on Randall's Island for his business meeting, that night goes to a Playboy restaurant and then to a Playboy theater where he sees a Playboy movie. That's the Playboy Environment. And while we don't have all those things yet, we have many of them and we're exploring the rest."

As I listened, Preuss's vision seemed curiously chilling, a world in which I knew I could never feel at home. After our interview I went back to my room at the adjacent Playboy Towers hotel, walking through the Playboy Walk, a shop-lined promenade that connects the 37-story Playboy Building to the 300-room hotel. I showered and shaved; then, because it was a typical Chicago winter night with the wind howling in from Lake Michigan, I decided not to go out to dinner. Instead, I wandered downstairs for a drink at the Towers Bar, a circular affair of burnished copper set in the middle of a dark lounge filled with brown Naugahyde couches and easy chairs. After a couple of drinks I went back through the Playboy Walk, stopping at the 24-hour-a-day newsstand to pick up an evening paper, and then, using my temporary Playboy key, went into the Playboy Club which nestles behind an 80-foot expanse of bronze glass between the Playboy Building and the hotel. I had dinner in the club's V.I.P. Room, wandered upstairs to catch the show at the Penthouse, had a nightcap in the Playmate Bar, then went back through the Playboy Walk, stopping this time at the Playboy Drugstore to pick up some toothpaste (Crest, not Playboy).

The next morning, I had breakfast at the sidewalk cafe in the Walk, then killed 10 minutes examining the Playboy products resting behind glass display cases (earrings, keychains, tieclips, cigarette lighters, cocktail shakers, billfolds, golf balls, putters, parkas and pillows). Then I took the elevator in the Playboy Building up to my first interview of the day, scarcely aware that I had not been outside in 24 hours. Later, I came across a release which described the Playboy Center—the term used to describe the Building, Hotel, Club and Walk—as "a total leisure-time environment."

Whatever his press releases or his subordinates may say, Hugh

9. The 'Alternative Life-Style' of Playboys and Playmates 107

Hefner doesn't like the term. "What kind of a dream is that? My dream isn't to create a Playboy Environment, or even a whole series of Playboy Environments, in which everybody would spend all their time, because if I were another person out there I would find that terribly dull."

Hugh Hefner is brighter, more sensitive and human than he is generally given credit for being. He also has a keen sense of just how much the public will take. "You don't lay Playboy emblems on the guy's shirts, shorts, wife, dog and children; the butter doesn't come shaped like a Playboy rabbit," he once said. And he is quick to sense the oppressive overtones of a term like "the Playboy Environment." He told me: "We don't want people to live inside our world all the time. For one thing, it's much harder to create the true Playboy Life-Style inside the necessarily artificial and commercial environment of a Playboy hotel, resort or club than it is in your own apartment."

Well, what if we call it the Playboy Life-Style rather than the Playboy Environment? "Sure, I'd say that we're trying to offer Americans an alternative life-style and some of the facilities and accouterments which will enable them to live it."

A Life-Style Empire? An industrial giant which conceives, communicates and popularizes a way of life [14] through its magazines, books, records and films and then provides many of the things needed to live that life? Or an entertainment cartel which goes beyond simply selling fantasies as an escape from life but tries to sell those very fantasies as a way of life? An intriguing idea. Can it work?

There is at least one precedent: the Walt Disney empire, which began by presenting a fantasy world in films, comic books, records and television; then licensed a whole line of Disney products (Mickey Mouse watches and hubcaps, Pluto snow-shovels, Peter Pan tea sets and Three Little Pigs toothbrush holders); and finally built controlled environments in which young and old could temporarily live out those fantasies: first, California's Disneyland; then Walt Disney World, which opened last year in Orlando, Fla., adding hotels, restaurants and other facilities ("to create an environment around the project which would be in keeping with its character and purpose," Disney explained before his death). As Aubrey Menen, the Anglo-Indian novelist, remarked after visiting Disneyland: "The strongest desire an artist knows is to create a world of his own where everything is just as he imagines it."

Hefner and other Playboy officials recognize the Disney parallel. For years they have referred to the Playboy Clubs—and now the resort hotels—as "Disneyland for adults." The two men never met and their public stands were very different (Disney was a Goldwater Republican, Hefner a liberal Democrat). But Hefner deeply admired Disney and his works—he paid a special visit to Disney World this spring—and he sees certain similarities in their careers, starting with their common passion for cartooning. (Throughout his youth, Hefner drew an autobiographical cartoon strip; to this day, he remains cartoon editor of *Playboy* and selects every cartoon in the magazine.)

But the Disney-Hefner parallel goes far deeper. Both men were quintessential Midwesterners, born in Chicago of farming heritage (Disney's parents came from Kansas, Hefner's from Nebraska). Playing out their boyhood fantasies in their productions, [15] both men somehow reflected the fantasies of millions of other Americans. (Of Tom Sawyer's Island at Disneyland, Disney once said, "I put in all the things I wanted to do as a kid—and couldn't"; Hefner says, "The magazine is a projection of my own adolescent dreams and aspirations.") Both retained a childlike sense of wonder and make-believe (Disney waxed rhapsodic about the "precious, ageless, absolutely primitive remnant of something in every world-racked human being which makes us play with children's toys and laugh without self-consciousness at silly things and sing in bathtubs"; Hefner urges his editors never to lose the magazine's "gee whiz" quality). Both were fascinated by toys (Disney lavished hours on the miniature railroad in his back yard; Hefner has a "game room" filled with pinball machines in each of his houses). Both extravagantly admired and utilized the wonders of modern technology ("If Disney had any genius at all it was for the exploitation of technological innovation," writes Richard Schickel in "The Disney Version"; Hefner lives amid a profusion of electronic gadgetry and his magazine reflects this preoccupation). Both were compulsive workers and meticulous perfectionists (Disney fussed over every story point, gag or animation in his films and over every detail in his construction projects; for years, Hefner drove his editors crazy by personally supervising every phase of the magazine, and he now inspects carpets, lighting and drapes in his hotels and resorts). Both project a cheerful, comforting, bland feeling about the world and their own place in it. (Disney once said, "I don't have any depressed moods and I don't want to have any. I'm happy, just very, very happy." And Hefner: "I quite literally would not trade places with anybody on earth. I'm a completely happy man.")

In "The Decline of the WASP," Peter Schrag draws another parallel. He sees Hefner and Disney as "the two great puritan entrepreneurs of culture in the 20th century," the two extreme expressions of white, Anglo-Saxon, Protestant cultural values. He has a point. For while Hefner displays none of the anti-Semitism which Schickel detects in Disney and although there are many Jews high in the Playboy organization, the tone and feel of Hefner's world is intensely WASP. During our airborne Monopoly game Barbi Benton (nee Barbara Klein) sniffed something from the galley. "It smells like matzoh-ball soup!" she cried.

9. The 'Alternative Life-Style' of Playboys and Playmates 109

"Oh boy! I haven't smelled that in years. Have you ever had matzoh-ball soup?" Then she caught herself. "Oh, but I know it can't be. It's just Hef's fried chicken."

Schrag's real point is that Disney and Hefner examplify the "puritanical compulsion to order the world, to control, to clean up." It is a keen insight. For if Schickel is right when he talks of Disney's "lifelong rage to order, control and keep clean any environment he inhabited," so is Schrag when he calls Hefner "a compulsive sanitizer."

Which brings us to Sex. For Disney's animals and Hefner's women are intriguingly similar. At first glance, Mickey Mouse may have seemed a curious choice for a starring role in Disney's bright, upbeat world. After all, mice are rodents: dirty, smelly denizens of the earth's dark places. But, as Schickel notes, "in the mouse, as he was conceived by Disney, all conflict that the animal's real nature might have caused was resolved by an act of creative will: reality was simply ignored. Mickey was a *clean* mouse."

Playboy's women are *clean* women. Just as Disney sanitized his rodents, so Hefner has sanitized his Playmates. No warts, wrinkles or other blemishes—and no internal wrinkles, quirks or complexities—mar their ivory perfection. Just as Disney's animals (particularly his ubiquitous chipmunks, squirrels and rabbits) are always bouncy, cuddly, cute and innocent, so are [72] Hefner's bunnies. And if Disney makes his animals behave not the way animals really behave in nature, but the way they would if they were human, so Hefner makes his women look and behave not like real women but the way adolescent men, in their fantasies, want women to be.

A recent article in *The Wall Street Journal* said *Playboy* was "in full flight from its origin as a 'girlie' magazine." This misses the point, which is that *Playboy* was never really one of the "girlies," those garish pulps named *Wink, Snicker* or *Leer* which distort women in another direction by decking them out in garter belts and suggestive looks.

From the start *Playboy* has shunned lingerie (occasionally a girlish white nightgown or slip, but never anything "kinky") In the early days, when it was hard to get a decent girl to pose in the nude, a few of the Playmates looked as though they might feel at home on a barstool in the Place Pigalle. But Hefner has always sought the "virginal cheerleader" look (the first Playmate was called "Sweetheart of the Month"), and today there is no shortage of snub-nosed cheerleaders, stewardesses and nursery-school teachers just dying to be Playmates. ("You have to fight them off with a baseball bat," says Dwight Hooker, a *Playboy* photographer.)

Occasionally *Playboy* encounters a case like that of Debbie Hanlon of Royal Oak, Mich., who had already been photographed as April's

Playmate when she backed out because her parents, both Jehovah's Witnesses, objected. ("A beautiful girl like her portrayed in the nude would be bound to give men unchristian thoughts," her mother explained.) But the mother of Leslie Bianchini, the January, 1969, Playmate, had a more typical reaction: "I had no negative feelings about it. Our society is moving away from the old puritan values. Magazines like *Playboy* are an accepted part of American life."

Playboy still runs into occasional legal problems in out-of-the-way places like McAlester, Okla., Hattiesburg, Miss., and Salem, Ore. Some major companies still steadfastly refuse to advertise in the magazine, among them airlines, automobile manufacturers, Coca-Cola and Gillette (a Gillette spokesman says the company has "reservations about its being an appropriate medium for our products"). The insurance industry is particularly leery about *Playboy:* Michael Arlen, a distinguished writer for *The New Yorker, Atlantic* and many other magazines, was recently told by one insurance company that they considered him "uninsurable" because he had written for *Playboy.* Several Wall Street brokerage houses declined to underwrite the *Playboy* stock before Loeb Rhoades & Co. finally consented. And then objections were raised to the nude figure of Willy Rey, the February, 1971, Playmate, which was to recline across the stock certificate. Miss Rey's red hair was coiled over her bosom to assuage the financial community's sensibilities.

But such scruples are rapidly melting away: Witness this story out of Houston, Tex. Last fall Mrs. Margaret McClean wrote a letter to *The Houston Chronicle* saying that her husband, a postman, had delivered copies of *Playboy* to George Garver, the city's former school superintendent, then waging a fight for reinstatement. "A man who reads *Playboy* should not have a position in the schools," Mrs. McClean wrote. "To a decent person, *Playboy* magazine is one of the most immoral, obscene and lewd-type publications and should not be found any place in a decent home and never near children." It was an argument which might have been expected to arouse considerable support in a community hardly known for its liberalism. Instead, the mail which poured in to Houston's papers overwhelmingly defended Mr. Garver's reading habits and condemned Mr. McClean for violating postal regulations by revealing the contents of his mailbag. (He was promptly suspended and transferred to the vehicle-maintenance division.) A few months later, after two new school board members were elected, the board voted to rehire Mr. Garver, who showed up for his first day back on the job in a green Playboy tie dotted with hundreds of little rabbits.

But *Playboy*'s relentless respectability is perhaps best demonstrated by the glacial circumspection with which it has met the first even moderately serious challenge in 20 years. *Penthouse,* the British-based mag-

9. The 'Alternative Life-Style' of Playboys and Playmates 111

azine which has been publishing here for nearly three years, now claims almost 1.65 million American readers, still only a fraction of *Playboy*'s circulation but much closer than any other competitor has ever come. Nobody [73] in Hefnerland will admit for the record that they are worried, but some will argue that *Playboy*'s well-scrubbed wholesomeness is outmoded, even downright dull compared with *Penthouse*'s "Continental" approach (its European "Penthouse Pets," unairbrushed and uninhibited, strike overtly erotic poses).

Partly in response to this challenge, *Playboy* has ever-so-slowly begun to relax its standards. In August, 1969—the very month *Penthouse* hit the stands here—*Playboy* offered its readers their first glimpse of pubic hair, caught fleetingly in a strobe-lighted photo sequence of actress Paula Kelly. "It was a very carefully thought-out experiment," says one staffer. "We wanted to test the water." Only 29 months later when fully satisfied that most of its readers were not offended, did *Playboy* go all the way: Last January's Playmate, Marilyn Cole, presented what a spokesman called "the first pose in which a girl displayed all her charms for a full frontal view."

But just so far and no farther. "We would be insane to tamper much more with a formula that has worked so well for us," confided one *Playboy* editor. And thus the new magazine scheduled to appear in September, *Oui,* an American adaptation of the immensely successful French men's magazine, *Lui.* Although naturally no reference was made to *Penthouse,* Hefner's announcement this spring made clear that the new venture was designed to meet the "Continental" competition: *"Oui* will be written and edited for a sophisticated American audience . . . will differ from *Playboy* in that it will have a European accent." The beauty of the project is that it enables *Playboy* to take on the insolent challenger indirectly without risking its own prestige. If it works, fine; if not, *Playboy* will still be able to pose decorously, her skirt hoisted a few inches above the gutter. [74]

10. A Vivacious Blonde Was Fatally Shot Today or How to Read a Tabloid
Otto Friedrich

There is a joke among newspapermen that if a woman is pretty, she is called "beautiful"; if she is plain, she is called "attractive"; and if she is hideous, she is called "vivacious." Half the joke is the exaggeration; the other half is that this is no exaggeration at all. In describing a woman involved in a murder or a robbery or a divorce case, the same technique is generally applied to every aspect of her appearance. If she is tall, she is "statuesque." If she is short, the word is "petite." Thin women are "slender," while fat ones are "curvaceous." Physical appearance is not so important in a man, and the emphasis shifts to financial appearance. "Socially prominent" is a popular description of any man who is murdered by his wife. Bookies and gigolos may be identified as "sportsmen." And one connoisseur has defined "socialite" as "a tabloid term meaning human being."

This form of wordmanship—the art of exaggerating without actually lying—is so common in tabloid newspapers that it may be termed tabloid prose, but it is by no means restricted to tabloids. Indeed, most newspapers and most wire services use it much of the time. Tabloid prose is not merely a corruption of the English language, however. Literary critics tell us that form cannot be disassociated [467] from content, and since many writers of tabloid prose are intelligent and cultivated people, the reason for the use of a word such as "curvaceous" may be found in the mentality of the person for whom it is written. More accurately, the reason lies in the editor's concept of the mentality of

Source: American Scholar 28, no. 4 (Autumn 1959): 467–73. Copyright © 1959 Otto Friedrich. Reprinted by permission of the author.

10. A Vivacious Blonde Was Fatally Shot Today or How to Read a Tabloid 113

the person who can be enticed by such words into surrendering his five or ten cents.

Despite all its pretenses of representing the public, the average newspaper is simply a business enterprise that sells news and uses that lure to sell advertising space. It is scarcely different from enterprises selling shoes or grass seed. Like any other business, a newspaper obeys the law of supply and demand, and most newspapers have discovered that a sex murder attracts more readers than does a French cabinet crisis. Murder, however, is a fairly commonplace event—one a day is the average in New York alone—and the tabloid editor therefore makes distinctions between what are known as "classy cases" and "cheap cases."

It is commonly believed that a reader's interest is attracted by a case with which he can identify himself—there but for the grace of God, et cetera. But if the average tabloid reader were murdered, his misfortune would not receive much coverage in the average tabloid. He would be a "cheap case." Essentially, a cheap case involves what tabloid editors consider to be cheap people. This includes all working-class people, such as factory hands, waitresses and the unemployed. It also includes farmers, usually brushed aside as "hillbilly stuff." Alcoholics, whose antics are sometimes extremely entertaining, come under the same ban. So do Negroes, Mexicans, Puerto Ricans and other "lesser breeds without the law." This causes some difficulties for the wire services since the current fashion is to delete any references to a criminal's race as "irrelevant." Thus an editor who might begin by showing great interest in a murder would cut the story down to a few paragraphs after learning that it involved a "Jig," but he would not publicly divulge the dread word that motivated his editing—and, of course, his editorial columns would continue to clamor for civil rights.

There is another subdivision of the cheap case that the editor generally describes as "too gruesome." Onto his spike go the stories, more common than the average newspaper reader realizes, of children [468] being raped or chopped to pieces, stories of burglars torturing their victims to make them reveal their cache. Both cheap and gruesome, in the minds of most editors, is the subject of homosexuality. A traveling salesman strangled by a boy he brought up to his room at the Y.M.C.A. would never deserve one-tenth the tabloid attention that he would attain if his assassin had been a girl.

Sadism, sodomy, tortures, drunken stabbings, certain adulteries—these things happen every day, but in a kind of nether world that lies beneath what the tabloids like to consider their dignity. In contrast to all this, there is the "classy case." What gives a murder "class"? Rich men, beautiful women, yachts, racing stables—everything, in short, that forms part of the dreamworld of the gum-chewing tabloid reader. For the secret of the whole tabloid formula is that the "classy" murder case is not one with which the reader *can* identify himself but one with which he *would like* to identify himself. The *New York Times* and the *Herald Tribune* provide society pages for social climbers to read; the tabloids provide society columns for day-dreaming shopgirls. The concept of class, in other words, represents the Hollywood-fed, all-American fantasy, and yet the "news" about this dreamworld is always at least implicitly disastrous. The stockbroker is discovered in his "love nest"; the heiress is a "love slave"; the playboy is sued for "heart balm." Thus the lower orders, in buying the news about the upper ones, are given satisfying accounts of their objects of envy committing depravities and defalcations, of their imminent descent to the readers' own level. Although reader-criminal identification may seem farfetched here, one can assume that the tabloid reader would like to be in a position to *have* a "love nest," even if it meant eventually being "exposed."

Once in a decade there is a case like the shooting of Jim Fisk or the kidnapping of the Lindbergh baby, a case in which all the rules of the tabloid form fit into place and a famous story virtually writes itself. But the tabloids are printed every day, and every day the readers are hungry for a new taste of high-class sensations. That is why the homely waitress strangled on the beach becomes a "shapely blonde" (the favored term "blonde" can apply to almost any color of hair, although obviously unblonde women are often [469] exoticized by terms such as "flame-haired" or "raven-tressed"). This is why the seedy sawbones who pinches his patients becomes a "distinguished physician" living in "a luxurious home in the fashionable suburb of Blank." Indeed, tabloid prose often reads like the same newspaper's real estate section for the simple reason that both the tabloid writer and the advertising writer are trying to make the shabby reality conform to the fantasy. Homes, in both cases, if not luxurious, are then spacious. Suburbs are always fashionable.

And houses are always "homes," for all the idealizing forces behind the tabloid writer require him to use the genteel euphemism in every case where the unidiomatic word will provide "class." Thus sons become heirs or scions. Doctors become physicians, carpenters become contracting executives, and even the lowest of the species may be "socially prominent."

The tabloid distortions represent so ubiquitous a fantasy that the tabloid writer occasionally discovers one of his subjects really acting out the transformation of human being into socialite. A few years ago, a New York millionaire was shot to death by his wife, and the tabloids

10. A Vivacious Blonde Was Fatally Shot Today or How to Read a Tabloid 115

set up a hue and cry for every detail of the story. One of the gaps was the background of the wife, who had been generally thought to be the orphaned daughter of a colonel. It took a tabloid reporter a considerable amount of time to determine that the colonel had never existed, and that the actual father was still very much alive as a streetcar motorman in Detroit. When the father was finally interviewed about his daughter's misfortunes, he expressed surprise that she had married a New York millionaire. He remembered that she had changed her name to become a model, but for many years he had been under the impression that his daughter was a well-known Hollywood actress with a similar *nom de guerre*. Here is a tabloid creation in the flesh.

Sex, as is well known, combines with crime to provide the tabloids with their huge circulations. But sex is as strangely distorted as crime, as strangely twisted to fit the American fantasies. The same bans apply —drunks, Negroes, workers, homosexuals, all these have no sex life of any news value. And yet the lowest "starlet" in Hollywood has her casual affairs broadcast to millions under such wonderful disguises as "friends wonder if so-and-so is secretly married [470] to so-an-so." Disguise is the essence of sex chronicles, for although sex sells newspapers, even the most lurid tabloid schizophrenically considers itself a "family newspaper." Although it may seem strange to a casual reader, the tabloid editor's desire to stimulate sales is handcuffed by a criterion known as "good taste." This criterion is so mysterious, so much a matter of "feel," that it can best be illustrated by an example.

An enterprising young lady once tried to achieve fame by going to a Cannes film festival, accosting a popular actor, stripping off all her clothes above the waist, and embracing the rather embarrassed actor while photographers frantically took pictures that could never be printed. From reporters' accounts of the scene, the girl achieved a certain small notoriety, enough to get her to Hollywood, where her misfortunes were usually reported as an excuse to run pictures of her. One day, this aspiring actress—or could it have been some other specimen of the familiar type?—appeared in a two-column picture, wearing a tiny crucifix that dangled down into a resting place between her luxurious breasts. The editor, who had been out of the office when the picture was first printed, returned to his desk and cried out in horror. At considerable expense, the picture was treated with an airbrush, which sprayed flesh-colored paint over the crucifix, so that a new engraving of the voluptuous bosom could be portrayed in the next edition without violating "good taste."

Perhaps one more incident would illustrate this strange concept further. A few years ago, a teen-age youth in a suburb of Boston murdered a girl with whom he had just had sexual intercourse on the front seat of an automobile. When the youth confessed to the police, he proudly repeated over and over the details of how he had become a man in the parked car, and the words he used to express that experience were: "Then I scored and then I scored again, that's where I scored." The childish boast embarrassed the same editors who normally want to emphasize every implication of sex, and when the story was finally printed the youth was quoted as saying that "intimacies had occurred" in the spotted front seat of the car.

Intimacies. This is the tabloid word for sex. It turns up over and over again. If any ingenuous tabloid writer tries to use a word like "sex," on the theory that an accurate term is always in better taste than a euphemism, the more experienced copy desk will change it to "intimacies." The reason for this involves the same fantasies that dominate Hollywood: Miss Blank, who has had three husbands, is cast as an ingénue stranded overnight on a mountain top with Mr. Blank, who has had three wives. There is much giggling as they pitch their separate tents, but at the end they will get married. The movie will be advertised with twenty-foot-high posters of Miss Blank lying panting on the mountain top in her chemise while Mr. Blank crouches nearby in the attitude of a neurotic gorilla. The movie-goer knows that he will not be actually shown anything that could offend the local archbishop, but he will be allowed his snicker. The snicker, the leer, that nervous substitute for the thwarted need, is the American emotional response to the so-called "popular culture."

Although the tabloids and the movies provide much the same outlet for the need to snicker, the tabloids push the whole process one step further than is possible in the movies. With an almost baroque stylization, the tabloids would take Mr. Blank and Miss Blank to the mountain top, and then, instead of fading out like a discreet movie camera, they would quote Miss Blank as saying that "intimacies occurred." Nor is that the only dainty disguise. Mr. Blank may also be said to have been "dallying" with Miss Blank, or maybe he was "romancing" her. He is her "sweetheart." No, says she, they are "just good friends," and everybody gets a good healthy snicker out of it.

Curiously enough, the chief trouble for the tabloid writer occurs in supposed sex cases where no sex has been enjoyed, as far as can be determined. The problem arises, for instance, in the periodic story of the "nice" teen-age girl running off with a boy. The tabloid editors enjoy a vicarious thrill at the prospect of a young girl's availability, but the writer finds that everything he can say about the errant couple has already been tinged with the implications of past cases. Were they just "close friends"? Were they "intimate friends"? Had there been, all virginally, a "romance"? Every word revives echoes of the old euphe-

10. A Vivacious Blonde Was Fatally Shot Today or How to Read a Tabloid 117

misms and the [472] old snickers. Denials are accepted as lies. The English language has been wrung out.

Are the tabloids hopeless? Perhaps, but not on the grounds of sensationalism. Having already become rich, they hunger nowadays after finer things, such as respectability and political influence. In New York, where the *Times* fills its half-size brothers with awe, the tabloids feel compelled to tell their uninterested readers about such portentous events as a Senate debate on farm parity, largely because the *Times* has or inevitably will do so. It is almost with shock that today's tabloid writer, looking back through clippings on the Lindberg case, finds Damon Runyon reporting the execution of Bruno Hauptmann in terms of near-hysteria: "The Wolf-man is dead." What amazement he feels, then, in looking at the old *Graphic*'s faked pictures of Peaches Browning in the bedroom with her aged husband, at the balloon that issues from Daddy's mouth and quotes him as quacking like a duck. To find such authentic trashiness now, one must leave America and take a look at the London *Mirror,* which is comparatively entertaining and consequently sells twice as many copies as its biggest New York counterpart. Although American tabloid circulations are in or near the millions, their sales are actually stagnant or declining, despite the increase in population. That is natural, however, when the popular touch has become the genteelism, when irreverence has given way to reverence, stuffiness, even pomposity.

One tabloid's saucy story about the preparations of a European princeling's long-anticipated marriage to a celebrated beauty was killed on the strength of a new managerial directive that the wedding had been handled too impertinently and was henceforth to be treated "with dignity." And so for one solid week, it printed fifteen "romantic" but "dignified" manuscript pages per day on one of the most laughable events of our time. The stories were laughable too, precisely because they accepted their subjects' social pretensions at face value. I wrote them myself. [473]

11. *From* Television and Growing Up: The Impact of Televised Violence

Surgeon General's Scientific Advisory Committee on Television and Social Behavior

Television's Effects

Television's popularity raises important questions about its social effects. There is interest and concern in regard to many segments of the population—ethnic minorities, religious groups, the old, the unwell, the poor. This committee has been principally concerned with one segment, children and youth, and in particular with the effects of televised violence on their tendencies toward aggressive behavior.

People ask behavioral scientists various questions about television and violence. In our opinion the questions are often far too narrowly drawn. For example:

(1) It is sometimes asked if watching violent fare on television *can* cause a young person to act aggressively. The answer is that, of course, under some circumstances it can. We did not need massive research to know that at least an occasional unstable individual might get sufficiently worked up by some show to act in an impetuous way. The question is faulty, for the real issue is how often it happens, [6] what predispositional conditions have to be there, and what different undesirable, as well as benign, forms the aggressive reaction takes when it occurs.

Source: Summary of Report to the Surgeon General, United States Public Health Service, from the Surgeon General's Scientific Advisory Committee on Television and Social Behavior (Washinton, D.C.: Government Printing Office, 1972), pp. 6–19.

(2) It is sometimes asked if the fact that children watch a steady fare of violent material on television many hours a day from early childhood through adolescence causes our society to be more violent. Presumably the answer is, to some degree, "yes," but we consider the question misleading. We know that children imitate and learn from everything they see—parents, fellow children, schools, the media; it would be extraordinary, indeed, if they did not imitate and learn from what they see on television. We have some limited data that conform to our presumption. We have noted in the studies at hand a modest association between viewing of violence and aggression among at least some children, and we have noted some data which are consonant with the interpretation that violence viewing produces the aggression; this evidence is not conclusive, however, and some of the data are also consonant with other interpretations.

Yet, as we have said, the real issue is once again quantitative: how much contribution to the violence of our society is made by extensive violent television viewing by our youth? The evidence (or more accurately, the difficulty of finding evidence) suggests that the effect is small compared with many other possible causes, such as parental attitudes or knowledge of and experience with the real violence of our society. [7]

The sheer amount of television violence may be unimportant compared with such subtle matters as what the medium says about it: is it approved or disapproved, committed by sympathetic or unsympathetic characters, shown to be effective or not, punished or unpunished? Social science today cannot say which aspects of the portrayal of violence make a major difference or in what way. It is entirely possible that some types of extensive portrayals of violence could reduce the propensity to violence in society and that some types might increase it. In our present state of knowledge, we are not able to specify what kinds of violence portrayal will have what net result on society.

What are the alternatives? If broadcasters simply changed the quantitative balance between violent and other kinds of shows, it is not clear what the net effect would be. People hunt and choose the kinds of stimulus material they want. Violent material is popular. If our society changed in no other way than changing the balance of television offerings, people, to some degree, would still seek out violent material. How much effect a modest quantitative change in television schedules would have is now quite unanswerable. More drastic changes, such as general censorship, would clearly have wide effects, but of many kinds, and some of them distinctly undesirable.

In our judgment, the key question that we should be asked is thus a complicated one concerning alternatives. The proper question is, "What kinds of changes, if any, in television content and practices could have a significant net effect in reducing the propensity to undesirable aggression among the audience, and what other effects, desirable and undesirable, would each such change have?" [8]

The state of our knowledge, unfortunately, is not such as to permit confident conclusions in answer to such a question. The readers of this report will find in it evidence relevant to answering such questions, but far short of an answer. The state of present knowledge does not permit an agreed answer.

Effects on Aggressiveness

Television is only one of the many factors which in time may precede aggressive behavior. It is exceedingly difficult to disentangle from other elements of an individual's life history.

Violence and aggressiveness are also not concepts on which there is unvarying consensus. This applies equally to events observed in real life or through the media and to behavior in which an individual may engage. Violence is a vague term. What seems violent to one may not seem so to another. Aggressiveness is similarly ambiguous, and its designation as antisocial depends not only on the act but also on the circumstances and the participants.

For scientific investigation, terms must be defined precisely and unambiguously. Although various investigators have used somewhat different definitions, generally both televised violence and individual aggressiveness have been defined as involving the inflicting of harm, injury, or discomfort on persons, or of damage to property. The translation of such a conception into measurement procedures has varied very widely, and whether antisocial activity is involved or implied is a matter for judgment in the specific instance. [9]

Effects on Aggressiveness: Evidence from Experiments

Experiments have the advantage of allowing causal inference because various influences can be controlled so that the effects, if any, of one or more variables can be assessed. To varying degrees, depending on design and procedures, they have the disadvantages of artificiality and constricted time span. The generalizability of results to everyday life is a question often not easily resolvable.

Experiments concerned with the effects of violence or aggressiveness portrayed on film or television have focused principally on two different kinds of effects: *imitation* and *instigation.* Imitation occurs when what is seen is mimicked or copied. Instigation occurs when what is seen is followed by increased aggressiveness.

Imitation. One way in which a child may learn a new behavior is through observation and imitation. Some twenty published experiments document that children are capable of imitating filmed aggression shown on a movie or television screen. Capacity to imitate, however, does not imply performance. Whether or not what is observed actually will be imitated depends on a variety of situational and personal factors.

No research in this program was concerned with imitation, because the fact that aggressive or violent behavior presented on film or television can be imitated by children is already thoroughly documented.

Instigation. Some thirty published experiments have been widely interpreted as indicating that the viewing of violence on film or television by children or adults increases the likelihood of aggressive behavior. This interpretation has also been widely challenged, principally on the ground that results cannot be generalized beyond the [10] experimental situation. Critics hold that in the experimental situation socially inhibiting factors, such as the influence of social norms and the risk of disapproval or retaliation, are absent, and that the behavior after viewing, though labeled "aggressive," is so unlike what is generally understood by the term as to raise serious questions about the applicability of these laboratory findings to real-life behavior.

The research conducted in this program attempted to provide more precise and extensive evidence on the capacity of televised violence to instigate aggressive behavior in children. The studies variously involve whole television programs, rather than brief excerpts; the possibility of making constructive or helping, as well as aggressive, responses after viewing; and the measurement of effects in the real-life environment of a nursery school. Taken as a group, they represent an effort to take into account more of the circumstances that pertain in real life, and for that reason they have considerable cogency.

In sum. The experimental studies bearing on the effects of aggressive television entertainment content on children support certain conclusions. First, violence depicted on television can immediately or shortly thereafter induce mimicking or copying by children. Second, under certain circumstances television violence can instigate an increase in aggressive acts. The accumulated evidence, however, does not warrant the conclusion that televised violence has a uniformly adverse effect nor the conclusion that it has an adverse effect on the majority of children. It cannot even be said that the majority of the children in the various studies we have reviewed showed an increase in aggressive behavior in response to the violent fare to which they were [11] exposed. The evidence does indicate that televised violence may lead to increased aggressive behavior in certain subgroups of children, who might constitute a small portion or a substantial proportion of the total population of young television viewers. We cannot estimate the size of the fraction, however, since the available evidence does not come from cross-section samples of the entire American population of children.

The experimental studies we have reviewed tell us something about the characteristics of those children who are most likely to display an increase in aggressive behavior after exposure to televised violence. There is evidence that among young children (ages four to six) those most responsive to television violence are those who are highly aggressive to start with—who are prone to engage in spontaneous aggressive actions against their playmates and, in the case of boys, who display pleasure in viewing violence being inflicted upon others. The very young have difficulty comprehending the contextual setting in which violent acts are depicted and do not grasp the meaning of cues or labels concerning the make-believe character of violence episodes in fictional programs. For older children, one study has found that labeling violence on a television program as make-believe rather than as real reduces the incidence of induced aggressive behavior. Contextual cues to the motivation of the aggressor and to the consequences of acts of violence might also modify the impact of televised violence, but evidence on this topic is inconsistent.

Since a considerable number of experimental studies on the effects of televised violence have now been carried out, it seems improbable [12] that the next generation of studies will bring many great surprises, particularly with regard to broad generalizations not supported by the evidence currently at hand. It does not seem worthwhile to continue to carry out studies designed primarily to test the broad generalization that most or all children react to televised violence in a uniform way. The lack of uniformity in the extensive data now at hand is much too impressive to warrant the expectation that better measures of aggression or other methodological refinements will suddenly allow us to see a uniform effect.

Effects on Aggressiveness: Survey Evidence

A number of surveys have inquired into the violence viewing of young people and their tendencies toward aggressive behavior. Measures of *exposure* to television violence included time spent viewing, preference for violent programming, and amount of viewing of violent programs. Measures of *aggressive tendencies* variously involved self and others' reports of actual behavior, projected behavior, and attitudes. The behavior involved varied from acts generally regarded as heinous (e.g.,

11. From Television and Growing Up: The Impact of Televised Violence

arson) to acts which many would applaud (e.g., hitting a man who is attacking a woman).

All of the studies inquired into the relationship between exposure to television violence and aggressive tendencies. Most of the relationships observed were positive, but most were also of low magnitude, ranging from null relationships to correlation coefficients of about .20. A few of the observed correlation coefficients, however, reached .30 or just above. [13]

On the basis of these findings, and taking into account their variety and their inconsistencies, we can tentatively conclude that there is a modest relationship between exposure to television violence and aggressive behavior or tendencies, as the latter are defined in the studies at hand. Two questions which follow are: (1) what is indicated by a correlation coefficient of about .30, and (2) since correlation is not in itself a demonstration of causation, what can be deduced from the data regarding causation?

Correlation coefficients of "middle range," like .30, may result from various sorts of relationships, which in turn may or may not be manifested among the majority of the individuals studied. While the magnitude of such a correlation is not particularly high, it betokens a relationship which merits further inquiry.

Correlation indicates that two variables—in this case violence viewing and aggressive tendencies—are *related* to each other. It does not indicate which of the two, if either, is the cause and which the effect. In this instance the correlation could manifest any of three causal sequences:

> that violence viewing leads to aggression;
> that aggression leads to violence viewing;
> that both violence viewing and aggression are products of a third condition or set of conditions.

The data from these studies are in various ways consonant with both the first and the third of these interpretations, but do not conclusively support either of the two. [14]

Findings consonant with the interpretation that violence viewing leads to aggression include the fact that two of the correlation coefficients at the .30 level are between *earlier* viewing and *later* measured aggression. However, certain technical questions exist regarding the measures employed, and the findings can be regarded as equally consonant with the view that both violence viewing and aggression are common products of some antecedent condition or conditions.

Various candidates for such a preceding condition can be identified in the data. These include preexisting levels of aggression, underlying personality factors, and a number of aspects of parental attitudes and behavior, among them parental affection, parental punishment, parental emphasis on nonaggression, and habitual types of parent-child communication patterns. Several of these variables failed to operate statistically in a manner consonant with common origin interpretations. At least two, "parental emphasis on nonaggression" and "family communication patterns," operated in manners consonant with such an interpretation, but the pertinent data were too limited to validate common origin status for either one.

The common origin interpretation remains viable, however. Improved measures might possibly change the picture, and there is need for further and more refined investigation of the role played by personality factors and by family and peer attitudes and behaviors.

General Implications

The best predictor of later aggressive tendencies in some studies is the existence of earlier aggressive tendencies, whose origins may [15] lie in family and other environmental influences. Patterns of communication within the family and patterns of punishment of young children seem to relate in ways that are as yet poorly understood both to television viewing and to aggressive behavior. The possible role of mass media in very early acquisition of aggressive tendencies remains unknown. Future research should concentrate on the impact of media material on very young children.

As we have noted, the data, while not wholly consistent or conclusive, do indicate that a modest relationship exists between the viewing of violence and aggressive behavior. The correlational evidence from surveys is amenable to either of two interpretations: that the viewing of violence causes the aggressive behavior, or that both the viewing and the aggression are joint products of some other common source. Several findings of survey studies can be cited to sustain the hypothesis that viewing of violent television has a causal relation to aggressive behavior, though neither individually nor collectively are the findings conclusive. They could also be explained by operation of a "third variable" related to preexisting conditions.

The experimental studies provide some additional evidence bearing on this issue. Those studies contain indications that, under certain limited conditions, television viewing may lead to an increase in aggressive behavior. The evidence is clearest in highly controlled laboratory studies and considerably weaker in studies conducted under more natural conditions. Although some questions have been raised as to

11. *From* Television and Growing Up: The Impact of Televised Violence

whether the behavior observed in the laboratory studies can be called "aggressive" in the consensual sense of the term, the studies point to [16] two mechanisms by which children might be led from watching television to aggressive behavior: the mechanism of imitation, which is well established as part of the behavioral repertoire of children in general; and the mechanism of incitement, which may apply only to those children who are predisposed to be susceptible to this influence. There is some evidence that incitement may follow nonviolent as well as violent materials, and that this incitement may lead to either prosocial or aggressive behavior, as determined by the opportunities offered in the experiment. However, the fact that some children behave more aggressively in experiments after seeing violent films is well established.

The experimental evidence does not suffer from the ambiguities that characterize the correlational data with regard to third variables, since children in the experiments are assigned in ways that attempt to control such variables. The experimental findings are weak in various other ways and not wholly consistent from one study to another. Nevertheless, they provide suggestive evidence in favor of the interpretation that viewing violence on television is conducive to an increase in aggressive behavior, although it must be emphasized that the causal sequence is very likely applicable only to some children who are predisposed in this direction.

Thus, there is a convergence of the fairly substantial experimental evidence for *short-run* causation of aggression among some children by viewing violence on the screen and the much less certain evidence from field studies that extensive violence viewing precedes some *long-run* manifestations of aggressive behavior. This convergence of the two types of evidence constitutes some preliminary indication of a causal [17] relationship, but a good deal of research remains to be done before one can have confidence in these conclusions.

The field studies, correlating different behavior among adolescents, and the laboratory studies of the responses by younger children to violent films converge also on a number of further points.

First, there is evidence that any sequence by which viewing television violence causes aggressive behavior is most likely applicable only to some children who are predisposed in that direction. While imitative behavior is shown by most children in experiments on that mechanism of behavior, the mechanism of being incited to aggressive behavior by seeing violent films shows up in the behavior only of some children who were found in several experimental studies to be previously high in aggression. Likewise, the correlations found in the field studies between extensive viewing of violent material and acting in aggressive ways seem generally to depend on the behavior of a small proportion of the respondents who were identified in some studies as previously high in aggression.

Second, there are suggestions in both sets of studies that the way children respond to violent film material is affected by the context in which it is presented. Such elements as parental explanations, the favorable or unfavorable outcome of the violence, and whether it is seen as fantasy or reality may make a difference. Generalizations about all violent content are likely to be misleading.

Thus, the two sets of findings converge in three respects: a preliminary and tentative indication of a causal relation between viewing violence on television and aggressive behavior; an indication [18] that any such causal relation operates only on some children (who are predisposed to be aggressive); and an indication that it operates only in some environmental contexts. Such tentative and limited conclusions are not very satisfying. They represent substantially more knowledge than we had two years ago, but they leave many questions unanswered.

Some of the areas on which future research should concentrate include: (1) Television's effects in the context of the effects of other mass media. (2) The effects of mass media in the context of individual developmental history and the totality of environmental influences, particularly that of the home environment. In regard to the relationship between televised violence and aggression, specific topics in need of further attention include: predispositional characteristics of individuals; age differences; effects of labeling, contextual cues, and other program factors; and longitudinal influences of television. (3) The functional and dysfunctional aspects of aggressive behavior in successfully adapting to life's demands. (4) The modeling and imitation of prosocial behavior. (5) The role of environmental factors, including the mass media, in the teaching and learning of values about violence, and the effects of such learning. (6) The symbolic meanings of violent content in mass media fiction, and the function in our social life of such content. [19]

12. The Press and the Bay of Pigs
Victor Bernstein and Jesse Gordon

Aside from its other meanings, the Bay of Pigs was "also important in the history of relations between the American press and the U.S. Government," Clifton Daniel, managing editor of the *New York Times,* told the World Press Institute last year. Mr. Daniel went on to reconstruct this history insofar as it involved his newspaper. This article attempts a reconstruction on a somewhat broader basis. Such a history has permanent relevance to the democratic process; and, in any case, it is always useful to remind the press that if it worried as much about its own credibility gap as about the Administration's the country would be well served.

Early in November, 1960, Carey McWilliams, editor of *The Nation,* received a phone call from Paul Baran, Stanford University economist. He said that Ronald Hilton, then director of Stanford's Institute of Hispanic American and Luso-Brazilian Studies, "is just back from Guatemala. In the current issue of his *Hispanic American Report,* he writes that it is common knowledge down there that the CIA is training Cuban exiles at a secret Guatemalan base in preparation for an invasion of Cuba." Mr. McWilliams checked back with Dr. Hilton, and the result was an editorial which appeared in *The Nation* of Saturday, November 19.

"Fidel Castro," the editorial began, "may have a sounder basis for his expressed fears of a U.S.-financed 'Guatemala-type' invasion than

---

Source: *Columbia Forum* 10, no. 3 (Fall 1967): 5–13. Copyright © 1967 by the Trustees of Columbia University in the City of New York. Reprinted by permission of the publisher.

most of us realize." It went on to give the gist of Dr. Hilton's story, which located the base near the mountain town of Retalhuleu and said that the whole affair had been aired on the front page of *La Hora,* Guatemala's leading newspaper. The editorial ended:

> We ourselves, of course, pretend to no first-hand knowledge of the facts. . . . If Washington is ignorant of the existence of the base, or, knowing that it exists, is nevertheless innocent of any involvement in it, then surely the appropriate authorities will want to scotch all invidious rumors. . . . On the other hand, if the reports as heard by Dr. Hilton are true, then public pressure should be brought to bear upon the Administration to abandon this dangerous and hare-brained project.
>
> There is a second reason why we believe the reports merit publication; they can, and should, be checked immediately by all U.S. news media with correspondents in Guatemala.

The issue containing the editorial went to press on Friday, November 11. On that day, 75 proofs, together with copies of a news release based upon the editorial, were distributed by Jesse Gordon to all major news media, including foreign news bureaus in New York. The more important local offices were serviced by messenger. Mr. Gordon followed the dispatch of the releases with telephone calls to various news desks.

The phone calls elicited some puzzling reactions. The Associated Press was called three times; each time a different desk man answered, professed interest in the story, but said he hadn't seen either the release or a proof of the editorial. Could duplicates be sent immediately? Three duplicates were sent in as many hours, apparently to end up on the desk of someone in the AP hierarchy who didn't want them to go any farther. In the end, neither the AP nor the United Press International used the story, nor did they request any check on it that weekend from their correspondents in Guatemala.

On Monday, Mr. Gordon was again in touch [5] with the UPI, this time speaking to Francis L. McCarthy, head of the service's Latin American desk. "Yes," said Mr. McCarthy, "there's a big base in operation in Guatemala and U.S. planes are flying in and out. But the Pentagon denies any knowledge and the State Department says 'no comment.' One story we hear is that the base is being built by the U.S. as a replacement for Guantánamo."

At this stage, knowledge of the base follows an interesting geographic distribution pattern. The readers of the Guatemalan newspaper *La Hora* knew there was a base. Indeed, according to Andrew Tully in his *CIA: The Inside Story,* "Practically everybody in Central America knew about this [Retalhuleu] training base and, of course, so did Fidel Castro." In the United States, however, where by repute exists the freest and most efficient press in the world, apparently the only people who knew about the base were Dr. Hilton, Mr. McCarthy, and the assorted readership (totaling fewer than 100,000) of the *Hispanic American Report, The Nation* and the *York* (Pa.) *Gazette and Daily* which—alone among the country's dailies—had published *The Nation's* release in its issue of November 12.

What of the *New York Times,* the *ultima Thule* of the publicist? Mr. Gordon sent four copies of the editorial to the *Times*—one each to the city and national editors, another to Herbert L. Matthews (editorial writer) and another to Peter Kihss (a staff reporter who was then covering domestic aspects of the Cuban situation). Additionally, the city and national desks of the *Times,* as well as those of other major news media, received copies over the PR Newswire, a private Teletype circuit. Mr. Gordon followed dispatch of the proofs by phone calls to Mr. Kihss and others; all professed interest in the story, and Mr. Gordon was asked where Dr. Hilton could be reached.

It took nine days for the *Times* to react. On page 32 of its issue of November 20, it printed an unsigned dispatch from Guatemala City based on its correspondent's interview with President Miguel Ydígoras Fuentes. The President was asked about "repeated reports" of a "base established with U.S. assistance as a training ground for military action against Cuba." The article continued:

> The President branded the reports as a "lot of lies." He said the base . . . was one of several on which Guatemalan Army personnel was being trained in guerrilla warfare. The object of the training, he said, was to combat invasions of the type that have occurred recently in Honduras, Nicaragua and Panama.

Five days later, on November 25, the *York Gazette and Daily* shed light on how the AP had been handling developments:

> The *Gazette and Daily* asked the AP . . . to check [*The Nation*'s] report. The AP said *The Nation* article ocemed "thin"—an adjective which, we think, fairly describes any story as it begins to develop from hearsay or second-hand sources . . . . But when we explained that we were not requesting a rewrite of *The Nation* article but rather a check in Guatemala, the AP went to work. Within a few days, the AP sent a story which was printed on page two of the *Gazette and Daily* on November 17, headlined: "Guatemala President Denies Reports of Anti-Castro Force." The headline reasonably sums up the story; the AP had interviewed President Ydígoras of Guatemala and he had "branded as false" the things *The Nation* had published.
>
> Now for the windup. In a letter from Stanford dated November 19, Dr.

Ronald Hilton writes as follows: "On Friday, November 18, Mr. [Lyman B.] Kirkpatrick [Jr.], the Inspector General of the CIA, spoke in San Francisco at the Commonwealth Club. . . . He was asked, 'Professor Hilton of Stanford says there is a CIA-financed base in Guatemala where plans are being made for an attack on Cuba. Professor Hilton says it will be a black day for Latin America and the U.S. if this takes place. Is this true?' After a long silence, Mr. Kirkpatrick replied: 'It will be a black day if we are found out.' "

In lying to both the *Times* man and the AP reporter, President Ydigoras displayed the virtue of consistency, at least. But there is another, more significant, observation to be made about these two dispatches. Neither reporter took the elementary journalistic step (or, if they took it, failed to report that they did so) of interviewing anyone on the staff of *La Hora,* which had published the story the previous October 30. At the very least, they should have seen—or reported an attempt to see— the newspaper's publisher, Clemente Marroquin Rojas, who was then a member of the Ydígoras cabinet (and is today Vice President of Guatemala). Moreover, according to Dr. Hilton, the base and its purposes were "common knowledge" in the country; should not the reporters have been instructed, at the very minimum, to test this "common knowledge"? [6] It is precisely for this purpose, as any journalist will tell you, that taxi drivers have been invented. But both correspondents chose to go to the one man in the country who would be sure to deny the story—the President.

There was, perhaps, some excuse for the AP correspondent, Albarao Contreras, who was a Guatemalan citizen and could hardly be expected to probe into government secrets for the meager space rates paid to him as a "stringer." But what of the *Times* man?

During April of the current year, while this article was being researched, Victor Bernstein wrote to Mr. Daniel at the *Times,* requesting identification of the author of the November 20, 1960, dispatch, and in general asking for clarification of what the *Times* had done after receiving The *Nation*'s original press release. Mr. Daniel replied promptly in a letter dated April 27, 1967:

> Emanuel Freedman, then our Foreign News Editor, wrote a memorandum on November 25, 1960, that referred to the denial interview with President Ydígoras published in *The Times* of November 20, and then provided this background: "We first investigated Dr. Hilton's allegations a few days earlier on the basis of a tear sheet sent to us in advance of *The Nation's* appearance on the newsstands. We talked with Dr. Hilton at Stanford University by telephone to determine whether he had anything more than the hearsay evidence attributed to him in *The Nation.* (He had not.) Then

we asked the Washington Bureau, which drew a blank, and our stringer in Guatemala, who reported that there had been rumors about a U.S.-organized training base, but that it had been impossible to get any confirmation. He denied that Ydígoras had gone on TV about the matter."

The Ydígoras interview was written by Paul Kennedy. He was in Nicaragua at the time that *The Nation* article reached us, and we asked him to go to Guatemala to look into the situation. . . . He met a blank wall in his inquiries and on the 19th sent the Ydígoras interview. Mr. Kennedy left Guatemala on the 21st.

Paul Kennedy was a *Times* expert on Latin America. If, for the nonce, his interview with Ydígoras satisfied the *Times'* editors, it did not satisfy the editors of the *St. Louis Post-Dispatch*, who a short time afterward sent one of their own men, Richard Dudman, into Guatemala. Mr. Dudman saw no purpose in collecting further denials, so he steered clear of the Presidential Palace and ran around asking questions. He confirmed the existence of a "secret, 1,200-foot airstrip" that had been cut out of the Guatemalan jungle, and of nearby barracks capable of housing 500 men. A Guatemalan civilian told him that many of the soldiers at the base spoke with a "Cuban accent"; he also conscientiously reported that an English-speaking Guatemalan soldier had dismissed all stories about the base as "Communist propaganda."

Even with these tentative conclusions, Mr. Dudman had censorship troubles and in the end filed his story not out of Guatemala, but out of neighboring El Salvador. This led the *Post-Dispatch* to print an editorial which should have galvanized the entire American press into action:

> What is going on in Guatemala? Who is trying to conceal what, and for what purpose? Why should Richard Dudman . . . have to go to neighboring El Salvador to send a dispatch to this newspaper about what he found in Guatemala?

These were what any journalist would call "gutsy" questions, crying for answers. Yet the AP and the UPI, upon whom the overwhelming bulk of the American press is utterly dependent for foreign news, still made no attempt to search out the answers. But around the middle of December the *Los Angeles Mirror* sent its aviation editor, Don Dwiggins, to Guatemala. He reported that American funds were involved in the airstrip and base construction. The AP picked up and distributed a three-paragraph summary of Mr. Dwiggins' long article, but again failed to show any reportorial initiative of its own. In an article that appeared in *The Nation* dated January 7, 1961, Mr. Dwiggins presented strong evidence in support of Dr. Hilton's "hearsay" reports:

> No one in an official position would explain why Guatemala, a country

without a single jet plane of its own, needs a jet airstrip for military use. ... A military base actually exists behind the green curtain of Retalhuleu. All access to the airfield is cut off. ... As there is no airline traffic into Retalhuleu, there is no question as to the airstrip's purpose. Guatemala's air force, it should be noted here, consists of corroding war-surplus Mustang fighters, AT-6 trainers and some war-weary, twin-engine bombers squatting like wounded birds at Guatemala City's La Aurora Airport.

And Mr. Dwiggins reported that, upon his return to Los Angeles, an anti-Castro pilot told him of a "fantastic air-raid operation scheduled for some time early in 1961." People "high up the government," the pilot said, were offering $25,000 to pilots to fly the mission. [7]

It would seem that, by now, things were beginning to add up, even if somewhat slowly. There is definitely a new airstrip and base of some kind in Guatemala; even the *Times* says so. Mr. Dudman has reported the possible presence at the base of soldiers who speak Spanish with a Cuban accent. Mr. Dwiggins has recorded that U.S. money is involved in construction of the base and has pointed out that Guatemala, which has no jets, obviously has no use for an airstrip capable of handling them. Unmentioned, so far, is the unmentionable CIA. Still, it would indeed seem that Castro had reasonable grounds for suspecting that the U.S. was planning something unpleasant for him.

But to the *Times,* nothing adds up to anything, yet. On January 3, the U.S. broke relations with Castro. "What snapped U.S. patience," said the *Times* "Review of the Week" for Sunday, January 8, "was a new propaganda offensive from Havana charging that the U.S. was plotting an 'imminent invasion' of Cuba, and a demand that the U.S. cut its Havana embassy to eleven." In nearly five columns of text on the Cuban situation, the only base mentioned by the *Times* is Guantánamo. Why, then, the writer asks plaintively, was Castro making all those invasion charges fulminating so against the U.S.? The writer answers his own question: "The Castro Government has become increasingly shrill with its anti-American propaganda to busy minds that otherwise would be preoccupied with dissatisfactions at home."

But two days later *Times* readers were to get more solid fare. In the January 10 issue there appeared a second and lengthy dispatch from Paul Kennedy, this one sent directly from Retalhuleu. (In the weeks following November 20, 1960, Clifton Daniel explained in his letter of April 27, 1967, "rumors and tangible pieces of information built up—including stories published in the *Los Angeles Mirror* and the *St. Louis Post-Dispatch*—and as a result we asked Mr. Kennedy to go back to Guatemala and get out of the capital to try to find out just what was going on.") In a sense, it can be said that this second Kennedy piece broke the log-jam on the story, and at a later date it was to be pinpointed by President Kennedy as an example of "premature disclosures of security information."

Actually, the *Times* article of January 10 was written with the utmost circumspection. "This area [around Retalhuleu] is the focal point," the story began, "of Guatemala's military preparations for what Guatemalans consider will be an almost inevitable clash with Cuba." This was not only circumspect; it was misleading. The base had nothing to do with the military preparations of Guatemala; it had to do with the military preparations of the U.S. and a group of Cuban exiles. That Mr. Kennedy knew this, or at least strongly suspected it, was apparent in his text; but each time he offered a sinister interpretation of events, he balanced it with an innocent one. Thus, while Guatemalan authorities insist that the purpose of the base was to "meet an assault, expected almost any day, from Cuba," the "opponents of the Ydígoras Administration" insist that the preparations are for an offensive against Castro. (What is the relevance of labeling those who suspect aggression as "opponents" of Ydígoras? Are we to believe them less?) Mr. Kennedy asserted flatly that at the base "commando-like forces are being drilled in guerrilla warfare tactics by foreign personnel, mostly from the United States," and that Americans are assisting with "matériel and ground and air facilities." But he carefully added, quoting an American official, that the United States is supplying only matériel needed for "defensive operations."

Nothing in the story identifies the nationality of the guerrillas under training; Cubans are mentioned only as being among the "experts from several nations" who are acting as trainers. The base, Mr. Kennedy observes (laughingly?), seems to be on the wrong side of Guatemala for efficient defense against a Cuban assault on the Caribbean coast; on the other hand, it is explained to him that its inland site gives it good capabilities for self-defense.

Mr. Dwiggins, it is now clear, came much closer to the truth than Mr. Kennedy. But a half-revelation in the *Times* carries more impact than full revelation elsewhere. With this dispatch, the country as a whole became aware that something peculiar was going on in Guatemala, to say the least. Those who had read Dr. Hilton's original "hearsay" reports found Mr. Kennedy somewhat less baffling; they had a key to the puzzle. But only readers of *Hispanic American Report, The Nation,* and the *York Gazette and Daily* were in that fortunate position. Still missing, however, was any echo of Dr. Hilton's [8] suggestion of CIA involvement. It was now to come from an unexpected source—the State Department. A few hours after the Kennedy story appeared in the *Times,* the afternoon *New York Post* described State officials as turning aside all questions about Retalhuleu with the observation, "Don't ask us about it, ask the spooks—the Central Intelligence Agency."

Meanwhile, beginning on January 8, the *New York Daily News* began a series of articles that pushed back the frontiers of our knowledge a little farther. The activities in Guatemala were definitely in preparation for an invasion of Cuba, the paper said; it quoted Manuel A. de Varona, head of "the most powerful anti-Castro" group in the United States, as saying: "Our invading force will land in Cuba. . . . They will take over as occupation troops. . . . A provisional government will be set up [which] will restore all properties to the rightful owners." Mr. de Varona was vague only about where all the money was coming from. The *Daily News* was less vague, but quite inaccurate. "It is an open secret," said the newspaper, "that the *Frente* [various anti-Castro groups in the U.S. had been organized into a Front] is being financed by American and Cuban industrial interests" who hoped to get their properties back from Fidel Castro. It was, of course, not industrialists who were paying for all the shenanigans going on; it was the American taxpayer via the CIA.

On January 11, the *Miami Herald,* located in the city where most of the Cuban refugees were living and where the anti-Castro activities were greatest, printed the first of a long series of articles on what was going on. The first story said forthrightly: "Recruiters, some American, have for months been selecting anti-Castro men in Miami for secret flights to Retalhuleu." But two days later *Time* magazine blandly referred to what it called Castro's "continued tawdry little melodrama of invasion." And about the same time, in the Security Council of the U.N., U.S. Ambassador James J. Wadsworth termed the latest Cuban charge of planned invasion as "empty, groundless, false and fraudulent."

The story continued to expand. *Time* magazine finally decided that Castro was not altogether a victim of hallucinations, and on January 27 declared that the *Frente* was getting up to $500,000 a month from the U.S. and boldly stated that the entire operation was in charge of a CIA agent known as "Mr. B." Dr. Hilton had had to wait ten weeks for the last of his "hearsay" reports to be confirmed by a major publication.

It is understandable that President Kennedy, Secretary of State Rusk, CIA Director Dulles and others in Washington were viewing this publicity with something less than enthusiasm. True, during the campaign the previous fall, Kennedy had complained that America had done too little for Castro's "democratic opposition" and said that if elected he would do more. But he had never spelled out just what he would do. Had he been thinking of presenting *bon voyage* baskets to any anti-Castro invaders departing our shores? Four days before the invasion actually began, he told a press conference: "There will not be under any conditions an intervention in Cuba by the U.S. armed forces. . . . The basic issue in Cuba is not one between the United States and Cuba. It is between the Cubans themselves. And I intend to see that we adhere to this principle. . . ."

But the deep American involvement could not be kept hidden—not after the Guatemala story had once broken. And it grew increasingly difficult to hide as recruiting agents scurried around New York and Miami, gathering sacrificial lambs for the planned invasion. By the second week in April the recruiting was so open that *El Diario,* a New York Spanish-language paper, and the *New York Mirror,* could print the addresses of local recruiting stations. Then there was the impossible problem of keeping the various leaders of the Cuban exile groups quiet. Right and Left factions filled the press with their mutual recriminations, or with complaints of discriminatory treatment at the hands of the Administration.

Still, there persisted in Washington the quaint notion that nothing was really happening unless it was reported in the *New York Times.* And, for many weeks following Paul Kennedy's somewhat equivocal report from Retalhuleu, the *Times* did nothing deeply distressing to Allen W. Dulles. Indeed, in some ways it seemed to be playing the Administration game. As late as April 5, just 12 days before the invasion began, James Reston wrote that "The Administration has reason to believe that there are now between 100 and 200 Cuban airmen in Czechoslovakia being trained to fly Soviet MIG fighters." Washington officialdom, aware that it could not stop [9] speculation on the invasion, had evidently decided on an alternative: to leak stories tending to justify it.

Then, on April 7, the *Times* printed a long dispatch from Miami by Tad Szulc, their able and experienced Latin-American correspondent. While there were few elements in this account that had not already appeared elsewhere, Mr. Szulc not only linked the CIA to the coming invasion but hinted strongly that the climax was "imminent." The handling given the story by the *Times,* and the crisis of conscience it provoked among its editors, were described at length by Mr. Daniel in his address last year before the World Press Institute. Orvil Dryfoos, then publisher of the *Times,* was described by Mr. Daniel as particularly upset: "He was gravely troubled by the security implications of Szulc's story. He could envision failure for the invasion, and he could see the *New York Times* being blamed for a bloody fiasco."

So Mr. Dryfoos, according to the Daniel account, came down from his fourteenth floor office to the news room on the third floor to see Turner Catledge, then managing editor. The two conferred and decided to turn to Mr. Reston, in Washington, for advice. The author of *The*

Artillery of the Press advised his superiors to spike the guns, more or less, and the upshot was that Mr. Szulc's account was edited to eliminate references to the CIA and to the "imminence" of the invasion. Instead of a four-column head, as had been originally planned, it was given a one-column head.

In justice to the *Times,* it must be noted that in addition to the consciences of Messrs. Dryfoos, Catledge, and Reston, there were other consciences at work that night. Lewis Jordan, news editor, and Theodore Bernstein, assistant managing editor, objected strenuously to this downgrading of the story as a violation of *Times* tradition; and Mr. Daniel, in his recounting of the episode, placed himself alongside the dissenters.

About a fortnight after the Bay of Pigs took its dismal place in history, a group of press executives met the President at the White House. Mr. Daniel told the World Press Institute what took place:

> President Kennedy ran down a list of what he called premature disclosures of security information. His examples were drawn mainly from the *New York Times.* He mentioned, for example, Paul Kennedy's story. . . .
>
> Mr. Catledge pointed out that this information had been published in *La Hora* in Guatemala and in *The Nation* in this country before it was ever published in the *Times.*
>
> "But it was not news until it appeared in the *Times,*" the President replied.
>
> While he scolded the *New York Times,* the President said in an aside to Mr. Catledge, "If you had printed more about the operation, you would have saved us from a colossal mistake." More than a year later, President Kennedy [told] Orvil Dryfoos, "I wish you had run everything on Cuba. . . . I am just sorry you didn't tell it at the time."

President Kennedy had changed his mind, but Mr. Reston never did. A year ago he told Mr. Daniel: "It is ridiculous to think that publishing the fact that the invasion was imminent would have avoided this disaster. I am quite sure the operation would have gone forward." Certainly he did nothing to prevent it. Four days before the invasion, he was publicly asking questions to which he already obviously knew most of the answers:

> How much will the U.S. Government help the Cuban refugees? Will it provide them with all the money and arms necessary to launch an invasion, not from American ports and airfields, but from somewhere else? Will it train the refugees in the arts of sabotage and guerrilla warfare in Guatemala or elsewhere?

Yet, in a larger sense, Mr. Reston was probably right. The President, in his astonishing asides to Messrs. Catledge and Dryfoos, seems merely to have been trying to share his monopoly of wrong decisions. In all likelihood, it would have done no good for the *Times* to have "told all" on April 7. At best, the telling might have forced the Administration to delay the invasion a couple of weeks (at added expense to the American taxpayers, who were footing the training bills); at worst, it might have enabled Castro to have been even better prepared than he was, and the invasion might have been totally crushed in one day instead of three.

The evidence is strong that by these final weeks, the affair was beyond aborting; planning had reached the point of no return. The time for arousing public opposition to the idiocy which was launched on April 17 was back in October, 1960, when *La Hora* first broke the story of the Retalhuleu base. The persistency with which the American press ignored the story still seems incredible. Its intrinsic plausibility should at once [10] have been recognized and acted upon; every informed journalist in the U.S. knew Guatemala as an old playground of the CIA. This is where the "spooks" from Washington had overturned the Arbenz regime in 1954.

About the press coverage of the invasion itself, the less said the better. The chief source of information was a Mr. Lem Jones who, according to Arthur M. Schlesinger Jr., in his *A Thousand Days*, "was putting out in the name of the [Cuban Revolutionary] Council press releases dictated over the phone by the CIA." The CIA, Mr. Schlesinger intimates wryly, had not even bothered to inform the Council that Mr. Jones had been hired to do the invasion publicity. Who was Mr. Jones? In Haynes Johnson's *The Bay of Pigs*, he is described this way: "The president of Lem Jones Associates, Inc., a Madison Avenue public relations firm . . . had done public relations work for such clients as a lay committee of the Armenian Apostolic Church and corporation stockholders waging proxy fights; but his present client, he told a reporter, was 'a very serious thing, too ' "

Mr. Jones was still in the proxy business, it appeared; this time he was proxying for the Cuban Revolutionary Council and the CIA. Largely on the basis of his news releases, headlines throughout the U.S. recounted mass uprisings by the Cuban people against Castro, Soviet MIGs blasting the invaders, rebel capture of the Isle of Pines, the surrender of Castro's brother. An eight-column banner in the *Miami News* screamed: CUBAN NAVY IN REVOLT. All this time the invading force of 1,400 men was being systematically destroyed by Castro's forces, and nowhere in the length and breadth of the island did a single Cuban raise a rifle in behalf of the "liberators." And four American pilots, members of the Alabama Air National Guard, assigned by the U.S. Air Force for special duty with the invasion, died in this affair which, in President Kennedy's words, was strictly one "between the Cubans themselves."

From beginning to end, the Bay of Pigs was as humiliating for the American press as it was for the country as a whole. In the aftermath, some editors recognized this. On May 10, the *New York Times* editorialized under the heading, "The Right Not To Be Lied To":

> The Cuban tragedy has raised a domestic question that is likely to come up again and again until it is solved. The cause may be something that is happening in Laos [or Vietnam?], in Central Africa or in Latin America, but the question remains the same: is a democratic government in an open society such as ours ever justified in deceiving its own people? . . . A democracy—our democracy—cannot be lied to. . . . The basic principle involved is that of confidence.

Newsweek posed the question: "To what degree was the press really to blame for the magnitude of the American propaganda defeat? The best answer is that the newsmen, like many others, became pawns in the intensifying conflict between Washington and Havana."

The press had a right to be angry. It had been lied to, again and again, by President Kennedy, Allen W. Dulles, Dean Rusk, and everyone else in the hierarchy of blunderers responsible for the Bay of Pigs. But it also had the duty to be ashamed. No law required it to swallow uncritically everything that officialdom said. On the very day the American-planned, American-equipped expedition was landing at the Bay of Pigs, Secretary Rusk told a group of newsmen: "The American people are entitled to know whether we are intervening in Cuba or intend to do so in the future. The answer to that question is no." Where was the editorial explosion that should have greeted this egregious lie? And even when the press had opportunity to strike a blow for truth, it failed. On April 19, while the shooting was still going on, the *Times* received a dispatch from its correspondent at the U.S. naval base at Guantánamo Bay. The last paragraph of the story read:

> The sensitive radar on Navy ships here have picked up no trace of high-speed Cuban or Communist aircraft. Officials, therefore, are confident that there have been no MIG fighters in this area of Cuba, at least. Nor has the Navy sighted any foreign submarines.

This last paragraph appeared only in the early edition of April 20. In the later editions, it was deleted. Mr. Daniel, asked about this, made this response in his letter of April 27: "I cannot at this date give the reason with certainty, but this sort of thing happens so routinely in

12. The Press and the Bay of Pigs 139

makeovers for late editions that the odds are that it was simply a matter of space for makeup purposes." In other words, all the news that fits. There is no reason to doubt Mr. Daniel's explanation, but an explanation is not a justification. Lem Jones' war bulletins out of Madison [11] Avenue had been replete with references to MIGs and Soviet submarines, the work of CIA fiction writers seeking to raise war fever in the American people. Surely so strong a doubt that they ever existed, expressed by so unimpeachable a source as our own Navy men, deserved a better play than a tail-end paragraph. And if it had been anywhere else in the story, it would not have had to be dropped for space.

How does one explain the malaise that afflicted so much of the press during the period? There is no doubt that, in many places, a covert if voluntary censorship was at work. The *Times* treatment of Szulc was one example. The *Miami Herald* openly acknowledged voluntary censorship. The *Herald* published its first story on the Miami-Retalhuleu airlift the day after Paul Kennedy's story from Guatemala appeared in the *New York Times*. A box alongside the *Herald*'s story explained:

> Publication of the accompanying story on the Miami-Guatemala airlift was withheld for more than two months by the *Herald*. Its release was decided upon only after U.S. aid to anti-Castro fighters in Guatemala was first revealed elsewhere.

This was on January 11. The *Herald* had apparently known all about Retalhuleu since November 10—just about the time Dr. Hilton was reporting the story to *The Nation*. President Kennedy should have chastized the *Herald*, not the *Times;* had the *Herald* printed the story at the outset, there might really never have been a Bay of Pigs.

This demented patriotism, the urge to play along with government at whatever cost to truth, struck elsewhere. Mr. Schlesinger (in *A Thousand Days*) reports that in March 1961 the *New Republic* set aside a detailed exposé of invasion preparations in Miami at the request of the White House. (Of the magazine's acceptance of the suggestion that the piece be dropped, Mr. Schlesinger comments that it was "a patriotic act which left me slightly uncomfortable.") And in the February 2, 1963, issue of *Editor & Publisher*, Alan J. Gould, on the occasion of his retirement as general manager of the AP, is quoted as saying:

> I think the people in Government should have learned a lesson for all time on the handling of the Cuban affair. Occasionally we have withheld stories for a time in the national interest. When the President of the United States calls you in and says this is a matter of vital security, you accept the injunction.

If the editors of the *Miami Herald* knew the significance of Retalhuleu, it is safe to say that the AP editors knew, too. Yet the AP never budged any part of its massive reportorial staff to get at the truth in behalf of its thousands of clients. Neither the AP, nor the UPI, nor the San Francisco papers ever seemed to have tried to follow through on the startling remark of that CIA official to a San Francisco Commonwealth Club gathering: "It will be a black day if we are ever found out."

The press is not normally so cooperative with government, even on matters touching on national security. In this instance, there was no security to be breached. Castro knew about Retalhuleu as soon as *La Hora* did, and quite likely sooner; and he was in the fortunate position of not having to verify his information with such as President Ydígoras. The early apathy of the press makes sense only when viewed as motivated not so much by patriotic reticence as by eager jingoistic collaboration. The fact is that most powerful American publishers wanted that damn Castro out of there as much as Allen W. Dulles did. So they kept silent until the few independent souls among them precipitated the news competition that is the normal lifeblood of the industry. But the damage had already been done: *public opinion had been eliminated as a factor in a major foreign policy decision.*

Even today most journalists, with some honorable exceptions, criticize the Bay of Pigs not as the wrong thing to have done, but as the wrong way to have done it. One is reminded of most current criticism of the Vietnam war: the cure suggested is always something other than the simple getting out. It is difficult to accept that there is no right way of doing the wrong thing.

Where, then, does the duty of the press lie? Must it always tell all that it knows? Or are there occasions when government, as representative of the people, has the moral right to call upon its discretion? President Kennedy was not alone in his feeling that the press should suppress news in the interest of the government (which is assumed to be identified with the national interest). But back in 1851 that old Thunderer, *The Times of London,* had something to say on this subject: [12]

> The purposes and duties of the [Ministers of the Crown and of the Press] are constantly separate, generally independent, sometimes diametrically opposite. . . . The Press can enter into no close or binding alliances with the statesmen of the day, nor can it surrender its permanent interests to the convenience of the ephemeral power of any Government. The first duty of the Press is to obtain the earliest and most correct intelligence of the events of the time, and instantly, by disclosing them, to make them the common property of the nation. The statesman collects his information secretly and by secret means; he keeps back even the current intelligence of the day with ludicrous precautions. . . . The Press lives by disclosures.

This is a generally admirable statement of a condition that should exist, perhaps, but doesn't. The fact is that most of the press decides for or against cooperation with government not on any basis of principle, but on the basis of the issue. Do we, the editor asks himself, approve or disapprove of what the government is asking us to help it do? So William F. Buckley Jr., alerted to secret peace negotiations between Washington and Hanoi, and fearing an outcome favorable to the Communists, might rush to wreck the talks by publicizing them. Walter Lippmann, in all likelihood, might keep his mouth shut. Who has best served journalism and the public weal? On the other hand, who best served journalism and the public weal in the months before the Bay of Pigs—those who talked, or those who kept silent? [13]

13. The Press and the Assassination
William L. Rivers

The reports of President Kennedy's assassination and its aftermath were swift, lengthy, appropriately couched in grief and boxed in black, and the various journals of the news business made it clear during the following weeks that the press was proud of them. The chronicle of reporters' actions and the advertisements acclaiming them in *Editor & Publisher*—the Associated Press bought two pages, United Press International bought four—were highly self-congratulatory. The analyses of press performance in *The Masthead* and in *The Bulletin* of the American Society of Newspaper Editors were similarly positive. Although W. S. Harrison of the *Toledo Blade* charged in *The Masthead* that the press must share in the blame for the murder of Lee Oswald, such questioning voices were muted. Other, louder voices in the same issue held that the Dallas police were responsible: they should not have given in to the demands, primarily from television, that Oswald be transferred publicly from jail to jail. And although television may have emerged from Dallas with honor for having given up millions to broadcast nothing but unsponsored news for nearly four days, Earl Johnson consoled the newspaper world in the *UPI Reporter* by pointing out that TV's sacrifice was more apparent than real: some sponsors paid for their broadcast time anyway, and others simply rescheduled commercials for a later date.

Source: Bradley S. Greenberg and Edwin B. Parker, eds., *The Kennedy Assassination and the American Public: Social Communication in Crisis* (Stanford, Calif.: Stanford University Press, 1965), pp. 51–60. Copyright © 1965 by the Board of Trustees of the Leland Stanford Junior University. Reprinted by permission of the publisher.

13. The Press and the Assassination   143

There seemed to be little change even when, months later, the Warren Commission report criticized the mass media for swamping Dallas in reporters. The report quoted one FBI agent as likening conditions at the police station to "Grand Central Station at rush hour," and pointed out that newsmen in the mass may influence events almost as decisively as [51] they cover them. The Commission called on the press to develop a code of ethics and practices embracing crime and court proceedings. This was a sobering indictment. Miles Wolff, President of the American Society of Newspaper Editors, called together newspaper and broadcasting representatives to discuss it. The group was concerned enough to select a five-man steering committee to study the Warren Commission recommendations, but made it clear that the sense of the meeting was not at all apologetic: "Within forty-eight hours, the print and electronic media reported the Dallas Story so accurately and completely that the Warren Commission, in ten months and with unlimited resources, did not alter the basic outlines of what the media had reported." All in all, if the assassination coverage was not a journalistic triumph but a chaotic encounter of the unprepared with the unforeseen, the press is not saying so.

Much of the self-congratulation seems deserved. The press associations and many metropolitan newspapers and mass magazines put platoons of editors and reporters on every aspect of the story everywhere without regard to cost. Some newspapers canceled columns of scheduled advertising to make room for sidebars to the assassination story. With only hours to go before their weekend deadlines, the news magazines were transformed. *U.S. News & World Report* junked its deadline along with many pages that were ready for printing, produced twenty new pages, and remade the entire issue. *Newsweek* produced twenty-five new pages. *Time* added seventeen pages, including a cover story on President Johnson. It was all worthwhile; not even hugely increased press runs could satisfy the demand. (In the first real test of the print media *versus* total news on television, the record indicates that electronic journalism is never likely to make newspapers and magazines obsolete.) In Dallas, the *Times-Herald* sold eighty thousand copies more than its daily norm. The first issue of *Life* after the assassination was quickly depleted; single copies were selling for as much as ten dollars in San Francisco.

Some of the individual reporting performances were remarkable. Tom Wicker of the *New York Times* stitched together a lengthy report that was at once a crisp news story, a detailed chronicle, and a stark revelation of mood and atmosphere. Merriman Smith of United Press International, who won the Pulitzer Prize for his work in Dallas that day, proved himself capable of distinguishing between the moving and the maudlin in a time of tragedy by writing an almost clinical account of what he heard and saw: [52]

> The President was face down on the back seat. Mrs. Kennedy made a cradle of her arms around the President's head and bent over him as if she were whispering to him.
> Gov. Connally was on his back on the floor of the car, his head and shoulders resting in the arms of his wife, Nellie, who kept shaking her head and shaking with dry sobs. Blood oozed from the front of the Governor's suit. I could not see the President's wound. But I could see blood spattered around the interior of the rear seat and a dark stain spreading down the right side of the President's dark gray suit.

And yet there is much more to say about press performance during the assassination period that is far less positive. And if nothing like a solution to the problem of crisis reporting emerges from saying it, it may nonetheless suggest some of the questions that might have accompanied the self-appreciation.

The story of the press and the assassination actually began several hours before a shot was fired. Early on the morning of November 22, the issue of *Editor & Publisher* dated November 23 came off the press carrying a curious article. Headlined "The S.S. Ruffians," it was a reporter's protest that the Secret Service is overprotective in guarding the President—and the writer's acidity creates the suspicion that the use of "S.S." was not so much designed to save space as to suggest an unpleasant analogy with Hitler's crack troops. The reporter, Thomas Del Vecchio, wrote as a veteran of 24 years of interviewing dignitaries who arrived at airports. His complaint was that reporters were often excluded from the groups that greeted President Kennedy at Idlewild:

> How come? What's happened here?
> It's all in the name of security.
> Now where does the problem of security end and the problem of a controlled press kept from access to the news begin?
> There is no question that the press and the Secret Service have reached that point and beyond.
> On top of all this is the rudeness and ruffian manner a good many of these agents assume toward the press under the guise of security.
> They often act as though newsmen were not Americans and did not have a record almost as impressive as theirs for respect for their President and his security.
> Just where do the rights under the First Amendment end and the assumed and overriding rights of the Secret Service take complete charge?

There was much more in the same outraged tone. Predictably, the

13. The Press and the Assassination 145

article provoked a strong reaction. One reader's reproving letter to the [53] editor of the magazine pointed out that even aside from the assassination Del Vecchio's article was bitter, petty, subjective, and poor journalism. Editor Robert U. Brown responded with a column entitled "Hindsight Criticism," holding, "If such articles have to be written with some intuition as to whether the President might not be alive tomorrow because of an assassin's bullet, there would be very little criticism." It was a predictable rejoinder, and perhaps a persuasive one, but it dealt not at all with the central question: Was Del Vecchio right? Brown might have decided this easily by pondering a related question: Would he have published the article after the assassination?

It would have been a curious article had there been no assassination. Despite charges that the Kennedy Administration "managed the news," the President's own relations with the press were open to the point of porosity. Never in history had so many reporters been so free to talk with the President and explore the presidency. In sharp contrast to his predecessor (who preferred the company of businessmen to journalists and preferred reading Luke Short to Walter Lippmann), Mr. Kennedy fostered such warm relations with many Washington correspondents that his press secretary once complained amiably that the comings and goings of reporters were creating a traffic problem in White House corridors.

Del Vecchio's article is chiefly notable for showing that some spokesmen for the press, not content with continuing dialogues with the President in Washington or with frequent confrontations elsewhere, demand unlimited access wherever the President touches ground. The President is not to be a public servant but public property. That this is something more than one peeved reporter's view is suggested by the fact that *Editor & Publisher,* which echoes the opinions and yearnings of a good many newspapers, chose to make "The S.S. Ruffians" its lead article. Copies of the issue were flown to Miami for distribution at an Inter-American Press Association meeting on November 22. Presumably, some editors and publishers were reading the article when they learned of the assassination.

The two issues of the *Dallas Morning News* that appeared immediately before the assassination are similarly interesting. Much has been made of the full-page advertisement purchased by the "American Fact-finding Committee" in the issue of November 22. Headed "Welcome Mr. [54] Kennedy," the advertisement posed questions like, *"Why* have you scrapped the Monroe Doctrine in favor of the Spirit of Moscow?" and *"Why* have you ordered or permitted your brother Bobby, the Attorney General, to go soft on Communists. . . ?" Incredibly,

Robert U. Brown of *Editor & Publisher* undertook, in a column entitled "More Hindsight," to defend the *News*. "In the first place," he wrote, "it was not a 'hate' ad. It was a political advertisement. . . ." Then, in a defense for which few editors and publishers will thank him, Brown held that not one of the questions in the advertisement "hasn't been asked in one form or another on the editorial page of some American newspaper."

The editors of the *News* have answered critics by pointing to the sweetly phrased editorial with which they greeted the President. One editorial could hardly change the image of a paper whose publisher, E. M. "Ted" Dealey, had become a national figure of sorts in 1961 by charging at a White House luncheon that Kennedy and his administration were "weak sisters." Dealey had interrupted the President to say that the nation needs a man on horseback, but "you are riding Caroline's tricycle." However, the most provocative aspect of Dealey's paper during Kennedy's tour of Texas was neither the advertisement nor the editorial but the news columns. The day before the President arrived, the top of the front page was covered almost five inches deep across seven columns with a story epitomized by the headline "JFK Visit Ires San Antonio Liberals." Three columns at the bottom were given over to "Rain Seen in Dallas During JFK Visit"—a "weather story" in the conventional sense only until it reached the third paragraph, where the reporter slid smoothly into the real subject with "political skies should remain dark" and went predictably on from there.

The *News* of the following morning, the day Kennedy was to arrive, was a strange celebration of a Presidential visit. The lead story on the front page ran across two columns that extended from the top almost to the bottom of the page. Headed in huge type across seven columns "Storm of Political Controversy Swirls Around Kennedy Visit," it was built largely on Senator Ralph Yarborough's complaint that Governor John Connally had not invited Yarborough to a reception at the Governor's Mansion. Nearly four columns at the bottom of the page were covered with a story headed "Yarborough Snubs LBJ." All eight columns at the top of page 12 were four inches deep with "President's Visit Seen Widening Democratic Split." [55]

One cannot know the extent to which the *News*, always passionate, excites the passions of Dallas. But surely Walter Lippmann is correct in contending that Dallas is the very atmosphere of violence and that it is only incidental that Lee Oswald turned left while those Dallasites who assaulted Lyndon Johnson and his wife in 1960 and those who hit and spat upon Adlai Stevenson a month before the assassination turned right. "The common characteristic of all of them," Walter Lippmann wrote, "was their alienation, the loss of their ties, the rupture of the community." On the morning that this analysis was published, Jack Ruby killed Lee Oswald. One could hardly ask for stronger confirmation. But one can commend these issues of the News to those who study conflict as it is promoted in the press. And one can venture that the News and similar papers, so many of them so noticeably devoted to seeking out political conflict, should consider the possibility that they are manufacturing it as well.

As for the coverage of the assassination, the problem for the reporter may be suggested by the fact that the most recent precedent was more than six decades in the past. The President is shot. The natural movement is toward him; this much is certain. But, the President is dead—bewilderment reigns. Does the reporter stay near the body to glean the details of death? Or does he try to attach himself to the police who seek the assassin? Or does he attempt to divine the next movements of the new President and move with him? And whatever his decision, what should be his manner, what are his rights and privileges, what is the priority of information in tragedy's hierarchy of values?

Above all, where in the midst of chaos does the reporter find incontrovertible fact? This is the most important question, for one who reviews the journalistic record of the assassination period can recognize the inevitable difficulties, award many high marks for enterprise and diligence, and yet be left with the inescapable conclusion that the press reported many more facts than there actually were.

Item: The rifle was found by a window on the second floor of the Texas School Book Depository. Or it was found in the fifth-floor staircase. Or it was hidden behind boxes and cases on the second floor. Ultimately, all reports agreed that it had been found on the sixth floor.

Item: The rifle was first reported to be a .30-caliber Enfield. Then it [56] was a 7.65 mm Mauser. But it was also an Army or Japanese rifle of .25 caliber. Finally, it became an Italian-made 6.5mm rifle with a telescopic sight.

Item: There were three shots. But some reports mentioned four bullets: one found on the floor of the President's car, one found in the President's stretcher, a third removed from Governor Connally's left thigh, and a fourth removed from the President's body. There was even one report of a fifth bullet found in the grass near the side of the street where the President was hit. Finally, there was general agreement that there were only three bullets.

So far, the mistakes seem to be of no great moment—small discrepancies fairly quickly resolved. But when these conflicting reports were coupled with some of the more mystifying details, the pivotal importance of absolute accuracy became evident:

Item: The first reports of the President's wounds described "a bullet in the throat, just below the Adam's apple" and "a massive, gaping wound in the back and on the right side of the head." The position of the President's car at the time of the shooting, seventy-five to one hundred yards beyond the Texas School Book Depository explains the head wound. But how can one account for the bullet in the throat?

Item: The shots were fired between 12:30 and 12:31 P.M., Dallas time. It was reported at first that Oswald dashed into the house at Oak Cliff where he was renting a room "at about 12:45 P.M." Between the time of the assassination and the time of his arrival at the rooming house, Oswald reportedly (1) hid the rifle, (2) made his way from the sixth floor to the second floor of the building, (3) bought and sipped a Coke (lingering long enough to be seen by the building manager and a policeman), (4) walked four blocks to Lamar Street and boarded a bus, (5) descended from the bus and hailed a taxi, and (6) rode four miles to Oak Cliff. How did he accomplish all this in fourteen minutes?

Item: Oswald was only an average marksman in the Marines. Yet gun experts who were meeting in Maryland at the time of the assassination held that, considering the rifle, the distance, the angle, and the movement of the President's car, "the assassin was either an exceptional marksman or fantastically lucky in placing his shots." The Olympic champion marksman, Hubert Hammerer, said upon being interviewed in Vienna that *one* shot could have been made under the conditions described, but he considered it unlikely that anyone could have triggered [57] three accurate shots within five seconds with a bolt-action rifle. How did Lee Oswald do it?

All this is the stuff of conspiracy theories. Given a mass of conflicting and mystifying detail about the actions of an accused assassin, it is natural to seek an easier explanation. One is that Oswald was not the assassin—except that so many of his actions were suspicious. Another is that he had an accomplice—"No one remembered for sure seeing Ruby between 12:15 and 12:45," one press report ran—and the mind leaps to the desired assumption. Small wonder that the Warren Commission's findings are unlikely ever to receive anything approaching total belief.

It is a curious fact that the most involved of the conspiracy theories sprang from those who are usually the sniffiest about press reports, the academicians. Some of them know that the press goes to the authorities for quotations on matters of moment. Deep down, they are likely to suspect authority more than they suspect the press. Thus it was that a political scientist and a historian, Jack Minnis and Staughton Lynd, wrote "Seeds of Doubt," which appeared in *The New Republic*.

"Seeds of Doubt" was by far the most remarkable article to appear

13. The Press and the Assassination 149

during the assassination period. Without ever actually saying that someone was suppressing information and rearranging evidence, Minnis and Lynd seemed to be saying nothing else. Their article was a catalogue of conflicting press reports from the time of the first news up to mid-December, and broadly hinted that the authorities were making changes as they went along in order to bring inconvenient facts into line with indisputable evidence. The tone was typified by the section dealing with the speed of the President's car:

> All early accounts of the assassination put the speed of the President's limousine at about 25 miles per hour, but now it has slowed to 15 miles per hour (*Life,* November 29), "no more than half the 25 miles per hour first estimated by authorities" (*Newsweek,* December 9), and 12 miles per hour (*U.S. News & World Report,* December 9). The latter magazine comments: "If President Kennedy's car had been moving even 20 miles per hour, the experts say, it might have made the lead time too difficult a problem for the sniper."

Assessing the Minnis-Lynd article and an accompanying sidebar that speculated about the throat wound and the whereabouts of Jack Ruby at the time of the assassination, one horrified reader commented, [58] "What can it all mean, except the insinuation that Oswald and Ruby *were* connected and that Oswald's death was part of a mysterious conspiracy in which both were engaged and which the authorities are trying to hush up?"

As it turned out, the structure of the Minnis-Lynd thesis came crashing down only a few days after the article appeared. The President's throat wound, it was finally determined, had not been caused by the entry of a bullet but by the exit of a fragment. Oswald had not made his trip in fourteen minutes but in thirty, having arrived in Oak Cliff at about 1:00. The exceptional marksmanship is perhaps best explained by Gertrude Himmelfarb: "But why . . . assume that each of the shots found its intended mark? It would appear that not three out of three but one out of three achieved its purpose (the first inflicting no serious injury and the second hitting Governor Connally). To know how extraordinarily successful or lucky an assassin is, one would have to know how often he was unsuccessful or unlucky." As if to confirm this diagnosis, it was later reported that Oswald had earlier shot at General Edwin Walker.

In the end, one must conclude that the press performed in *its* best tradition. The *news* of the assassination was made up almost entirely of authoritative reports. After all, reporters did not say that a bullet entered the President's throat; they quoted Drs. Malcolm Perry and

Kemp Clark of the Parkland Memorial Hospital in Dallas. The Dallas police first identified the rifle as a .30-caliber Enfield and a 7.65mm Mauser. A Secret Service man said he thought the weapon was a .25-caliber Army or Japanese rifle. The housekeeper at the Oak Cliff rooming house said that Oswald had come dashing in at about 12:45. And so on.

But the central question is whether the best tradition of the press is good enough. To blame a quoted authority is not a defense of the press but an explanation of two errors: the authority's for making a mistake and the press's for publishing it. The lesson of Dallas is actually an old one in responsible journalism: reporting is not democratic to the point that everything posing as fact has equal status.

It must be said immediately that some errors were inevitable. Governor Connally says that the car had just made the turn at Elm and Houston Streets when the firing began. Mrs. Connally says that the car was nearing [59] the underpass—220 yards from the turn. Both cannot be right—in fact, the consensus indicates that both were wrong—but where can a reporter find better authorities than those who were in the car at the time?

Putting aside the discrepancies that are never likely to be resolved, one must ask whether the press was too eager to satisfy the hunger for detail and to beat the competition. It is one thing to report certainties such as that the President has been shot and is dead, and quite another to quote a seeming authority—the nearest Secret Service man, a flustered housekeeper—whose speculations breed suspicion. Is satisfying the public desire for a story adequate reason for rounding it out with supposition? Is it possible that the proud Age of Instant Communication sparks competition that debases journalism? These are questions, in any case, that might be debated at the next meeting of the American Society of Newspaper Editors. [60]

14. The "Orthodox" Media under Fire: Chicago and the Press
Nathan B. Blumberg

> Mrs. Humphrey said the Chicago protesters had received entirely too much attention, presumably from the press, radio and television. She said that they were "noisy and rude." And she said she, her husband and their children certainly wanted to hear young America's views, but that they already were aware of them.
> "Our youngsters are all over talking with young executives and young Jaycees," she explained.
> —Charlotte Curtis in the *New York Times,* Aug. 31, 1968

The primary journalistic—and ultimately, perhaps, historical—lesson of Chicago is that the news media of general circulation have been guilty of a massive failure, especially [54] during the past decade, to describe and interpret what has been happening in the United States and in the world.* The "orthodox" press, essentially satisfied with the prevailing conditions of life, has resisted or ignored the inequities of our society and has attempted to perpetuate governmental, economic and social abuses. It is not enough to open the columns and the electronic channels for a few hours or days to report what is really happening as they were opened during the battle of Chicago; the reports Americans saw and heard and read in much of the orthodox media should be their steady diet. Significantly, the "underground" newspapers had little to add to what happened in what it termed "Czechago" except for accounts of speeches delivered in Lincoln and Grant parks. In effect, by doing its job, the orthodox media briefly made the underground press irrelevant.

No valid purpose is served by attempting to analyze the political situation in the United States as most editorial writers, columnists and

---

* This section incorporates most of the address of the author at the opening session of the Association for Education in Journalism convention at the University of Kansas in 1968. It was delivered approximately two hours before the Chicago police made their first sweep of Lincoln Park on Sunday evening, August 25.

Source: Montana Journalism Review, no. 12 (1969): 54–60. This piece is a final portion of an extensive study on press performance on Chicago. Reprinted by permission of the author.

commentators employed by the orthodox press persist in viewing it. It is an acute form of journalistic self-deception (which, especially in recent years, has been the gravest single sin of commission by our press) to write and speak of Democrats and Republicans, Wallaceites and McCarthyites, or the maneuverings and machinations of politicians and bureaucrats as if these are the significant and ultimate crucial divisions in our society. It emphatically is not simplistic to suggest that the central political fact of our times is that there are only two sides: Those who do not want to see any fundamental change in the status quo are pitted violently against those who find the status quo intolerable. Of course there are degrees and nuances on both sides, but it is useless to deny that when large numbers of our citizens are frustrated and angry with the established system, those who are not on their side are against them. Thus: "You are either part of the problem or part of the solution."

[*And there, on the last page of* Newsweek, *is poor Stewart Alsop's column which begins: "There is no more dismaying experience for a political writer than being confronted with an important political phenomenon he really doesn't understand. I had this experience on a Wednesday afternoon during Chicago's hell week." Intended to be a disarming admission, it is in fact a damning indictment. All he had done was cross the street from the Hilton Hotel to Grant Park, there to stage his personal confrontation with the political realities of contemporary America. And how does he view the scene? He sees with the same old eyes he has used for years, in which everything is adjusted to the context of traditional (and essentially trivial) political maneuvering. He suggests that we always have had a "generational conflict" and right now we have one because a kid, if he's 18, has "passively watched a television screen for some 22,000 hours" (if you think this is all made up, see for yourself on page 108 of* Newsweek, *Sept. 16, 1968), and we suffer from affluence, to which other empires have succumbed, "vide the Roman Empire." Then the peroration: Something bad is happening—"some political poison, some Virus X" that "is beyond the capacity of the middle-aged to understand, or the young to explain." Finally, he is staggered by the possibilities: "In Chicago, for the first time in my life, it began to seem to me possible that some form of American Fascism may really happen here." (He stopped there, choosing not to roast the one remaining chestnut: Huey ·Long's observation that if Fascism ever came to the United States it would come in the name of Americanism.) It should be added, however, that Alsop is no more irrelevant than many other political columnists and commentators who have demonstrated in their premises and their conclusions that they live in a world of political* phenomena they really don't understand, a world that has swept past them, a world to which they respond ritualistically, burdened by experience that no longer applies and accrued wisdom that provides no answers to current questions. To point out that Eric Sevareid, for example, to the very moment of this writing has never had a beginning understanding of what the dissent movement is all about is to state the obvious. If one accepts the frame of reference and the pattern of logic of the politician in the traditional posture of "making it," one cannot understand and thereby interpret even a Eugene McCarthy, much less an Abbie Hoffman. And it matters not whether the columnist is "liberal" or "conversative." Examine the following:

—After the dust had settled in Chicago, Newsweek columnist Kenneth Crawford saw the whole thing as a television plot in which the networks were out to get his boys. In what must rank among the most paranoiac pronouncements on the entire Chicago affair, Crawford pondered what would have happened "had Daley acted on the notion he once entertained of supporting Kennedy instead of Humphrey." Wondrous things would have happened, Crawford concluded. Television reporters would have made no references to mysterious security men following them around; excuses would have been found for police excesses and the news would have been spread that "Ribicoff's innocents were responding to agitators bent upon raiding the convention's hall or at least its biggest hotel." Of such stuff is nonsense fabricated. But there was in Crawford's column a single startlingly suggestive sentence, which revealed far more than he probably had intended; finally, he wrote, if Daley had appeased the networks by rejecting Humphrey and adopting Edward Kennedy, "parallels would have been found between the Chicago riots and earlier bloodlettings decreed and brought off by some of the [55] same leaders at the Pentagon and at Columbia." He obviously ached for the good old days when dissenters got what was coming to them with the full approval of the networks and the print media, including the news magazine that publishes his column.

—Max Lerner, smarting over criticism of coverage of the week in Chicago, was driven in his fashion to examine the deficiencies of the American press and came up with an extraneous assortment of failures. "Mostly," he wrote, "our sins are lack of analysis in depth, lack of venturesomeness in the realm of ideas, lack of historical background, a tendency to treat every isolated event as equal to every other event in a kind of democracy of news, a fear of hurting fat cats, a chasing-off after every new fad and a vulgarization of sensitivity and taste." Note that in every case with the possible exception of one—"a fear of hurting fat cats"—he averted his eyes from the major flaws of the news media. This frustrated and frustrating analysis was so palpably meretricious that it was, of course, picked up and run in Time magazine. And the way it was run tells all that anyone needs to know about that particular publication. It not only altered Lerner's words within quotation marks, but without showing ellipsis put a period after "democracy of news" and then went on to quote other parts of the column. Thus Time readers were not informed of Lerner's other listed sins of the press—"a fear of hurting fat cats, a chasing-off after every new fad and a vulgarization of sensitivity and taste." The editors of Time know when someone is hitting too close to home.

—James J. Kilpatrick, one of the leading exponents of the right-wing viewpoint: "If the police and troops had not done their job, these pug-ugly scavengers would have torn the Hilton to the ground," a sentence that leaves even more unanswered questions than usual for our friend from the South. "Almost no one," he concluded incredibly, "has said thanks to the mayor and thanks to the cops. I do." If he meant that almost no one who had witnessed the horror in Chicago had afterwards dropped by to thank the police, he certainly was correct; but if he meant that approving letters, telegrams and telephone calls had not flooded Mayor Daley's office and police headquarters, he was badly misinformed.

(When it was all over, only two signs of property damage were visible along Michigan Avenue. One was the plate glass window of the Haymarket Lounge of the Conrad Hilton, which had been shattered by terrified bystanders backing away from a group of club-swinging police. The other was the glass front of an office which had been pelted with stones. Some student demonstrators obviously had been selective; the damaged establishment was that of IBM.)

—James Reston's incredible column on the day following the climactic battles in the streets and parks: "The Democratic party was deeply hurt politically by the vicious clashes between demonstrators and police on the streets of Chicago. Though the party itself had no direct responsibility for the incidents, it held its convention here knowing of the dangers of violence and counted on Mayor Daley and his police to handle the situation without embarrassment to the party. This gamble failed. . . ." And so forth. One can look into the future and visualize 100,000 white students streaming into Chicago to aid West Side ghetto residents who had barricaded the streets and declared war on half a million troops flown into the city the previous day, and then Reston's column in the New York Times and other daily newspapers: "Sen. Edward Kennedy's drive for the Democratic presi-

14. The "Orthodox" Media under Fire: Chicago and the Press 155

dential nomination suffered what may be a serious setback yesterday as events transpired in Chicago. President Nixon still holds one of the two keys to this puzzle. . . ."

Some columnists and commentators of the orthodox media, on the other hand, went out on the streets to see what was happening and reported the story. Notable among these was John S. Knight, editorial chairman of the Knight newspapers, who probably has been more accurate down through the years about the war in Vietnam than any other American journalist and who has demonstrated a remarkable understanding of young people and what is happening in this country. He is, unfortunately, a rarity among publishers ("I know from personal observation," he later wrote, "that some of the editors who defended Daley to the hilt never left their safe shelters in the Hilton Hotel"). In his interpretive coverage of Chicago, he emphasized that most of the demonstrators were "of good presence and surprisingly well dressed . . . in no way resembled the hippies and yippies of the cartoons . . . displayed no hostility and were eager to talk when not chanting anti-war songs and slogans." He wrote that for his part he "could not see that their assembling in the park constituted any threat to anyone. The police took another view. . . . Abuse of police power only raised tensions when a firm but fair policy could have controlled any real or threatened mob action. . . . If these kids came to their rally skeptical of government and duly constituted authority, they must have left it completely disillusioned on all counts." The hostile response to Mr. Knight's views predictably was heavy, but the following Sunday in his weekly "Notebook" he held firm, continuing to deplore "the overkill used by Chicago police in clubbing innocent people." Another exception to the columnar pap poured daily into the editorial pages of the orthodox press was Tom Wicker, whose lucid and accurate analyses from Chicago under deadline pressures emphasized both the specific and general significance of unleashed and unrestricted police power. A few excerpts: [56] "The marchers were political dissidents, some radical, most idealistic, determined to exercise the right of free speech and free assembly and—as Edmund Muskie recognized in his acceptance speech—to have something to say about the kind of future they will inherit. . . . Contrary to Humphrey's banalities, the lesson is that raw, unchecked police power is not the answer to anything. It is not the answer to the race problem, which is real, nor the answer to the crisis of American youth, which also is real. It is the last resort, instead, of angry and fearful old men who see 'order' as a rigid freezing of the America they have made, and who think 'law' has no higher function than to preserve that order. . . ." Still another columnist (now lost to the profession) who on the night of the nomination of the Democratic candidate for president chose the streets instead of the convention hall was Jimmy Breslin. He looked back on 20 years of "having policemen in the family, riding with policemen in cars, drinking with them, watching them work in demonstrations and crowds in cities all over the world," and concluded that "the performance of the police of Chicago on Michigan Avenue last night was the worst one I ever have seen." He documented his case fully.]

A Rarely Spoken Truth

And it is time, too, for recognition of the stark, naked but almost never spoken truth that hundreds—perhaps thousands—of reporters and copy editors and even editors who draw their pay from the owners of the orthodox press are disgusted with the politics of their employers, but the economic necessities of their situation force them to vent their frustrations in the bars, in letters to friends, in their homes or wherever they gather with fellow professionals. What, finally, can they do? Where, finally, can they go? With the orthodox press dominated by the Hearsts, the Scripps-Howards, the Pulliams, the Ridders, the Copleys, the McCormick heirs, they stick grimly and unhappily with their jobs. And even if they could go to the *New York Times,* the *Washington Post,* the *St. Louis Post-Dispatch,* the Cowles or the Knight or the Field papers—to name a few of the newspapers that display at least some significant measure of decency, fairness and respectability—they have discovered they still are up against editors and publishers who order stories killed, or buried, or covered up when the pressures of the business community or the country club are applied. The men and women of the working press know better than anyone the truth of A. J. Liebling's essentially accurate aphorism that without a school for publishers no school of journalism can have meaning.

All of us need desperately to look with fresh eyes at some of the ways in which the news media have helped to stifle reforms and perpetuate injustices. Until illegal and brutal conduct by some members of police forces is reported regularly in our press, the residents of our ghettos and those who seek legitimate redress of grievances will continue to suffer at the hands of their tormentors. What Americans saw and read during those four days in Chicago is a 24-hour reality every day, perhaps in lesser quantity but in undiminished quality, in hundreds of localities. The police reporters know it, the city editors know it, the editors and the publishers know it. It is known to many of those who control the content of magazines, radio and television. Many persons have died or suffered

14. The "Orthodox" Media under Fire: Chicago and the Press 157

terribly from mistreatment, but only the underground press reports it regularly. It has been the unwritten code of the orthodox press that stories of police beating up people or otherwise violating the law don't get into the paper—unless, of course, the scandal becomes so obvious, as the not-so-funny joke has it, that people are afraid to call the police.

[One of the few blessings emerging from the events in Chicago was the massive breakthrough made in police reporting not only by newspapers and wire services but by magazines. Especially noteworthy among the news magazines was Newsweek, which in contrast to its limited and orthodox coverage of the march on the Pentagon the preceding October reported and interpreted at length what had occurred in Chicago. "Miraculously," Newsweek stated, "no one was killed by Chicago Mayor Richard Daley's beefy cops, who went on a sustained rampage unprecedented outside the unreconstructed boondocks of Dixie. 'Kill 'em! Kill 'em!' they shouted as they charged the harum-scarum mobs of hippies, yippies, peace demonstrators and innocent onlookers in the parks and on the streets outside the convention headquarters hotel, the vast Conrad Hilton. Time and again, the police singled out reporters and photographers for clubbing—attacking more than a score. . . . In the midst of all the bloodletting, a middle-aged man in a dark business suit pleaded with an onrushing cop. 'I'm only watching,' he cried. 'You don't belong here, you bastard,' retorted the cop—and clubbed him across the shoulder. . . . Pushed up against a wall by a phalanx of cops, a pretty blonde begged for mercy. No one listened. Instead, a group of police prodded her in the stomach with their clubs, sending her to her knees, her face in her hands, screaming: 'Please God, help me. Please help me.' When a neatly dressed young man tried to help, the police beat him over the head—leaving boy and girl, blood-drenched and whimpering, wrapped in each other's arms. 'You're murderers,' screamed a youth —[57] until a cop silenced him with a rap across the face." The same kind of reporting marked other accounts in the post-convention issue, capped by extraordinary pictorial coverage of events on the streets (27 photographs, seven of them in gory color). Time also reflected its stunned reaction to Chicago by forgoing its customary flippant style for a serious attempt at significant interpretation. Nothing changed, however, at U.S. News & World Report, which weighted its article heavily in favor of Mayor Daley and what it termed "the city's tough policy on law enforcement" and concluded with an approving quotation of a sentence in a Chicago Tribune editorial. Nothing more should be expected from a magazine which, in discussing possible Supreme

Court appointments in the same issue, could assert: " 'Liberals' seem to show more concern for rights of suspected criminals; 'conservatives' tend to show most concern for rights of law-abiding people."

General interest magazines and opinion magazines, almost without exception, expressed shock at the behavior of the Chicago administration and police. Four of these magazines merit special notice:

—Life in its post-convention issue published what is unquestionably the outstanding example of group coverage and interpretation in its history. It ran four articles, two editorials and several revealing photographs devoted to the confrontation in Chicago and left no doubt where it believed the blame rested for the ugly events. Especially dramatic was its editorial departure from bland acceptance of the status quo, including a bristling indictment of Mayor Daley and a memorable last sentence: "But has Chicago now learned that he is an anachronism and an embarrassment?"

—The New Yorker, not noted for timeliness or concern with current affairs of social or political importance, rushed into print in its Sept. 7 issue two articles on Chicago and a highly sympathetic account in "Talk of the Town" of a protest demonstration outside Humphrey's New York headquarters. In one article Michael J. Arlen described a police action he had witnessed ("You can have only a partial idea of how rotten it was") and in the second article Richard H. Rovere, although not as successful as when he examines the innards of the political establishment, lacerated Chicago's mayor and police force ("This is a peculiarly violent city; there may be no higher ratio of brutes among the police here than among the police anywhere, though it certainly seemed as if there were to those who watched them in action the last two nights").

—Business Week, considerably sobered in its coverage and opinion by the actions of Chicago's authorities, placed the blame for the disaster on "Daley's extreme security precautions and the heavy-handedness of his police." Editorially, it moved even farther away from its established position. Examining in the wake of events in Chicago why the nation has seen "things turn sour," it noted that "something of a consensus has developed on the key issue of Vietnam. The U.S. wants to get out."

—The National Review confirmed the suspicion that something mighty peculiar is going on at William Buckley's place when it featured an article by Gary Wills sympathetic to the dissenters. Wills, who in an earlier article on the Republican convention patently mocked the sacred cows of the conservative pasture, deplored "Mayor Daley's untenable first-line toughness" and chastised him for giving the

14. The "Orthodox" Media under Fire: Chicago and the Press 159

protesters "no place to stay and demonstrate peacefully." The article was illustrated, furthermore, with drawings clearly anti-police and just as clearly not anti-demonstrators. The "New Politics," Wills concluded, "is unworkable in the long run; but Daley made it work, beautifully, in Chicago." He even made the ultimate admission for a National Review writer when he ruefully observed that "the convention in the streets may have been of more lasting importance than that held in the Amphitheater."]

Similarly documented is the fact that the news media have been guilty of a generally uncritical acceptance and often advocacy of the established policy in foreign affairs (i.e., the policy of the President and his State Department) through successive administrations during the past 20 years. That is the primary reason why it took so many months and years for millions of Americans and, at long last, for many American publications to be upset about the war in Vietnam. That calamitous conflict stands as confirmation of the fact that a major portion of the orthodox press was hesitant to question or provoke the governmental-industrial-military complex of which President Eisenhower gave the first warning signals. Our foreign policy has been controlled and militarized by the huge bureaucracies in the State Department and the Pentagon, which have effectively promoted the need for an arms race which has no visible end. Part of the revolution that is taking place concerns not only the necessity for a fresh look at the American commitment in Vietnam but the need for a comprehensive revision of the entire American foreign policy. It is not enough that we escape from the current quagmire; there simply must be no more Vietnams. Bismarck observed that every nation eventually must pay for the windows broken by its press, and we are paying a dear price at this time. Despite the massive reversal of position in the editorial pages and columns of orthodox publications on the issue of the war in Vietnam, it is a rare sight indeed to read or hear of any questioning of State Department and/or Pentagon policies in other areas of Southeast Asia, in the Middle East, in Latin America, in Africa, or in Western Europe, to name a few places where we are likely to be fighting new battles with the blood of young Americans.

Furthermore, if the white majority does not sleep well these nights, in too many cases the reason is that the news media have warned of agitators and militants, rioters and looters, but have not pointed out sufficiently the genuine grievances of our black brothers. If—or, more accurately, when—the United States becomes an apartheid society, the [58] blame will rest in large part on a blind and selfish and unconscionable white power establishment and its almost unfailing and subservient ally, the orthodox media. There has been, and there remains, a curious curtain of silence dropped by the white press to keep white people from knowing about events and conditions concerning black people. The record of reporting black attitudes and activities during the fifties and sixties is so dismal that it is openly admitted by many executives in high places of the media. Attempts to remedy that situation, no matter how worthy and how noble, cannot erase the record. We should refuse, for example, to join in the applause for *Newsweek* magazine for its analysis of "The Negro in America" and its advocacy of a program for action— "That in order to deal with the racial crisis effectively, there must be a mobilization of the nation's moral, spiritual and physical resources and a commitment on the part of all segments of U.S. society, public and private, to meet the challenging job." That 23-page report, which subsequently was awarded a journalistic prize, had one major flaw: The date on the cover. It was November 20, 1967, when it was probably too late, rather than November, 1957, when there was still time. The orthodox press too often squarely faces up to societal pressures and issues only to prevent the greater of evils. And we should not fall victim to the hypocrisy of many organs of the news media which finally have begun their examinations of black history, black heritage, black culture and the centuries of repression of black people. Even the *Chicago Tribune* now attempts to paint over a history of unremitting indifference to the sufferings of black people in its city by publishing—in May, 1968—a special section on the history of the Negro in America. Beyond and beneath comment is the pious pronouncement of the American Newspaper Publishers Asociation Foundation that grants-in-aid totaling a miserable $14,340 had been awarded to 26 Negro college journalism majors. The fund was established by a $100,000 contribution announced by the publisher of the *Chicago Tribune* last April and the grants were announced in August by Eugene S. Pulliam, thus keeping the record clear: Penance, such as it is, by the publishers of papers which rank among the most racist in the United States.

The orthodox press has failed, consciously or otherwise, to report and inform effectively in many other areas where we now face or soon will face critical problems. In large measure the failures resulted from a lack of gutsy local and state reporting, the glossing over of underlying conditions, the reporting of social abuses only when they no longer can be kept hidden. And even if publishers do not seek to slide over the sordid details of our society, the incontrovertible fact (ask almost any reporter or any former reporter now in public relations) is that newspapers in this country, with rare exceptions, simply have been unwilling to commit a reasonable portion of their profits to the production of effective, probing, well-researched investigative reporting. Thus, for example, the comfortable and unafflicted probably would be astonished to learn of the blazing hatred with which our judicial system is regarded by the poor and aspiring as a powerful weapon of the establishment to maintain order by using law as a bludgeon. The corruption and brutality of our courts, especially the lower courts, is not a subject of discussion in the ghettos of our land; it is accepted by the imprisoned inhabitants as a part of their hopelessness. Yet this corruption, witnessed daily not only by the victims but by the reporters for the media, is rarely reported. Well within the restrictions and penalties of "contempt of court," it is possible for the media in their day-by-day reporting to report newsworthy —but unpleasant—items reflecting on the integrity of our judicial system and the right of every person to equal treatment and equal penalty under the law.

Threats Hidden or Played Down

Still another revealing and damning indictment of the orthodox press is the steadily deteriorating quality of the American environment under a man-made miasma. It is not surprising that the orthodox press has splendidly lifted the mask of science and technology to reveal the horrible face of nuclear war; the catastrophic consequences of an atomic holocaust would be about as severe for the establishment as for the rest of us. But in other areas where science has revealed the depth of the crises we are in, the news media have not been nearly so eager to report facts that threaten to shake the existing economic order. Well reported are the technological triumphs that make it possible for us to enjoy the magnificent material base of our society, but kept hidden or played down or explained away until very recently have been the threats to human health and survival, because to solve the problems would necessitate grave economic, political and social disruptions opposed by those who derive economic profit from contaminating our environment. It was bad enough in the nineteenth century when the predator industries—especially mining and lumbering plundered our natural resources to make possible a new industrial society. The results of their rape of the land are visible from one end of the country to the other. But that was child's play compared with what is happening in this century as industries dare to destroy not only our land but the basic necessities of life: Our air and our water.

One can dwell on air pollution, on water polution by urban and industrial wastes, on the barbaric desecration of land called strip mining, the noise levels of our cities to which can be added the barely explored dangers of sonic booms, the radiation hazards from nuclear fallout, lead poisoning, the several ways we can get cancer of the lung, the shockingly unrestricted use of insecticides, herbicides and fungicides, military experiments with gas and chemical warfare (of which the Utah story stands as a monumental example of the complaisance of the news media), not to mention the possible synergistic effects of various manmade poisons, chemical and pollutants. Bluntly, the coverage of the California grape strike is a continuing national journalistic disgrace, and the superficial handling of campus dissent and demonstrations has alienated large numbers of university and college students who understand what is happening. As for younger students, it was George Beebe, [59] senior managing editor of the *Miami Herald*, writing in *APME News* last July, who said he had studied what interests young minds and concluded: "It is pretty obvious that only the sheltered child could enjoy the teen-age sections I have seen." Most segments of the orthodox media not only lag behind the Supreme Court in their definitions of "obscenity" but are wildly out of touch with millions of young people who see the genuine obscenities of the world about them and are not upset by some words regarded as taboo by their elders.

[Among the curious arguments used against the demonstrators by Humphrey, Daley and others was that they were "obscene." Nonetheless, as anyone who was there can categorically confirm and as quotations in the Walker Report to the National Commission on the Causes and Prevention of Violence make abundantly clear, a majority of the audible "obscenities" were uttered by police, most of whom appeared unable to address even each other without employing scatological or sexual allusions. Let it be noted, too, that several general-circulation magazines—including Life—*published some of these "obscenities" and William Buckley's* National Review *in its Chicago coverage exposed that magazine's readers for the first time to two words that previously had been withheld from them. It was Buckley himself who, in full view of millions of television viewers on ABC, lashed out at Gore Vidal with the following words: "Shut up, you queer. Don't call me a crypto-Nazi again or I'll sock you in your goddamn face. Go back to your pornography writing." Vidal, author of a novel that features a hero or heroine who is a hermaphrodite, simply responded the next day: "I've always tried to treat Buckley like the great lady that he is." Then there was Mayor Daley, paragon of virtue, who publicly deplored alleged excremental excesses: "When I ask you as a law-abiding citizen not to proceed any further, and you linked arms and someone in your outfit kicks them in the groin or spits at him in the face or hits them with a bag of urine or a bag that begins with 's' and ends with 't,' what would you do? I just wonder what you*

14. The "Orthodox" Media under Fire: Chicago and the Press 163

would do?" Esquire *magazine gave the answer the question deserved:* "Duck."]

Fortunately, some hopeful signs can be noted. We know what the industrial establishment and the orthodox press did to Rachel Carson when in *Silent Spring* she exposed the surface of this putrescent problem. But just as it is now becoming fashionable to explore the urban crises and the conditions of the black people, so it is now permissible to report on our noxious air and our filthy water—even *Life* magazine has come to that. Again too little, too late. The acquiescence and even the cooperation and approbation of the orthodox press in the pollution of our environment constitute one of the darker chapters in the history of the American press.

The many other examples that could be cited would only serve to emphasize that pragmatic modifications of the structure, operation, function and purposes of the press no longer are enough. If Xerox can demonstrate that it has received the message from McLuhan when it announces that it is not in the business of selling copiers but is "in the business of making it easier for people to understand one another," then it is time for the orthodox press to recognize that it is not in the business of selling papers and perpetuating the status quo but is in the business of telling what is really happening in our society. Journalism by paroxysm has been a way of muddling through, but we are paying a terribly high price for covering up and explaining away our problems. There may still be time for the United States if the press fulfills the mission assigned it two centuries ago as the estate that stands above and often against the three other estates.

But not much time remains. Let no one minimize the fact that only small incalculables and coincidences—acts of God, if you will—kept Chicago from becoming the scene of an imponderable catastrophe. During the beautifully cool days and nights of convention week the temperature peaks ranged from 69 to 78 degrees. Temperatures during the week preceding the convention hit highs of 89 to 94, but the heat wave broke on the Sunday eve of the gathering and did not return until four days after the delegates departed. In that kind of heat and humidity, how many would have been killed? What we now debate would be as nothing compared to what might have been. [60]

15. Television and the Press in Vietnam; or, Yes, I Can Hear You Very Well—Just What Was It You Were Saying?
Michael J. Arlen

There's still rubber, of course—the rubber that finds its way from the large French plantations in the south and in the Central Highlands into Michelin and other Free World tires—but, aside from that, probably the largest and most valued single export item from South Vietnam these days is American journalism. The stuff pours out of Saigon each day in a torrent of television film, still photographs, and words—the film and the photographs heading east toward relay stations in Tokyo or San Francisco on the now daily jet flights out of Tan Son Nhut Airport, and the words rushing along the new cable that links Saigon, Guam, Honolulu, and the West Coast and that makes a phone conversation between Saigon and Chicago infinitely clearer than anything that can usually be managed between one Saigon hotel room and another. General William Westmoreland has a telephone in his quarters that enables him to speak instantly with the Commander-in-Chief in Washington. Simmons Fentress, of *Time-Life,* has a telephone that enables *him* to communicate instantly with the *Time-Life* news bureau in Rockefeller Center. Most bureaus are not quite that up-to-the-minute; in fact, many bureaus, the *Times* among them, borrow the Reuters lease line, the *Times* men trudging up to their small office on Tu-Do Street after dinner in order to file their three or four daily stories by one or two in the morning, which is one or two in the afternoon (the previous afternoon) in New York, and thus get them there in time [103] for the next morning's edi-

Source: Michael J. Arlen, *Living-Room War* (New York: Viking Press, 1969), pp. 103–22. Copyright © 1967 by Michael J. Arlen. All rights reserved. Originally appeared in the *New Yorker.* Reprinted by permission of The Viking Press, Inc.

tion. All the same, there is a staggering amount of communication going on in Vietnam: the military, with all its field radios and private telephones and teletype machines, communicating within the military; the embassy and the CIA and USAID and so forth communicating within "the mission"; all of them communicating, when they choose to, with the journalists; the journalists communicating with their editors, and the editors with the public—hundreds of teletypes and Telexes clackety-clacking away all over the bloody country, roughly five-hundred working journalists (and working pretty hard for the most part, too), and where it all ends up, where it all ends up is Fred leans forward in his chair at eleven-thirty in the evening, stares briefly and intensely at the floor, sticks his chin out a bit, adopts a thoughtful look, and, speaking somewhere in the direction of his left shoe, declares, "Well, it's certainly, um, you have to say, ah . . . a very . . . *complex* situation."

After even a little time in Vietnam, a couple of things seem fairly clear. One is that although in a certain sense one can hardly avoid calling the situation in Vietnam "complex" (for that matter, the cell structure of the Arizona tree frog is complex), on a number of possibly more useful levels (for instance, the level of operable communication, of what can be sent out and what can be received) it isn't so complex after all. (The word "complex" tends to be one of our contemporary talismans; whatever you touch with it becomes somehow embalmed and unreachable, and the "complexity" itself is likely to become more interesting or important than the subject it is supposed to enfold.) The situation in Vietnam is obviously composed of many different parts— parts involving such seemingly disparate elements as power politics, South Vietnamese peasant life, the United States Congress, military firepower and tactics, local politics, and corruption—but the parts themselves are relatively simple, or, at any rate, relatively comprehensible. One will never know everything there is to know about politics in the United States. One will never know everything there is to know about politics in Vietnam. Still, if one had the time, or took the trouble, to get in touch with a certain [104] number of reliable Vietnamese political authorities and ask them what was actually happening as a result of such-and-such a power alignment, or what might happen if such-and-such a Cabinet change was effected, they could probably tell one enough so that one could put together a fairly concrete, useful analysis of the subject, so that, for example, in the aftermath of the recent Vietnamese elections, with the Buddhists marching and the students getting beaten up and the Assembly threatening to throw out the vote, one wouldn't get stuck, as most of the American television stations and newspapers got stuck, with trying hastily to explain to the public at the end of September what it was that had been going on for more than a month and had been pointing in the direction of such an outburst (and for the most part not even trying to explain, just giving the bare facts or running around trying to illustrate them), and with the public, responding to yet another over-quick, undercooked explanation, once again nodding its head and muttering, "I told you so. Another mixed-up South American republic."

Vietnam may be the Number 1 story, but journalists don't have that smooth a time covering it. Virtually none of them speaks Vietnamese. Most newspapermen and TV men are here nowadays on only six-month tours of duty, which is hardly enough time to find out the name of the province chief in Binh Dinh, let alone ask him how the corruption situation is coming along—and, in any case, most of the six months is usually spent in chasing Vietnamese fire engines for the New York desk. When somebody gets on to a story, as CBS did with Con Thien early in September, then everyone goes chasing after it—wire services, newspapers, rival networks—the Saigon bureau chiefs receiving "rockets" from New York to get competitive (not really much different from the way the papers and TV cover a fast-breaking news event back home). The trouble is, Vietnam isn't a fast-breaking news event most of the time. The papers back home have their deadlines; the TV stations have their scheduled news broadcasts. The journalists here try to feed the stuff back—there's usually some kind of stuff to feed back, some of it technically [105] useful, and now and then it's good (R. W. Apple had a fine long piece in the *Times* this August on the "stalemate" in the war); sometimes it's ridiculous (as are the solemn transmissions of enemy casualty figures that are often obtained by a pilot looking down from a spotter plane a couple of thousand feet in the air)—and a lot of chatter comes out of the newspapers and picture tubes, but sometimes nothing really happens. Or, when it does happen, it happens in a time and space that often isn't very meaningfully evoked in terms of standard hard-news copy. People have this feeling that they're not getting the "true picture" of Vietnam from daily journalism. (Just about the first thing anyone asks a returning visitor from Vietnam is "What's *really* going on there?") People are, on the whole, right, and what makes the failure of the press to communicate the reality of the Vietnam war something well worth looking into is that the Vietnam war isn't such an isolated phenomenon as many people seem to think it is. "Not like the Second World War," people say. Indeed it isn't: no formal front lines, no supportive religious illusions about a Holy War, no happy embrace of propaganda ("We're all in this together, Fred. Hang the Kaiser. Down with Tojo. Here's a toast to Winnie, Uncle Joe, and Madame Chiang"). A different world now, a different war. The Detroit riots of 1967 are qualitatively, not just chronologically, different from the Detroit riots of 1943. The waves of energy emanating from the hippies in California are

15. Television and the Press in Vietnam 167

qualitatively different from those that emanated from the Lindy Hoppers that short while ago. It isn't, perhaps, that the world is deeper in chaos than it used to be, but that the element of chaos which has always been there in life, which really *is* life (after all, there were minority groups and emerging nations in the eleventh century too), is now coming more and more out from under wraps: Father has left the house, and the children have some new toys and are threatening to knock the house to pieces, and that would be all right, it would be manageable, if we could somehow get inside the house and really find out what was going on, could sit down and try to understand the children, listen to them, at any rate if we could [106] confront what it was that they were doing (let alone thinking about), but, as things are, we make this big thing about how we know everything that's going on—*nothing* escapes us, because we too have new toys, which tell us things—but what really happens is that we sit outside the house and every now and then a maid comes out onto the porch and stamps one foot lightly for attention and then reads us a brief announcement, and we sit there looking thoughtful or impatient and listening to the sounds of breaking furniture from somewhere on the second story. We have this great arrogance about communications. We've given up much of our capacity for first-hand experience—certainly for first-hand sensory experience—cheerfully sitting at home shrouded in plastic, film, magnetic tape, peering out at the world through lenses, electronic tubes, photographs, lines of type. And we've also, at a time when the ability of a people to order and enhance its existence depends increasingly on its ability to know what is really going on (no more just getting the word from Father or the King; no more milling around in front of Whitehall to find out what really gives with Kitchener in the Sudan)—we've also given up the ideal of knowing first hand about ourselves and the world in favor of receiving sometimes arbitrary and often nearly stenographic reports through a machine system we call "communications," which for the most part neither recognizes the element of chaos in the world for what it is nor is able to make contact with it except on a single narrow-beam wavelength.

It's ironic, maybe, that, among the methods men have devised for usefully reflecting the world back to themselves, only those methods that the population at large doesn't really take very seriously—one thinks especially of the novel and the film—have made any significant attempt to cope with the evolving human experience. Not so long ago, in the nineteenth century, when the world was held in place by nuts and bolts, when the doors to all the upstairs rooms were locked up tight, when Father was home and brooked no nonsense—in those days, because it seemed relevant and interesting to find out about the things in people's [107] lives, what work they did, what trolley car they took from where to where, and whom they married, novelists wrote book after book after book that covered these things in an orderly way, and that often appeared to describe the universe largely in terms of stationary articles of furniture. Nowadays it seems more relevant to write about the inside of people's heads (or at least the writers' heads) and about how they really live—about how life doesn't always go in a straight line from here to there but moves forward, backward, upside down, inside the head, and outside. The nervier writers—the Mailers, the Pynchons, the Updikes—go reaching out and grabbing at how things seem to be right now. A book by Mailer, or a film by Antonioni, may not define the world, and you may not like it, but, taken all in all, the novels and films being turned out today seem to attempt to reflect more of the shifting dynamism of present-day life than does even the best of daily journalism (both press and television), which we take *very* seriously and defer to for most of our public and private impressions of the world and, one imagines, of ourselves. Daily journalism, in fact, seems to have changed very little over the last few decades—as if nobody quite knew what to do with it (except for adding more white space, syndicating Clayton Fritchey, and "livening up" the women's page), as if its conventions were somehow eternal. The *Times,* which has editors and reporters with sufficient imagination and sense of history to recognize that there is more to be reflected upon in our evolving experience in Vietnam than the daily bombing reports, continues for the most part to treat the war as an accounting exercise—and "treat" is right, for the hurly-burly of the world emerges in the pages of the *Times* somehow ordered and dignified, a bit the way a man's ridiculous life emerges as so splendidly established (all those "estate"s and "issue"s and so forth) when he listens to the lawyer read him out his will. Television, with all its technical resources, with all the possibilities of film and film-editing for revealing fluid motion, continues for the most part to report the war as a long, long narrative broken into two-minute, three-minute, or four-minute [108] stretches of visual incident. Now, it's obvious that there are plenty of events in the war, or anywhere, that ought to be treated in an accountant's manner, and also that there are plenty of incidents that are inherently visual and can most accurately be revealed on film. If there's an important battle, it ought to be put down, covered—just that. The thing is, though, that it doesn't take one very long in Vietnam to realize—perhaps "feel" would be closer than "realize"—that there is a crucial difference between what seems to be *here* and what is reflected of it back home on television and in newspapers. It isn't so much a matter of the press distorting the picture (one of the favorite themes of our embassy in Saigon), because, although there's a certain amount of that—a certain amount of deferring to official pronouncements that one knows are biased, a certain amount of translating battles in which we lost a cruel number of men into gallant actions that were "gallant" because we took so many losses—somehow the concept of press distortion implies a demonology that for the most part just doesn't exist. What really seems to be standing in the way of an accurate reflection of Vietnam right now isn't that the press is "lying" or not telling all it knows. It's partly that much of the press, especially the wire services and television, just doesn't have either the time or the inclination to investigate the various parts of the Vietnam picture—what's the true military situation, what's being done with new technology, what can't be done, how solid is the government's hold on the villages, how solid is the government, how good or bad is the ARVN, and so on. And, more important, when they do get hold of one of these parts, neither most of the newspapers nor most of television seems to be able to do anything more with it than to treat it as an isolated piece of detail —maybe an important piece of detail, maybe unimportant, but isolated in any case, cut off by the rigors and conventions of journalism from the events and forces that brought it into being, cut off, too, from the events and forces that it will in turn animate. The other week, as a small example, a crew from ABC flew in here to do an interview with Ambassador Ellsworth Bunker. The ambassador sat behind his desk and, in [109] response to questions gently shoved at him by ABC's John Scali, discoursed at length on such matters as the "new stability" that would, he said, result from the Thieu-Ky election, and on the fine prospects for Thieu and Ky to work well together in the new government ("They have worked together very well in the last two years."). The program was presented a few days later in the United States—presented, naturally, at face value. At the end of the next week, Buddhists were marching in the streets here, students were getting clubbed by the police, reporters and TV crews (including ABC's) were tearing around Saigon trying to cover a situation that was, after all, a fairly predictable result of the unpopularity of the recent elections, of the fact that the "new stability" we are so hopefully committed to in many instances seems to depend largely on the ability of General Loan to hold down the lid on the kettle, even of the fact that Thieu and Ky have trouble staying in the same room with each other, let alone in the same government. The point isn't that Mr. Bunker shouldn't have said what he said, or that journalists shouldn't have been chasing after riot coverage, but that in life, after all, events don't sit stiffly, separately upon a page, don't take place in terms of three-minute narrative slices of film; they push and jostle and flow and mix against one another, and the process of this mixing is often a more important and revelatory part of what is really going on (this continuing reality that we so proudly call history when it has gone past us) than the isolated announcements that we usually have to make do with. It's obviously not fair—or, at any rate, not realistic—to expect a consistent resourcefulness in writing, political analysis, and so forth from a profession (journalism) that has traditionally been longer on energy than on anything else. But it seems true to say that most journalists here convey a more firmly realized picture of Vietnam in a couple of hours of conversation in the evening (with all those elisions made, the separate parts connected) than they've achieved sometimes (in complicity with their editors and their public) in six months of filing detached, hard-news reports. And it seems even truer to say that one of the notable results of all this has been the [110] almost tangible inability of people back home to pay any very rigorous attention to Vietnam. It obsesses people, certainly, but more as a neurosis (which it's become, it often seems, largely as a result of this inability to confront it) than as a very real, evolving attempt of a large, important nation to relate outward to a large, important sector of the world, which, whether one finds the attempt good or bad, moral or immoral, useful or useless, is what it's all about.

People often refer to television's coverage of Vietnam as "television's war" (as one could probably describe television's coverage of civil rights as "television's civil war"), and although it seems fair to say that in general television has done very well strictly in terms of what it has set out to report about Vietnam—in terms of those usually combat-oriented film clips that appear on the morning and evening news programs—it also seems fair to say that for the most part television in Vietnam has operated on a level not much more perceptive than that of a sort of illustrated wire service, with the television crews racketing around the countryside seeking to illustrate the various stories that are chalked on the assignment boards in Saigon ("4th Div. Opn.," "Chopper story," "Hobo Woods Opn.," "Buddhist march"), constantly under pressure to feed the New York news programs new stories (ideally, combat stories), moving in here, moving out, moving in there the next day. Recently, the major effort of the military war has been taking place up north in the I Corps area, and, as a result, many of the television and newspaper correspondents are now working out of the Danang press center. Ordinarily, though, much of the work is done almost in bankerish fashion from Saigon, and one says "bankerish" not to disparage the factor of risk-taking in their covering of various operations (a factor that ranges from slight to very considerable), but as an indication of how difficult it is to get close to a strange war in an unfamiliar country by a process that more often than not consists in your having breakfast at the Hotel Caravelle at seven-thirty, driving out to a helicopter base, going by chopper to where some [111] military operation is occurring (say, a search of an area where a Vietcong ammunition dump supposedly exists, the possible picture value being in the blowing up of the ammo dump), wandering around in the woods taking pictures until three-thirty, maybe getting shot at a bit and maybe not, then taking the chopper back, doing all your paperwork and film-shipment arrangements, and meeting friends in the Continental bar at seven o'clock. The correspondents tend to have mixed feelings about all this themselves. Many of them, to be sure, are older men with families and are not crazy about spending more time than necessary out in the field, and, doubtless like journalists everywhere, they complain of not having enough time to cover the "right stories," and of the pressure from New York to provide combat coverage. Of the newspapermen and magazine correspondents, in fact, except for a couple of people like Peter Arnett and Henri Huet of the AP, and David Greenway of *Time*, and Dana Stone of UPI, virtually none are doing the combat work that television is now doing almost on a routine basis (a seemingly routine basis, anyway). And although it's true that the Vietnam story is more than the story of men shooting at one another (the television people themselves refer to it as "bang-bang" coverage, and have a healthy respect for what goes into the getting of it), it's also true that American men (and Vietnamese men) are indeed getting shot and killed, and are shooting and killing others, and one would have to be a pretty self-indulgent pacifist to say that it wasn't somebody's job to record and witness something of that. The trouble is that television doesn't do much more than that. It doesn't try. There are the highly structured news programs, with correspondents from around the world coming on for a few minutes at a time. And then, as a way of circumventing this limitation, there are the "news specials," which up to now have generally been done with the same hasty, unfeeling, technically skillful professionalism that (more justifiably) characterizes the shorter film clips. For the most part, "television's war" is a prisoner of its own structure, a prisoner of such facts as that although television is the chief source of news and information for [112] the majority of the people, the News & Information act is still just another aspect of the world's greatest continuous floating variety show; that the scope and cost of television news require an immense weight of administrative managing from above; that for TV the newsworthiness of daily events is still so restrictively determined by visual criteria. For example, people watching an evening news show about an ammo dump being blown up in the Hobo Woods might reasonably conclude, on a day, say, when a nationwide strike was averted in San Diego, when a rebel army was captured in Nigeria, when the Pope fell sick, and when Indonesia broke relations with Red China, that there was some special significance to the blowing up of this particular ammo dump, or not even anything special about it, just some significance—that its presentation on the screen in front of one said something useful about the war. In all too many cases, though, what the blowing up of the ammo dump says is that when you blow up an ammo dump it goes boom-boom-boom and there is a lot of smoke, and that is about it. Daily journalism in general seems to be virtually rooted in its traditional single-minded way of presenting the actuality of daily life, as if some invisible sacred bond existed between the conventional structures of daily journalism and the conventional attitudes of so many of the people whom daily journalism serves. This has been increasingly noticeable in journalism's severely conventional covering of most of the major matters of our time— covering civil rights, for instance, with its technically proficient battle-action accounts of rioting, and its distracted, uncomprehending, essentially uninterested sliding over of the dark silences that fill the empty spaces in between the riots. It is now especially evident, and damaging, in Vietnam, where, for the most part, American journalism has practically surrendered itself to a consecutive, activist, piecemeal, the-next-day-the-First-Army-forged-onward-toward-Aachen approach to a war that even the journalists covering it know to be non-consecutive, non-activist, a war of silences, strange motions, where a bang on the table gets you nothing and an inadvertent blink causes things to happen in rooms you haven't even looked into yet, where there is no Aachen, and "onward" is a word that doesn't seem to translate very well into the local language. The journalists reorder the actuality of Vietnam into these isolated hard-news incidents for the benefit of their editors. The editors say that that's what the public wants, and, to a great extent, the editors are right about that. The public does indeed want and need hard news, something concrete amid the chaos, something you can reach out to over the morning coffee and almost touch— a hill number, for example. Hill 63. Hill 881. It's a truism, especially among wire-service reporters in Vietnam, that if you can somehow get a hill number attached to a military operation (most operations start at one latitude-longitude point and move to another), regardless of the number of casualties, regardless, especially, of the relevance of this operation to the rest of the war, the story will run on for days, particularly in the pages of the small-to-medium-circulation newspapers that buy most of the wire-service copy. The public also presumably wants and needs a sense of progress, and since this is a public that tends to measure progress numerically—so many yards gained rushing, so many villages pacified, earnings per share up, body counts down, carloadings

15. Television and the Press in Vietnam 173

steady—there is a tendency on the part of the dispensers of information, the military and the government, to scour Vietnam for positive statistics and dole them out to newsmen, who are always under pressure to supply copy, and who know that there is nearly always a market back home for these firm-sounding stories that seem to be about numbers, which in turn seem to mean something, but in fact are often just about the numbers. One of the better *Catch-22* effects over here is to pick up the daily *Stars & Stripes* and read the wire-service lead, datelined Saigon—"Hurtling out of an overcast sky, warplanes of the United States Seventh Fleet delivered another massive air strike against the port city of Haiphong," and so on—and try to recall the atmosphere and the phrasing when the source information was delivered in the course of the daily briefing, the famous "five-o'clock follies" held each day at the Mission Press Center. A couple of dozen correspondents are slouched in chairs in the briefing room, a [114] bored Air Force major is reading aloud in a flat, uninflected voice the summary of the various air strikes conducted that morning and earlier that afternoon: "Airplanes of the United States Seventh Fleet flew 267 missions against targets in the south. . . . Airplanes of the 12th Tactical Fighter Wing flew 245 missions and 62 sorties against selected targets, including the warehouse system outside Hanoi and bridges in the Loc Binh area. . . ." Everybody has been dozing along, except that now someone asks, "Say, Major, isn't that Loc Binh just five miles from the Chinese border?" The major will acknowledge that it is. "Say, Major, isn't that the closest we've yet come to the Chinese border?" The major will acknowledge that it is. "Major," another voice will ask, "wouldn't you say that was a 'first'—I mean in proximity terms?" The major looks thoughtful for a moment. "In proximity terms," he will reply, "I would say 'affirmative.' "

Television correspondents try to get around the limitations, not of their medium but of what they are structurally required to cover (at least, the more political and thoughtful among them do), by inserting some sort of verbal point of view in the taped narrative they send off with their brief film reports, as though to say, Okay, fellows, here's your bang-bang footage, but if I put a little edge in my voice maybe it will come out a bit closer to the way things were. Morley Safer used to do this with a vengeance on CBS, and CBS's David Schoumacher and NBC's Dean Brelis do it to a certain degree now, and in some ways it's effective—it sharpens a point of view, if there should be one to begin with, and it allows for a slight intrusion of irony into a war that most news organizations are attempting to report without irony. (Trying to report a war without irony is a bit like trying to keep sex out of a discussion of the relations between men and women.) The fact is, though, that if you show some film of, say, half a dozen helicopters whirring in onto the ground, our men rushing out with rifles at the ready amid sounds of gunfire here and there, a platoon commander on the radio, men running by with stretchers amid more gunfire, what you are really doing is adding another centimeter or milimeter to what is often no more than an illusion [115] of American military progress (our boys rushing forward, those roaring helicopters, the authoritative voice of the captain). And to stand up there afterward, microphone in hand, and say, with all the edge in your voice you can muster, as Safer used to do, "Another typical engagement in Vietnam. . . . A couple of battalions of the Army went into these woods looking for the enemy. The enemy was gone. There was a little sniper fire at one moment; three of our men were hit, but not seriously. It was pretty much the way it usually goes," doesn't pull the picture back quite straight—or perhaps, to be a bit more accurate, it focuses one's eyes on a picture that may not really have any useful connection with the situation it claims to be communicating about. Communications. One is so terribly serious about some things. One has a direct circuit installed between Rockefeller Center and the Hotel Caravelle. One can whoosh eight cans of 16-millimeter film two-thirds of the way around the world in less than twenty hours. For around seventy-five hundred bucks, one can buy thirty minutes' worth of satellite time and relay the film in from Tokyo. The television people work like hell in Vietnam—Saturdays, Sundays, all the time, really. Many of the journalists there work like hell—able men, responsible men, pasting detail upon detail into some sort of continuing scrapbook of stories about bombing raids, and pacification programs, and bombing raids, and about the Buddhist march, and the new infrared searchlight, and bombing raids, and about the fact that forty thousand Vietcong defected in the last six months. And the detail accretes, day in, day out; paragraphs clatter out over the cable, film by the bagload heads home for processing, detail, detail, detail, and people back home, who have been fed more words and pictures on Vietnam than on any other event in the last twenty years, have the vague, unhappy feeling that they still haven't been told it straight. And, of course, it's true. When President Johnson stands behind the podium in the East Room, looks into the cameras, and declares that he has "read all the reports" and that the reports tell him "progress is being made," it isn't that he's lying. He doesn't need to lie for the situation to be potentially [116] disastrous; all he needs to do is defer to the authority of a reportorial system (one is thinking especially of the government's) that, in terms of the sensitivities, the writing skill, and the general bias of the reporters, is unlikely to be automatically accurate, or anywhere near it. Patriotism doesn't have much to do with it, any

15. Television and the Press in Vietnam 175

more than inaccuracy or distortion has much to do with whatever it is that gives old Fred—after three years in which he has read 725,000 words about Vietnam—the feeling that he couldn't write three intelligible sentences about the subject on a postcard to his mother.

There are a couple of things one could probably do to improve the situation. In television, the most likely would be to loosen up and expand the evening news programs so that the correspondents could handle larger themes, and then be less restrictively visual about the assignments. (The networks might also get some correspondents whose interest in daily events wasn't entirely confined to hustling 450 feet of film into a can.) In newspapers (the best of which are far less limited, obviously, than television), one might conceivably do the same sort of thing—loosen the paper up, get some new writers, encourage them to at least allow themselves the possibility of breaking through the barriers of the orthodox good-newspaper-writing declarative sentence ("McCormick Place, the huge exposition center that draws more than a million visitors a year to Chicago, was ravaged by fire today. Damage was estimated at $100 million" is the way *The New York Times* sings it). In television, again—although this, admittedly, isn't very likely, at least in this Golden Age—it might even happen that a network official would someday have the nerve and imagination to call on a few of the really inventive movie-makers, like Godard, Antonioni, and Richardson, or, since they might be a bit hard to get, on some of the young inventive movie-makers like Stan Vanderbeek, Shirley Clarke, Donn Pennebaker, and say, "How about you and you and you going in there for a while, to Vietnam, Harlem, Texas, and bringing back some film of what you think is going on?" After all, there *are* these really inventive [117] movie-makers, and one of the reasons they're in movies, and not TV, is that TV tends to remain so consistently nerveless and conventional in its use of film. And both the papers and TV could stand being a great deal more investigative, because if the emperor doesn't have any clothes on you're surely not doing the empire much of a favor by saying he does. Right now, for example, there's a big public-relations push going on among the military and the embassy people here to get across the idea that the ARVN is a fine, competent, reliable modern army, which it certainly isn't—partly because we spent three years (between 1959 and 1961) training it to be an old-fashioned army, and partly for reasons having to do with corruption and such matters. With the exception of Peter Arnett of the AP, and Merton Perry of *Newsweek,* and a very few others, however, nobody has really gone into the ARVN story, which isn't to say that everyone has been praising the ARVN; even *Time* qualifies its statements about it to the extent of acknowledging that the ARVN hasn't yet fully "found itself." Still, it's an important story to do (many of the things you find out about the ARVN are inextricably connected with the rest of Vietnamese life), and it's here, it's here all the time (maybe a bit the way Negro slums are there all the time back home), and nobody really looks into it until something happens—a victory, a defeat, a campaign. Or, when somebody does, he does it the way ABC looked into the ARVN the other day, which was to run a three-minute film clip on one of its few decent battalions receiving a Presidential citation from General Westmoreland, concluding with a few well-chosen words from the general on the great improvement he had lately detected in the South Vietnamese Army—all presented absolutely straight. The thing is, one takes note of these various deficiencies, inabilities, disinclinations, one dutifully nudges forward one's little "constructive suggestions"—but they're no more than that. We're all prisoners of the same landscape, and it hardly seems realistic to expect that we'll ever derive a truly intelligent, accurate, sensitive reflection of actuality from a free-market communications system that is manned and operated by people like us, and that will, [118] inevitably, tell us for the most part what we want to know. In Vietnam recently the war has shifted—superficially, maybe, but shifted anyway—up into the I Corps area, where, just below the DMZ, we have some batteries of Marine artillery, which were placed there last February in an aggressive move to fire upon the enemy infiltration routes, and which have now become exposed, potentially isolated, and subjected to extremely heavy shelling from the enemy's guns, these being in the main well camouflaged, dug in behind the hills within the DMZ, and hard to hit. The other day, after a month-long period in which Con Thien in particular had taken as many as a thousand rounds of artillery fire in a single day, the military headquarters in Saigon (four hundred miles to the south) suddenly announced that the enemy had pulled back from his positions, that we had in fact won at Con Thien, had punished him too severely with our artillery and bombers, and instantly there was a great outpouring of cables and messages back home. U.S. GUNS BATTER REDS AT CON THIEN, headlined the *New York Post*. REDS FLEE GUN POSTS; CON THIEN SIEGE ENDS, said the *Denver Post*. The AP put a big story on the wire which began, "Massive American firepower has broken the back of the Communists' month-long artillery siege of Con Thien," and went on to quote General Westmoreland as having said, "We made it a Dien Bien Phu in reverse." One of the few exceptions was Charles Mohr of the *Times*, who had recently been up there and who filed a long piece to his paper two days later to the effect that Con Thien was still extremely exposed, that "aerial photos confirmed a limited withdrawal but did not necessarily prove that the bulk of the gun pits—most of which have never been located—were hit by B-52 bombing raids and United States artillery," and that "few sources believe that more than a respite has been gained." There is disagreement among journalists here as to the real likelihood of our suffering a military defeat in I Corps, at a place, say, such as Con Thien. There are those who point out that two weeks ago eighteen inches of rain fell on Con Thien in two days, that air strikes could not get in, that trucks could not supply the base with ammunition, or even with water, that it is not totally implausible, [119] considering the fact that the enemy has superior forces in the area, for a combination of circumstances to occur in which the enemy might indeed overrun Con Thien, destroy the guns, raise hell, get out—and then you really would have a sort of mini-Dien Bien Phu disaster. There are also those—the majority—who regard a successful enemy attack on Con Thien as very unlikely, who think that Con Thien could never get that exposed, and who cite as evidence the fact that the enemy is as impeded by monsoon weather as we are. The majority view is probably right. ("The United States Command disclosed today that about 4000 men of the First Air Cavalry Division had been moved north to within 20 miles of Danang," the AP filed a few days later, forgetting perhaps to disclose that Danang is the central staging area for I Corps and the outposts near the DMZ, or that the reinforcement of the Marine Corps by the Army is not yet an everyday occurrence in Vietnam or anywhere else.) But, in either case, most journalists who have been up north (some of the same men, indeed, who seem to have so blithely passed along those "Victory at Con Thien" announcements) recognize that the shifting situation in I Corps, and notably around Con Thien (where for the first time Vietnam has turned into a conventional war; in fact, not just a conventional war—a small-scale replica of the First World War), not only says a great deal about the military possibilities in Vietnam right now but, even more important, raises a good many questions about the limits of technology as a cure-all in every modern military situation, about the hazards of trying to fight what appears increasingly to be a ground war with insufficient troops, about the possibilities of negotiating a peace settlement with an enemy who seems to be able to effectively increase his infantry capabilities more than we can. ("Long-range Communist artillery and Red mortars opened up again yesterday and today on U.S. Marine positions south of the Demilitarized Zone," the AP dispatch began on October 11, as if the previous ones had never existed.) Con Thien—lately, anyway—raises these sorts of questions, but, with few exceptions, such as Mohr, and Lee Lescaze of the *Washington Post,* nobody seems to even hear [120] the questions, let alone try to pass them on. (Television, it should be pointed out, first broke the Con Thien story, first took note of the fact that the situation had shifted from an aggressive gun emplacement last February to a defensive battery holding on for dear life in the fall, but, in terms of the three-minute film clips on the evening news, it hasn't done much beyond showing what the place is like—no mean trick itself.) Back home now, one gathers, the tide of impatience and unhappiness with the war keeps growing. Governor Reagan, one reads, advises that we should use the "full technological resources of the United States" to win the war. An eminent Midwestern senator visiting Saigon the other day slammed his thick hand upon the table and declared in anguish and frustration (the special anguish and frustration of eminent people) that he could see "no alternatives remaining" except that we "step up the bombing" or "pack up and leave." A journalist was talking here recently, a young man who works for television and who has been up to Con Thien. "The real hazard about Con Thien," he was saying, "is that we'll get so frustrated trying to win a ground war without enough troops that we'll indeed step up the technology, whatever that means. I hate to think what that means." There are so many real and possible tragedies connected with Vietnam—the tragedies of men and women dead, of men and women dying, of nations dying. (Perhaps there's no worse tragedy than people dying.) But sometimes, listening to the note of anger and impatience that arises above the towns and cities in our country, that hovers over daily life, feeling the growing swell of semi-automatic hawkishness and doveishness that pushes so many people nowadays, and seems to say less for what they rigorously, intelligently believe is right than for the inability of many persons to stand in uncertainty much longer when there are firm choices to be seen on either side, sometimes one has the sense that maybe as great a tragedy as any other will be that we will indeed *do* something shortly (this nation of men and women that always has to be doing something to keep sane), distracted, numbed, isolated by detail that seemed to have been information but was only detail, isolated [121] by a journalism that too often told us only what we thought we wanted to hear, isolated, in fact, by communications—expressing pieties, firmness, regrets, what you will, citizens patting each other on the back ("We did the right thing, Fred."), and not know what we did. Or why. And, once again, will have learned nothing. [122]

16. The Media Barons and the Public Interest: An FCC Commissioner's Warning

Nicholas Johnson

Before I came to the Federal Communications Commission my concerns about the ownership of broadcasting and publishing in America were about like those of any other generally educated person.

Most television programming from the three networks struck me as bland at best. I had taken courses dealing with propaganda and "thought control," bemoaned (while being entertained by) *Time* magazine's "slanted" reporting, understood that Hearst had something to do with the Spanish-American War, and was impressed with President Eisenhower's concern about "the military-industrial complex." The changing ownership of the old-line book publishers and the disappearance of some of our major newspapers made me vaguely uneasy. I was philosophically wedded to the fundamental importance of "the marketplace of ideas" in a free society, and a year as law clerk to my idol, Supreme Court Justice Hugo L. Black, had done nothing to weaken that commitment.

But I didn't take much time to be reflective about the current significance of such matters. It all seemed beyond my ability to influence in any meaningful way. Then, in July, 1966, I became a member of the FCC. Here my interest in the marketplace of ideas could no longer remain a casual article of personal faith. The commitment was an implicit part of the oath I took on assuming the office of commissioner, and, I quickly learned, an everyday responsibility.

Source: *The Atlantic Monthly*, June 1968, pp. 43–51. Copyright © 1968 by The Atlantic Monthly Company, Boston, Massachusetts. Reprinted by permission of the author and the publisher.

Threats to the free exchange of information and opinion in this country can come from various sources, many of them outside the power of the FCC to affect. Publishers and reporters are not alike in their ability, education, tolerance of diversity, and sense of responsibility. The hidden or overt pressures of advertisers have long been with us.

But one aspect of the problem is clearly within the purview of the FCC—the impact of *ownership* upon the content of the mass media. It is also a part of the responsibility of the Antitrust Division of the Justice Department. It has been the subject of recent congressional hearings. There are a number of significant trends in the ownership of the media worth examining—local and regional monopolies, growing concentration of control of the most profitable and powerful television stations in the major markets, broadcasting-publishing combines, and so forth. But let's begin with a look at the significance of media ownership by "conglomerate corporations"—holding companies [43] that own, in addition to publishing and broadcasting enterprises, other major industrial corporations.

During my first month at the FCC I studied the cases and attended the meetings, but purposefully did not participate in voting on any items. One of the agenda items at the July 20 commissioners' meeting proposed two draft letters addressed to the presidents of International Telephone and Telegraph and the American Broadcasting Company, ITT and ABC, Messrs. Harold Geneen and Leonard Goldenson. We were asking them to supply "a statement specifying in further detail the manner in which the financial resources of ITT will enable ABC to improve its program services and thereby better to serve the public interest." This friendly inquiry was my first introduction to the proposed ITT-ABC merger, and the Commission majority's attitudes about it. It was to be a case that would occupy much of my attention over the next few months.

There wasn't much discussion of the letters that morning, but I read carefully the separate statements filed with the letter by my two responsible and experienced colleagues, Commissioners Robert T. Bartley and Kenneth A. Cox, men for whom I was already feeling a respect that was to grow over the following months.

Commissioner Bartley, a former broadcaster with the deep and earthy wisdom one would expect in a Texas-born relative of the late Speaker Sam Rayburn, wrote a long and thoughtful statement. He warned of "the probable far-reaching political, social and economic consequences for the public interest of the increasing control of broadcast facilities and broadcast service by large conglomerate corporations such as the applicants." Commissioner Cox, former lawyer, law professor, counsel

16. The Media Barons and the Public Interest 181

to the Senate Commerce Committee, and chief of the FCC's Broadcast Bureau, characterized the proposed merger as "perhaps the most important in the agency's history." He said the issues were "so significant and far-reaching that we should proceed immediately to designate the matter for hearing."

Their concerns were well grounded in broadcasting's history and in the national debate preceding the 1934 Communications Act we were appointed to enforce. Precisely what Congress intended the FCC to do was not specified at the time or since. But no one has ever doubted Congress' great concern lest the ownership of broadcasting properties be permitted to fall into a few hands or to assume monopoly proportions.

The 1934 Act was preceded by the 1927 Radio Act and a series of industry Radio Conferences in the early 1920s. The conferences were called by then Secretary of Commerce Herbert C. Hoover. Hoover expressed concern lest control over broadcasting "come under the arbitrary power of any person or group of persons." During the congressional debates on the 1927 Act a leading congressman, noting that "publicity is the most powerful weapon that can be wielded in a republic," warned of the domination of broadcasting by "a single selfish group." Should that happen, he said, "then woe be to those who dare to differ with them." The requirement that licenses not be transferred without Commission approval was intended, according to a sponsoring senator, "to prevent the concentration of broadcast facilities by a few." Thirty years later, in 1956, Senate Commerce Committee Chairman Warren G. Magnuson was still warning the Commission that it "should be on guard against the intrusion of big business and absentee ownership."

These concerns of Congress and my colleagues were to take on fuller meaning as the ITT-ABC case unfolded, a case which eventually turned into an FCC *cause célèbre*. It also demonstrated the enormity of the responsibility vested in this relatively small and little-known Commission, by virtue of its power to grant or withhold membership in the broadcast industry. On a personal level, the case shook into me the realization, for the first time in my life, of the dreadful significance of the ownership structure of the mass media in America.

The ITT-ABC Merger Case

ITT is a sprawling international conglomerate of 433 separate boards of directors that derives about 60 percent of its income from its significant holdings in at least forty foreign countries. It is the ninth largest industrial corporation in the world in size of work force. In addition to its sale of electronic equipment to foreign governments, and operation of foreign countries' telephone systems, roughly half of its domestic income comes from U.S. Government defense and space contracts. But it is also in the business of consumer finance, life insurance, investment funds, small loan companies, car rentals (ITT Avis, Inc.), and book publishing.

This description of ITT's anatomy is taken (as is much of this ITT-ABC discussion) from opinions written by myself and Commissioners Bartley and Cox. We objected, vigorously, to the four-man majority's decision to approve the merger. So did some senators and congressmen, the Department of Justice, the Commission's own staff, the American Civil Liberties Union, a number of independent individuals and witnesses, and a belated but eventually insistent chorus of newspaper and magazine editorialists.

What did we find so ominous about the take-over of this radio and television network by a highly successful conglomerate organization? [44]

In 1966, ABC owned 399 theaters in 34 states, 5 VHF television stations, 6 AM and 6 FM stations (all in the top 10 broadcasting markets), and, of course, one of the 3 major television networks and one of the 4 major radio networks in the world. Its 137 primary television network affiliates could reach 93 percent of the then 50 million television homes in the United States, and its radio network affiliates could reach 97 percent of the then 55 million homes with radio receivers. ABC had interests in, and affiliations with, stations in 25 other nations, known as the "Worldvision Group." These, together with ABC Films, made the parent corporation perhaps the world's largest distributor of filmed shows for theaters and television stations throughout this country and abroad. ABC was heavily involved in the record production and distribution business, and other subsidiaries published three farm papers.

The merger would have placed this accumulation of mass media, and one of the largest purveyors of news and opinion in America, under the control of one of the largest conglomerate corporations in the world. What's wrong with that? Potentially a number of things. For now, consider simply that the integrity of the news judgment of ABC might be affected by the economic interests of ITT—that ITT might simply view ABC's programming as a part of ITT's public relations, advertising, or political activities. This seemed to us a real threat in 1966, notwithstanding the character of the management of both companies, and their protestations that no possibility of abuse existed. By 1967 the potential threat had become reality.

ITT's Empire

ITT's continuing concern with political and economic developments in foreign countries as a result of its far-flung economic interests was

16. The Media Barons and the Public Interest 183

fully documented in the hearing. It showed, as one might expect, ITT's recurrent concern with internal affairs in most major countries of the world, including rate problems, tax problems, and problems with nationalization and reimbursement, to say nothing of ordinary commercial dealing. Its involvement with the United States government, in addition to defense contracts, included the Agency for International Development's insurance of 5.8 percent of all ITT assets.

Testimony was offered on the fascinating story of intrigue surrounding "Operation Deep Freeze" (an underwater cable). It turned out that ITT officials, using high-level government contracts in England and Canada, had brought off a bit of profitable international diplomacy unknown to the United States State Department or the FCC, possibly in violation of law. Further inquiry revealed that officers and directors of ITT's subsidiaries included two members of the British House of Lords, one in the French National Assembly, a former premier of Belgium, and several ministers of foreign governments and officials of government-owned companies.

As it seemed to Commissioners Bartley and Cox and to me when we dissented from the Commission's approval of the merger in June, 1967, a company whose daily activities require it to manipulate governments at the highest levels would face unending temptation to manipulate ABC news. Any public official, or officer of a large corporation, is necessarily clearly concerned with the appearance of some news stories, the absence of others, and the tone and character of all affecting his personal interests. That's what public relations firms and press secretaries are all about. We concluded, "We simply cannot find that the public interest of the American citizenry is served by turning over a major network to an international enterprise whose fortunes are tied to its political relations with the foreign officials whose actions it will be called upon to interpret to the world."

Even the highest degree of subjective integrity on the part of chief ITT officials could not ensure integrity in ABC's operations. To do an honest and impartial job of reporting the news is difficult enough for the most independent and conscientious of newsmen. Eric Sevareid has said of putting on a news program at a network relatively free of conglomerate control: "The ultimate sensation is the feeling of being bitten to death by ducks." And ABC newsmen could not help knowing that ITT had sensitive business relations in various foreign countries and at the highest levels of our government, and that reporting on any number of industries and economic developments would touch the interests of ITT. The mere awareness of these interests would make it impossible for those news officials, no matter how conscientious, to report news and develop documentaries objectively, in the way that they would do if ABC remained unaffiliated with ITT. They would advance within the news organization, or be fired, or become officers of ABC—perhaps even of ITT—or not, and no newsman would be able to erase from his mind the idea that his chances of doing so might be affected by his treatment of issues on which ITT is sensitive.

Only last year CBS was reportedly involved, almost Hearst-like, in a nightmarish planned armed invasion of Haiti. It was an exclusive, and would have made a very dramatic start-to-finish documentary but for the inglorious end: U.S. Customs wouldn't let them leave the United States. Imagine ITT, with its extensive interests in the Caribbean, engaged in such undertakings. [45]

The likelihood of at least some compromising of ABC's integrity seemed inherent in the structure of the proposed new organization. What were the *probabilities* that these potentials for abuse would be exercised? We were soon to see the answer in the bizarre proceedings right before our eyes.

During the April, 1967, hearings, while this very issue was being debated, the *Wall Street Journal* broke the story that ITT was going to extraordinary lengths to obtain favorable press coverage of this hearing. Eventually three reporters were summoned before the examiner to relate for the official record the incidents that were described in the *Journal*'s exposé.

An AP and a UPI reporter testified to several phone calls to their homes by ITT public relations men, variously asking them to change their stories and make inquiries for ITT with regard to stories by other reporters, and to use their influence as members of the press to obtain for ITT confidential information from the Department of Justice regarding its intentions. Even more serious were several encounters between ITT officials and a *New York Times* reporter.

On one of these occasions ITT's senior vice president in charge of public relations went to the reporter's office. After criticizing her dispatches to the *Times* about the case in a tone which she described as "accusatory and certainly nasty," he asked whether she had been following the price of ABC and ITT stock. When she indicated that she had not, he asked if she didn't feel she had a "responsibility to the shareholders who might lose money as a result of what" she wrote. She replied, "My responsibility is to find out the truth and print it."

He then asked if she was aware that I (as an FCC Commissioner) was working with a prominent senator on legislation that would forbid any newspaper from owning any broadcast property. (The *New York Times* owns station WQXR in New York.) In point of fact, the senator and I had never met, let alone collaborated, as was subsequently made clear in public statements. But the ITT senior vice president, according to the *Times* reporter, felt that this false information was something she "ought to pass on to [her] . . . publisher before [she wrote] . . . anything further" about the case. The obvious implication of this remark, she felt, was that since the *Times* owns a radio station, it would want to consider its economic interests in deciding what to publish about broadcasting in its newspaper.

To me, this conduct, in which at least three ITT officials, including a senior vice president, were involved, was a deeply unsettling experience. It demonstrated an abrasive self-righteousness in dealing with the press, insensitivity to its independence and integrity, a willingness to spread false stories in furtherance of self-interest, contempt for government officials as well as the press, and an assumption that even as prestigious a news medium as the *New York Times* would, as a matter of course, want to present the news so as to serve best its own economic interests (as well as the economic interests of other large business corporations).

But for the brazen activities of ITT in this very proceeding, it would never have occurred to the three of us who dissented to suggest that the most probable threat to the integrity of ABC news could come from *overt* actions or written policy statements. After the hearing it was obvious that that was clearly possible. But even then we believed that the most substantial threat came from a far more subtle, almost unconscious, process: that the questionable story idea, or news coverage, would never even be proposed—whether for reasons of fear, insecurity, cynicism, realism, or unconscious avoidance.

Concentration of Control over the Media

Since the ITT-ABC case left the Commission I have not ceased to be troubled by the issues it raised—in many ways more serious (and certainly more prevalent) for wholly domestic corporations. Eventually the merger was aborted by ITT on New Year's Day of this year, while the Justice Department's appeal of the Commission's action was pending before the U.S. Court of Appeals. However, I ponder what the consequences might have been if ITT's apparent cynicism toward journalistic integrity had actually been able to harness the enormous social and propaganda power of a national television network to the service of a politically sensitive corporate conglomerate. More important, I have become concerned about the extent to which such forces *already* play upon important media of mass communication. Perhaps such attitudes are masked by more finesse than that displayed in the ITT-ABC case. Perhaps they are even embedded in the kind of sincere good intentions which caused former Defense Secretary (and former General Motors president) Charles Wilson to equate the interests of his company with those of the country.

I do not believe that most owners and managers of the mass media in the United States lack a sense of responsibility or lack tolerance for a diversity of views. I do not believe there is a small group of men who gather for breakfast every morning and decide what they will make the American people believe that day. Emotion often outruns the evidence of those who argue a conspiracy theory of propagandists' manipulation of the masses.

On the other hand, one reason evidence is so [46] hard to come by is that the media tend to give less publicity to their own abuses than, say, to those of politicians. The media operate as a check upon other institutional power centers in our country. There is, however, no check upon the media. Just as it is a mistake to overstate the existence and potential for abuse, so, in my judgment, is it a mistake to ignore the evidence that does exist.

In 1959, for example, it was reported that officials of the Trujillo regime in the Dominican Republic had paid $750,000 to officers of the Mutual Radio Network to gain favorable propaganda disguised as news. (Ownership of the Mutual Radio Network changed hands once again last year without any review whatsover by the FCC of old or new owners. The FCC does not regulate networks, only stations, and Mutual owns none.) RCA was once charged with using an NBC station to serve unfairly its broader corporate interests, including the coverage of RCA activities as "news," when others did not. There was speculation that after RCA acquired Random House, considerable pressure was put on the book publishing house's president, Bennett Cerf, to cease his Sunday evening service as a panelist on CBS's *What's My Line?* The Commission has occasionally found that individual stations have violated the "fairness doctrine" in advocating causes serving the station's economic self-interest, such as pay television.

Virtually every issue of the *Columbia Journalism Review* reports instances of such abuses by the print media. It has described a railroad-owned newspaper that refused to report railroad wrecks, a newspaper in debt to the Teamsters Union which gave exceedingly favorable coverage to Jimmy Hoffa, the repeated influence of the DuPont interests in the editorial functions of the Wilmington papers which it owned, and Anaconda Copper's use of its company-owned newspapers to support political candidates favorable to the company.

Edward P. Morgan left ABC last year to become the commentator on the Ford Foundation-funded Public Broadcasting Laboratory. He has always been straightforward, and he used his final news broadcast to be reflective about broadcasting itself. "Let's face it," he said. "We in this trade use this power more frequently to fix a traffic ticket or get a ticket to a ballgame than to keep the doors of an open society open

16. The Media Barons and the Public Interest 187

and swinging. . . . The freest and most profitable press in the world, every major facet of it, not only ducks but pulls its punches to save a supermarket of commercialism or shield an ugly prejudice and is putting the life of the republic in jeopardy thereby."

Economic self-interest *does* influence the content of the media, and as the media tend to fall into the control of corporate conglomerates, the areas of information and opinion affecting those economic interests become dangerously wide-ranging. What *is* happening to the ownership of American media today? What dangers does it pose? Taking a look at the structure of the media in the United States, I am not put at ease by what I see.

Most American communities have far less "dissemination of information from diverse and antagonistic sources" (to quote a famous description by the Supreme Court of the basic aim of the First Amendment) than is available nationally. Of the 1500 cities with daily newspapers, 96 percent are served by single-owner monopolies. Outside the top 50 to 200 markets there is a substantial dropping off in the number of competing radio and television signals. The FCC prohibits a single owner from controlling two AM radio, or two television, stations with overlapping signals. But it has only recently expressed any concern over common ownership of an AM radio station and an FM radio station and a television station in the same market. Indeed, such ownership is the rule rather than the exception and probably exists in your community. Most stations are today acquired by purchase. And the FCC has, in part because of congressional pressure, rarely disapproved a purchase of a station by a newspaper.

There are few statewide or regional "monopolies"—although some situations come close. But in a majority of our states—the least populous—there are few enough newspapers and television stations to begin with, and they are usually under the control of a small group. And most politicians find today, as Congress warned in 1926, "woe be to those who dare to differ with them." Most of our politics is still state and local in scope. And increasingly, in many states and local communities, congressmen and state and local officials are compelled to regard that handful of media owners (many of whom are out-of-state), rather than the electorate itself, as their effective constituency. Moreover, many mass media owners have a significant impact in more than one state. One case that came before the FCC, for example, involved an owner with AM-FM-TV combinations in Las Vegas and Reno, Nevada, along with four newspapers in that state, seven newspapers in Oklahoma, and two stations and two newspapers in Arkansas. Another involved ownership of ten stations in North Carolina and adjoining southern Virginia. You may never have heard of these owners, but I imagine the elected officials of their states return their phone calls promptly.

National Power

The principal national sources of news are the wire services, AP and UPI, and the broadcast networks. Each of the wire services serves on the [47] order of 1200 newspapers and 3000 radio and television stations. Most local newspapers and radio stations offer little more than wire service copy as far as national and international news is concerned. To that extent one can take little heart for "diversity" from the oft-proffered statistics on proliferating radio stations (now over 6000) and the remaining daily newspapers (1700). The networks, though themselves heavily reliant upon the wire services to find out what's worth filming, are another potent force.

The weekly newsmagazine field is dominated by *Time, Newsweek,* and *U.S. News.* (The first two also control substantial broadcast, newspaper, and book or publishing outlets. *Time* is also in movies (MGM) and is hungry for three or four newspapers.) Thus, even though there are thousands of general and specialized periodicals and program sources with significant national or regional impact, and certainly no "monopoly" exists, it is still possible for a single individual or corporation to have vast national influence.

What we sometimes fail to realize, moreover, is the political significance of the fact that we have become a nation of cities. Nearly half of the American people live in the six largest states: California, New York, Illinois, Pennsylvania, Texas, and Ohio. Those states, in turn, are substantially influenced (if not politically dominated) by their major population-industrial-financial-media centers, such as Los Angeles, New York City, Chicago, and Philadelphia—the nation's four largest metropolitan areas. Thus, to have a major newspaper or television station influence in *one* of these cities is to have significant national power. And the number of interests with influence in *more* than one of these markets is startling.

Most of the top fifty television markets (which serve approximately 75 percent of the nation's television homes) have three competing commercial VHF television stations. There are about 150 such VHF commercial stations in these markets. Less than 10 percent are today owned by entities that do not own other media interests. In 30 of the 50 markets at least one of the stations is owned by a major newspaper published in that market—a total of one third of these 150 stations. (In Dallas-Fort Worth *each* of the network affiliates is owned by a local newspaper, and the fourth, an unaffiliated station, is owned by Okla-

16. The Media Barons and the Public Interest 189

homa newspapers.) Moreover, half of the newspaper-owned stations are controlled by seven groups—groups that also publish magazines as popular and diverse as *Time, Newsweek, Look, Parade, Harper's, TV Guide, Family Circle, Vogue, Good Housekeeping,* and *Popular Mechanics.* Twelve parties own more than one third of all the major-market stations.

In addition to the vast national impact of their affiliates the three television networks each *own* VHF stations in all of the top three markets—New York, Los Angeles, and Chicago—and each has two more in other cities in the top ten. RKO and Metromedia each own stations in both New York City and Los Angeles. Metromedia also owns stations in Washington, D.C., and California's other major city, San Francisco—as well as Philadelphia, Baltimore, Cleveland, Kansas City, and Oakland. RKO also owns stations in Boston, San Francisco, Washington, Memphis, Hartford, and Windsor, Ontario—as well as the regional Yankee Network. Westinghouse owns stations in New York, Chicago, Philadelphia *and* Pittsburgh, Pennsylvania, Boston, San Francisco, Baltimore, and Fort Wayne. These are but a few examples of today's media barons.

There are many implications of their power. Groups of stations are able to bargain with networks, advertisers, and talent in ways that put lesser stations at substantial economic disadvantage. Group ownership means, by definition, that few stations in major markets will be locally owned. (The FCC recently approved the transfer of the last available station in San Francisco to the absentee ownership of Metromedia. The only commercial station locally owned today is controlled by the San Francisco *Chronicle.*) But the basic point is simply that the national political power involved in ownership of a group of major VHF television stations in, say, New York, Los Angeles, Philadelphia, and Washington, D.C., is greater than a democracy should unthinkingly repose in one man or corporation.

Conglomerate Corporations

For a variety of reasons, an increasing number of communications media are turning up on the organization charts of conglomerate companies. And the incredible profits generated by broadcast stations in the major markets (television broadcasters *average* a 90 to 100 percent return on tangible investment annually) have given FCC licensees, particularly owners of multiple television stations like the networks, Metromedia, Storer Broadcasting, and others, the extra capital with which to buy the New York Yankees (CBS), Random House (RCA), or Northeast Airlines (Storer). Established or up-and-coming conglomerates regard communications acquisitions as prestigious, profitable, and often a useful or even a necessary complement to present operations and projected exploitation of technological change.

The national problem of conglomerate ownership of communications media was well illustrated by the ITT-ABC case. But the conglomerate problem need not involve something as large as ITT-ABC [48] or RCA-NBC. Among the national group owners of television stations are General Tire (RKO), Avco, Westinghouse, Rust Craft, Chris Craft, Kaiser, and Kerr-McGee. The problem of *local* conglomerates was forcefully posed for the FCC in another case earlier this year. Howard Hughes, through Hughes Tool Company, wanted to acquire one of Las Vegas' three major television stations. He had recently acquired $125 million worth of Las Vegas real estate, including hotels, gambling casinos, and an airport. These investments supplemented 27,000 acres previously acquired. The Commission majority blithely approved the television acquisition without a hearing, overlooking FCC precedents which suggested that a closer examination was in order. In each of these instances the potential threat is similar to that in the ITT-ABC case—that personal economic interests may dominate or bias otherwise independent media.

Concentration and Technological Change

The problem posed by conglomerate acquisitions of communications outlets is given a special but very important twist by the pendency of sweeping technological changes which have already begun to unsettle the structure of the industry.

President Johnson has appointed a distinguished task force to evaluate our national communications policy and chart a course for realization of these technological promises in a manner consistent with the public interest. But private interests have already begun to implement their own plans on how to deal with the revolution in communications technology.

General Sarnoff of RCA has hailed the appearance of "the knowledge industry"—corporate casserole dishes blending radio and television stations, networks, and programming; films, movie houses, and record companies; newspaper, magazine, and book publishing; advertising agencies; sports or other entertainment companies; and teaching machines and other profitable appurtenances of the $50 billion "education biz."

And everybody's in "cable television"—networks, book publishers, newspapers. Cable television is a system for building the best TV antenna in town and then wiring it into everybody's television set—for a fee. It improves signal quality and number of channels, and has proved popular. But the new technology is such that it has broadcasters and newspaper publishers worried. For the same cable that can bring off-the-air television into the home can also bring programming from the cable operator's studio, or an "electronic newspaper" printed in the home by a facsimile process. Books can be delivered (between libraries, or to the home) over "television" by using the station's signal during an invisible pause. So everybody's hedging their bets—including the telephone company. Indeed, about all the vested interests can agree upon is that none of them want us to have direct, satellite-to-home radio and television. But at this point it is not at all clear who will have his hand on the switch that controls what comes to the American people over their "telephone wire" a few years hence.

What Is to Be Done?

It would be foolish to expect any extensive restructuring of the media in the United States, even if it were considered desirable. Technological change can bring change in structure, but it is as likely to be change to even greater concentration as to wider diversity. In the short run at least, economics seems to render essentially intractable such problems as local monopolies in daily newspapers, or the small number of outlets for national news through wire services, newsmagazines, and the television networks. Indeed, to a certain extent the very high technical quality of the performance rendered by these news-gathering organizations is aided by their concentration of resources into large units and the financial cushions of oligopoly profits.

Nevertheless, it seems clear to me that the risks of concentration are grave.

Chairman Philip Hart of the Senate Antitrust and Monopoly Subcommittee remarked by way of introduction to his antitrust subcommittee's recent hearings about the newspaper industry, "The products of newspapers, opinion and information, are essential to the kind of society that we undertake to make successful here." If we are serious about the kind of society we have undertaken, it is clear to me that we simply must not tolerate concentration of media ownership—except where concentration creates actual countervailing social benefits. These benefits cannot be merely speculative. They must be identifiable, demonstrable, and genuinely weighty enough to offset the dangers inherent in concentration.

This guideline is a simple prescription. The problem is to design and build machinery to fill it. And to keep the machinery from rusting and rotting. And to replace it when it becomes obsolete.

America does have available governmental machinery which is capable of scotching undue accumulations of power over the mass media, at least in theory and to some extent. The Department of Justice has authority under the antitrust laws to break up combinations which "restrain trade" or which "tend to lessen competition." These laws apply to the media as they do to any other industry.

But the antitrust laws simply do not get to where the problems are. They grant authority to block [49] concentration only when it threatens *economic* competition in a particular economic *market*. Generally, in the case of the media, the relevant market is the market for advertising. Unfortunately, relatively vigorous advertising competition can be maintained in situations where competition in the marketplace of ideas is severely threatened. In such cases, the Justice Department has little inclination to act.

Look at the Chicago *Tribune*'s recent purchase of that city's most popular and most successful FM radio station. The *Tribune* already controlled two Chicago newspapers, one (clear channel) AM radio station, and the city's only independent VHF television station. It controls numerous broadcast, CATV, and newspaper interests outside Chicago (in terms of circulation, the nation's largest newspaper chain). But, after an investigation, the Antitrust Division let this combination go through. The new FM may be a needless addition to the *Tribune*'s already impressive battery of influential media; it could well produce an unsound level of concentration in the production and supply of what Chicagoans see, read, and hear about affairs in their community, in the nation, and in the world. But it did not threaten the level of competition for advertising money in any identifiable advertising market. So, it was felt, the acquisition was not the business of the Justice Department.

Only the FCC is directly empowered to keep media ownership patterns compatible with a democracy's need for diversified sources of opinion and information.

In earlier times, the Commission took this responsibility very seriously. In 1941, the FCC ordered NBC to divest itself of one of its two radio networks (which then became ABC), barring any single network from affiliating with more than one outlet in a given city. (The Commission has recently waived this prohibition for, ironically, ABC's four new national radio networks.) In 1941 the Commission also established its power to set absolute limits on the total number of broadcast licenses any individual may hold, and to limit the number of stations any individual can operate in a particular service area.

The American people are indebted to the much maligned FCC for establishing these rules. Imagine, for example, what the structure of

16. The Media Barons and the Public Interest 193

political power in this country might look like if two or three companies owned substantially all of the broadcast media in our major cities.

But since the New Deal generation left the command posts of the FCC, this agency has lost much of its zeal for combating concentration. Atrophy has reached so advanced a state that the public has of late witnessed the bizarre spectacle of the Justice Department, with its relatively narrow mandate, intervening in FCC proceedings, such as ITT-ABC, to create court cases with names like *The United States vs. The FCC.*

This history is an unhappy one on the whole. It forces one to question whether government can ever realistically be expected to sustain a vigilant posture over an industry which controls the very access of government officials themselves to the electorate.

I fear that we have already reached the point in this country where the media, our greatest check on other accumulations of power, may themselves be beyond the reach of any other institution: the Congress, the President, or the Federal Communications Commission, not to mention governors, mayors, state legislators, and city councilmen. Congressional hearings are begun and then quietly dropped. Whenever the FCC stirs fitfully as if in wakefulness, the broadcasting industry scurries up the Hill for a congressional bludgeon. And the fact that roughly 60 percent of all campaign expenses go to radio and television time gives but a glimmer of the power of broadcasting in the lives of senators and congressmen.

However, the picture at this moment has its more hopeful aspect. There does seem to be an exceptional flurry of official concern. Even the FCC has its proposed rulemaking outstanding. The Department of Justice, having broken into the communications field via its dramatic intervention before the FCC in the ITT-ABC merger case, has also been pressing a campaign to force the dissolution of joint operating agreements between separately owned newspapers in individual cities, and opposed a recent application for broadcasting properties by newspaper interests in Beaumont, Texas. It has been scrutinizing cross-media combinations linking broadcasting, newspaper, and cable television outlets. On Capitol Hill, Senator Phil Hart's Antitrust and Monopoly Subcommittee and Chairman Harley Staggers' House Interstate and Foreign Commerce Committee have both summoned the Federal Communications Commission to appear before them in recent months, to acquaint the Commission with the committees' concern about FCC-approved increases in broadcast holdings by single individuals and companies, and about cross-ownership of newspapers, CATV systems, and broadcast stations. Representatives John Dingell, John Moss, and

Richard Ottinger have introduced legislation which would proscribe network ownership of any nonbroadcast interests. And as I previously mentioned, President Johnson has appointed a task force to undertake a comprehensive review of national communications policy.

Twenty years ago Robert M. Hutchins, then chancellor of the University of Chicago, was named chairman of the "Commission on Freedom of the [50] Press." It produced a thoughtful report, full of recommendations largely applicable today—including "the establishment of a new and independent [nongovernmental] agency to appraise and report annually upon the performance of the press," and urged "that the members of the press engage in vigorous mutual criticism." Its proposals are once again being dusted off and reread.

What is needed now, more than anything else, is to keep this flurry of interest alive, and to channel it toward constructive reforms. What this means, in practical fact, is that concern for media concentration must find an institutional home.

The Department of Justice has already illustrated the value of participation by an external institution in FCC decision-making. The developing concept of a special consumers' representative offers a potentially broader base for similar action.

But the proper place to lodge continuing responsibility for promoting diversity in the mass media is neither the FCC nor the Justice Department nor a congressional committee. The initiative must come from private sources. Plucky Nader-like crusaders such as John Banzhaf (who single-handedly induced the FCC to apply the "fairness" doctrine to cigarette commercials) have shown how responsive government can be to the skillful and vigorous efforts of even a lone individual. But there are more adequately staffed and funded private organizations which could play a more effective role in policy formation than a single individual. Even the FCC, where the public interest gets entirely too little representation from private sources, has felt the impact of the United Church of Christ, with its interest in the influence of broadcasting on race relations and in the programming responsibility of licensees, and of the American Civil Liberties Union, which submitted a brief in the ITT-ABC case.

Ideally, however, the resources for a sustained attack on concentration might be centered in a single institution, equipped to look after this cause with the kind of determination and intelligence that the Ford Foundation and the Carnegie Corporation, for example, have brought to bear in behalf of the cause of public broadcasting and domestic satellites. The law schools and their law reviews, as an institution, have performed well in this way for the courts, but have virtually abdicated responsibility for the agencies.

16. The Media Barons and the Public Interest

Such an organization could devote itself to research as well as representation. For at present any public body like the FCC, which has to make determinations about acceptable levels of media concentration, has to do so largely on the basis of hunch. In addition, private interest in problems of concentration would encourage the Justice Department to sustain its present vigilance in this area. It could stimulate renewed vigilance on the part of the FCC, through participation in Commission proceedings. And it could consider whether new legislation might be appropriate to reach the problem of newspaper-magazine-book publishing combinations.

If changes are to be made (or now dormant standards are to be enforced) the most pressing political question is whether to apply the standards prospectively only, or to require divestiture. It is highly unlikely, to say the least, that legislation requiring massive divestiture of multiple station ownership, or newspaper ownership of stations, would ever pass through Congress. Given the number of station sales every year, however, even prospective standards could have some impact over ten years or so.

In general, I would urge the minimal standard that no accumulation of media should be permitted without a specific and convincing showing of a continuing countervailing social benefit. For no one has a higher calling in an increasingly complex free society bent on self-government than he who informs and moves the people. Personal prejudice, ignorance, social pressure, and advertiser pressure are in large measure inevitable. But a nation that has, in Learned Hand's phrase, "staked its all" upon the rational dialogue of an informed electorate simply cannot take any unnecessary risk of polluting the stream of information and opinion that sustains it. At the very least, the burden of proving the social utility of doing otherwise should be upon him who seeks the power and profit which will result.

Whatever may be the outcome, the wave of renewed interest in the impact of ownership on the role of the media in our society is healthy. All will gain from intelligent inquiry by Congress, the Executive, the regulatory commissions and especially the academic community, the American people generally, and the media themselves. For, as the Supreme Court has noted, nothing is more important in a free society than "the widest possible dissemination of information from diverse and antagonistic sources." And if we are unwilling to discuss *this* issue fully today we may find ourselves discussing none that matter very much tomorrow. [51]

17. The Film Generation: Celebration and Concern
Stanley Kauffmann

Some of the following remarks were included, in differing forms, in talks delivered recently at several universities, colleges, and seminars. In one of the audiences were a distinguished poet and a critic of the graphic arts. Afterward, the critic came up to me and said, "You destroyed us. You wiped out our professions. You rendered my friend and me obsolete." I said that I neither believed nor intended that. Then he said wryly, stroking his chin, "On the other hand, if I were twenty years younger, I know I'd go into films."

His dismal reaction had been prompted by my assertion that film is the art for which there is the greatest spontaneous appetite in America at present, and by my reasons for thinking so. I must be clear that this is not to say that it is the art practiced at the highest level in this country; the film public depends more on imports today than does any other art public. But observation and experience, and the experience of others, make me believe that this uniquely responsive audience exists.

Or, in another phrase, there exists a Film Generation: the first generation that has matured in a culture in which the film has been of accepted serious relevance, however that seriousness is defined. Before 1935 films were proportionately more popular than they are now, but for the huge majority of film-goers they represented a regular weekly or semiweekly bath of escapism. Such an escapist audience still

Source: Stanley Kauffmann, *A World on Film* (New York: Harper and Row, 1966), pp. 415–28. Copyright © 1966 by Stanley Kauffmann. Reprinted by permission of Harper & Row, Publishers.

17. The Film Generation: Celebration and Concern 197

exists in large number, but another audience, most of them born since 1935, exists along with it. This group, this Film Generation, is certainly not exclusively grim, but it is essentially serious. Even its appreciations of sheer entertainment films reflect an over-all serious view. [415] There are a number of reasons, old and new, intrinsic and extrinsic, why this generation has come into being. Here are some of the older, intrinsic reasons.

1. In an age imbued with technological interest, the film art flowers out of technology. Excepting architecture, film is the one art that can capitalize directly and extensively on this century's luxuriance in applied science. Graphic artists have used mechanical and electronic elements, poets and painters have used computers, composers use electronic tapes. These are matters of choice. The film-maker has no choice: he must use complicated electronic and mechanical equipment. This fact helps to create a strong sense of junction with his society, of membership in the present. American artists have often been ashamed of—sometimes have dreaded—a feeling of difference from the busy "real" American world around them. For the filmmaker the very instruments of his art provide communion with the spirit of his age. I think that the audience shares his feeling of union, sometimes consciously (especially when stereophonic sound, special optical effects, or color processes are used). The scientific skills employed are thus in themselves a link between the artist and the audience, and are a further link between them all and the unseen, unheard but apprehended society bustling outside the film theater.

There is a pleasant paradoxical corollary. In an era that is much concerned with the survival of the human being as such, in an increasingly mechanized age, here a complicated technology is used to celebrate the human being.

2. The world of surfaces and physical details has again become material for art. Just as the naturalistic novel seems to be sputtering to a halt, overdescribed down to the last vest button, the film gives some of its virtues new artistic life. A novelist who employs the slow steam-roller apparatus of intense naturalism these days is asking for an extra vote of confidence from the reader, because the method and effects are so familiar that the reader can anticipate by pages. Even when there is the interest of an unusual setting, the reader is conscious that different nouns have been slipped into a worn pattern. The "new" French novel of Robbe-Grillet, Duras, Sarraute attempts to counteract this condition by intensifying it, using surfaces as the last realities, the only dependable objective correlatives. Sometimes, for some readers, this works. But both the old and the latter-day naturalisms [416] must

strain in order to connect. Rolf Hochhuth, the author of *The Deputy,* has said:

> When I recently saw Ingmar Bergman's *The Silence,* I left that Hamburg movie house with the question, "What is there left for the novelist today?" Think of what Bergman can do with a single shot of his camera, up a street, down a corridor, into a woman's armpit. Of all he can say with this without saying a word.

Despite Hochhuth's understandable thrill-despair, there is plenty left for the novelist to say, even of armpits, but the essence of his remark rightly strips from fiction the primary function of creating material reality. The film has not only taken over this function but exalted it: it manages to make poetry out of doorknobs, breakfasts, furniture. Trivial details, of which everyone's universe is made, can once again be transmuted into metaphor, contributing to imaginative act.

A complementary, powerful fact is that this principle operates whether the film-maker is concerned with it or not. In any film except those with fantastic settings, whether the director's aim is naturalistic or romantic or symbolic or anything else, the streets and stairways and cigarette lighters are present, the girl's room is at least as real as the girl—often it bolsters her defective reality. Emphasized or not, invited or not, the physical world through the intensifications of photography never stops insisting on its presence and relevance.

This new life of surfaces gives a discrete verity to many mediocre films and gives great vitality to a film by a good artist. Consciously or not, this vitality reassures the audience, tangentially certifying and commenting on its habitat. Indeed, out of this phenomenon, it can be argued that the film discovered pop art years go, digested this minor achievement, then continued on its way.

3. The film form seems particularly apt for the treatment of many of the pressing questions of our time: inner states of tension or of doubt or apathy—even (as we shall see) doubts about art itself. The film can externalize some psychical matters that, for example, the theater cannot easily deal with; and it can relate them to physical environment in a manner that the theater cannot contain nor the novel quite duplicate. The film can dramatize post-Freudian man, and his habitat—and the relation between the two. One does not need to believe in the death of the theater or the novel—as I do not—in order to see these special graces in the film. [417]

4. Film is the only art besides music that is available to the whole world at once, exactly as it was first made. With subtitles, it is the only art involving language that can be enjoyed in a language of which one

is ignorant. (I except opera, where the language rarely needs to be understood precisely.)

The point is not the spreading of information or amity, as in USIA or UNESCO films, useful though they may be. The point is emotional relationship and debt. If one has been moved by, for instance, Japanese actors in Japanese settings, in actions of Japanese life that have resonated against one's own experience, there is a connection with Japan that is deeper than the benefits of propaganda or travelogue. No one who has been moved by *Ikiru* can think of Japan and the Japanese exactly as he thought before.

Obviously similar experience—emotional and spiritual—is available through other arts, but rarely with the imperial ease of the film. As against foreign literature, foreign films have an advantage besides accessibility in the original language. The Japanese novelist invites us to recreate the scene in imagination. The Japanese film-maker provides the scene for us, with a vividness that our minds cannot equal in a foreign setting. Thus our responses can begin at a more advanced point and can more easily (although not more strongly) be stimulated and heightened.

This universality and this relative simultaneity of artistic experience have made us all members of a much larger empathetic community than has been immediately possible before in history.

5. Film has one great benefit by accident: its youth, which means not only vigor but the reach of possibility. The novel, still very much alive, is conscious of having to remain alive. One of its chief handicaps is its history; the novelist is burdened with the achievements of the past. This is also true of poetry. It flourishes certainly; as with fiction, the state of poetry is far better than is often assumed. But poetry, too, is conscious of a struggle for pertinent survival. In painting and sculpture, the desperation is readily apparent; the new fashion in each new season makes it clear. But the film is an infant, only begun. It has already accomplished miracles. Consider that it was only fifty years from Edison's camera to *Citizen Kane,* which is rather as if Stravinsky had written *Petrouchka* fifty years after Guido d'Arezzo developed musical notation. Nevertheless the film continent has only just been discovered, the boundaries are not remotely in [118] sight. It is this freshness that gives the young generation—what I have called the Film Generation—not only the excitement of its potential but a strong proprietary feeling. The film belongs to them.

These, I think, are some of the reasons for the growth of that new film audience. But they raise a question. As noted, these reasons have been valid to some degree for a long time, yet it is only in about the last twenty years that the Film Generation has emerged. Why didn't this happen sooner? Why have these reasons begun to be strongly operative only since the Second World War?

In that period other elements have risen to galvanize them. Some of these later elements come from outside the film world: the spurt in college education; political and social abrasions and changes; moral, ethical, religious dissolutions and resolutions. All these have made this generation more impatient and more hungry. But, since the Second World War, there have also been some important developments within the film world itself.* These developments have been in content, not in form. Three elements are especially evident: increased sexuality, an increase in national flavor, and an increased stress on the individual. The latter two are linked.

As for the first, sex has been important currency in the theater since *The Agamemnon,* and with the first films came the first film idols. In fact there are scenes in many silent films that would have censor trouble today. But apart from sexual display or the sex appeal of any actor or actress, there is now—in many foreign films and some American ones— a sexual attitude that can be respected: an attitude closer to the realities of sexual life than the mythology that is preached by clergy of every faith, by mass media, by parents. This relative sexual freedom, long established in fiction and the theater, has been slower to arrive in films because of their wider availability [419] to all ages and mentalities, and the consequent brooding of censors. Now, in a more liberal time, this freedom makes films even more pertinent to this generation. The mythology that still passes for sexual morality is prescriptive, these films are descriptive; but there is more to their merit than verisimilitude. Not by nudity nor bedroom calisthenics nor frank language but by fidelity to the complexities of sexual behavior, these films provide more than recognition. By accepting and exploring complexities, they provide confidence in the fundamental beauty of those complexities, in the desirability of being human, even with all the trouble it involves.

---

* These do not include linguistic developments. Nothing has changed the language of film as, for example, electronics has changed music or abstract expressionism has altered the vision of painting. There have been many technical film developments—wide screens, stereophonic sound, color refinements—but so far they have largely been peripheral to the art itself. They, and the improved hand-held camera and recorder, may affect the basic language of film in future; they have not yet markedly done so. This fact can be taken as an implied strength. Experiments in artistic technique are usually a sign that a boundary has been reached with old techniques. In film there is no hint of exhaustion in the techniques that were known to Griffith and Eisenstein forty years ago.

17. The Film Generation: Celebration and Concern 201

The second element, national flavor, has been described by the English critic Penelope Houston in *The Contemporary Cinema* (1963):

However partial or distorted an image one gets of a society through its cinema, it is still possible to discern the national face behind the screen. It is difficult to conceive of a neorealist idealism [in Italy] without the jubilant preface of the liberation of Rome; or to look at Britain's films of the past few years without reference to our redbrick radicalism; or to ignore the effect of the political climate on a French cinema which declares its awareness of strain in the very insistence with which it puts private before public life and creation for creation's sake before either.

It would be easy to add a similar sentence for almost every major film-producing country. Japanese films are concerned with contemporary unrest, directly and indirectly. Many of their costume pictures about samurai swordsmen are set in the 1860s when the feudal system was crumbling and immense social metamorphosis was taking place. The Soviet film has deepened in lethargy as revolutionary fervor wore off, as Stalinist despotism made it nervous, as some subsequent economic and scientific successes made it smug. It has become, with a few exceptions, either war glory or the ideologic equivalent of the petty bourgeois confection. As for America, the poor boy and rich girl story (or rich boy and poor girl) which was the staple of the popular film before the Second World War has disappeared. Money as romance, the Gatsby dream, has receded, not because everyone is now rich but because the middle-class image has replaced both the poor image and the rich image. What American would now relish the ancient compliment "poor but honest"? And what is the difference *in appearance* between the clerk's car and the boss's? The much-mooted [420] ascendancy of the middle class has reached the point where it is strong enough to control cultural forms, to magnify its own image in art.

With this ascendancy we have seen the emergence of a new romantic hero, posed against this bourgeois background, since all such heroes must contrast with their societies. The new romantic is the liberated prole, with a motorcycle or a Texas Cadillac, seeking his life by assaulting convention and morality, rather than by striving for success in accepted modes, either with money or with women. This hero scoffs at ideals of excellence and aspiration at the same time that he wants to dominate. There are signs that this hero may have run his course, but in the last twenty years or so he was pre-eminent.

A lesser companion of his still continues: the Frank Sinatra-Dean Martin figure, the smart, cool operator just inside the law, a philanderer righteously resentful of any claims on him by women. His casual *persona* derives in part from the night-club microphone, which was first a necessity, then became a prop, then a source of power and ease for those who had little power and could achieve nothing but ease. The invisible hand-held microphone accompanies the crooner-as-hero wherever he goes. His oblique, slithering solipsism seems likely to persist after the Brando figure, more directly descended from the proletarian rebel and Byronic individualist, has passed. Mere "coolness" persists; purposeful rebellion fades.

All the national colors described above apply both to popular and serious films. If we concentrate on serious film—film made primarily as personal expression, not as contractual job or money-spinner—then we often find, besides intensified national color, an intensified introspection. This is the third of our elements: a concern with the exploration of the individual as a universe. It is not a novelty in films. No more introspective films have ever been made than Wiene's *The Cabinet of Dr. Caligari* (1919) or Pabst's *Secrets of a Soul* (1926). But merely to mention such names as Bergman, Antonioni, Fellini, Ozu, Torre Nilsson, Olmi, Truffaut is to see that, for many outstanding directors, there has lately been more reliance on inner conflict than on classic confrontation of antagonists. These men and others, including some Americans, have been extending the film into the vast areas of innermost privacy, even of the unconscious, that have been the province of the novel and of metaphysical poetry. Saul Bellow has complained that the modern novelist doesn't tell us what a human being *is* today. Bellow is a notable exception to his own complaint; [421] but whether we agree or not, we can see that many contemporary film-makers have tried to answer that question, with a more consistent application than ever before in the history of the art.

These two elements—national color and the exploration of the individual—are obviously inseparable. Society and the man affect each other, even if it is in the man's withdrawal. These elements are further linked in a curious contradictory motion against our time. In an age when internationalism is promulgated as a solution to political difficulties, national colors have become more evident in films. In an age when social philosophers have begun to question the durability of individualism—which is, after all, a fairly recent concept in history and almost exclusive to the West—the film is tending to cherish the individual. Does this indicate a time lag between the film and the advances of political and social philosophy? On the contrary, I believe it indicates a perverse penetration to truth. The truth of art sometimes runs counter to what seems politically and intellectually desirable; that is always a risk of art. I think the film is showing us that nationalism, in the purely cultural sense, is becoming more necessary to us as jet plane and Telstar threaten to make us one world. I think that just at the time when technological and power structures challenge individualism, our own minds and souls have become more interesting to us. Up to now, technology has outraced self-discovery. Only now—in this postreligious, self-dependent age—are we beginning to appreciate how rich and dangerous each one of us is.

These elements have led, directly and by implication, to the phenomenon we are examining; the historical moment for the rise of the Film Generation, a surge of somewhat nostalgic revolution; a reluctance to lose what seems to be disappearing, accompanied by an impulse to disaffection, an insistence on an amorphous cosmos. ("Stay loose." "Swing.") Doubtless that nostalgia is sentimental, an unwillingness to be banned from an Eden of individualism that in fact never existed. But much of the revolution is clearheaded; not so much an attempt to halt change as to influence it; a natural and valuable impulse to scratch on the chromium fronts of the advancing tanks of factory-society "Kilroy was here."

The divided attitude toward social change leads to another, crucial polarity. This generation has an ambivalent view of cultural tradition. On the one hand there is a great desire for such tradition, admitted or not. Everyone wants to know that he came from somewhere; it's less [422] lonely. But this desire is often accompanied by a mirror attitude that looks on the past as failure and betrayal. It is of course a familiar indictment, the young accusing the old of having made a mess, but now the accusation is more stringent and more general because of the acceleration of change and the diminutions of choice.

This ambivalence toward tradition—this polarity that both wants and rejects it—has created a hunger for art as assurance of origins together with a preference for art forms that are relatively free of the past. Outstanding among these is film. Even though it has been on hand for sixty-five years or so, the film seems much more of the present and future than other forms. It has its roots of content and method—in older arts: drama, literature, dance, painting; yet it is very much less entailed by the past than these arts. It satisfies this generation's ambivalent need in tradition.

So far, this inquiry has been almost all celebration; now a concern must be raised. So far, we have discussed certain phenomena as cultural dynamics and social facts: now a word must be said in value judgment of the revolutionary standards involved. Not all the films that the Film Generation venerates seem worth its energy and devotion. It is not my purpose to lay down an artistic credo: I could always think of too many exceptions. Taste is a matter of instances, not precepts. One forms an idea of another's taste—or of one's own—from the perspective of many instances of judgment and preference, and even then, general deductions must be drawn delicately. But, drawing them as delicately as I am able, I am left with a concern to posit against the foregoing celebration.

There are enthusiasms of this Film Generation that I do not share, there are many enthusiasms of mine that they seem not to share. For the most part this is nobody's fault and probably nobody's virtue. But there is one enthusiasm in particular that has taken many members of this generation—not all, but a large proportion—that seems potentially deleterious and therefore to need discussion.

On college campuses around the country, in some film societies and small theaters (there are at least three in New York at this writing), much is being made of certain experimental films. The passion for experiment, as such, is eternal and necessary, but out of disgust with much commercial and fake-serious fare, there is a strong tendency to value experiment for its own sake, to regard it as a value instead of a means to value. And since, at this period in social and political affairs, a passion for these films has been taken to have other significances as well, the phenomenon is especially important.

The films to which I refer are often called underground films. In America a large proportion of them come from a group centered in New York but not confined there, variously called New American Films or the Film-maker's Cooperative. It is an association of dedicated film-makers and dedicated apostles. (The apostles carry the word widely. Two minutes after I met Federico Fellini in Rome, he asked me whether I had seen Jack Smith's *Flaming Creatures*.) The group also has a circle of apostolic critics.

Predictably, this group considers itself the element of poetry in an otherwise prosaic film situation in this country and the world. Also predictably, its works are difficult to describe because it is not a school like neorealism or surrealism. It includes these and many more styles. It welcomes anyone who uses film as a form of personal expression. The most lucid general statement about this group that I know was written by Ken Kelman (*The Nation*, May 11, 1964). He divides their works into three main categories. First, "outright social criticism and protest" (Dan Drasin's *Sunday*, Stan Vanderbeek's *Skullduggery*). Second, "films which suggest, mainly through anarchic fantasy, the possibilities of the human spirit in its socially uncorrupted state" (Jack Smith's *Flaming Creatures* and *Normal Love*). The third group "creates, out of a need to fill our rationalistic void, those actual inner worlds which fall within the realm of myth" (Kenneth Anger's *Scorpio Rising*, Stan Brakhage's *Anticipation of the Night* and *Window Water Baby Moving*). Kelman's article, like others on the subject, is a ringing statement written with inner consistency and a fire that outstrips mere sincerity. The difficulty is that, when one sees these films (I have seen all those cited and numerous others), one finds small consonance between the descriptions and the works. Not to belabor individual films, one can say that most of them represent the attitudes and intents that Kelman describes but that their acceptance as acomplishment reflects a deliberate disconnection from cultural and social history. For me, most of the "new" techniques are dated, most of the social criticism is facile or vacuous, the mythic content undernourishing, the general quality of inspiration tenuous, strained, trite. Much of the work seems made for a young audience that insists on [424] having its *own* films, at any critical or cultural price.

One of the grave liabilities in the situation is that writing like Kelman's and the attitudes it promotes tend to encourage the symbiotic state that exists today in the graphic arts. There is not much direct relation between film and audience, nothing so simple as the audience coming to the theater and being affected, or not, by what it sees. The audience exists jointly with these films in a highly verbalized critical environment; its preformed attitudes are eager dramatizations of credos and exegeses. Much of modern painting—op, pop, collage, latter-day abstraction—seems to have its life almost as much in what is written about it as on canvas. Indeed many of the paintings seem to have been made to evoke aesthetic disquisition, to exist verbally and in viewers' attitudes. The underground film has entered this territory—of art as "position"— a position sustained as much by the polemic-conscious audience as by the material on the screen. It has long been an indictment of Broadway and Hollywood hits that the audience is preconditioned, whipped into line by newspaper raves. Here is very much the same situation at a higher intellectual altitude.

Another grave liability is the pressure brought to bear by the underground movement for disconnection from cultural history. Generally, as has been noted, the Film Generation has at least an ambivalent attitude toward tradition: this underground movement pushes—by implication and otherwise—for complete rejection of the standards that have been continuingly evolved through some centuries of Western art. They are not to be evolved further, they are to be discarded. It is easy to chuckle patronizingly at this belief as one more instance of the perennial artistic rebellion of the young, but current social upheavals give it a momentum that takes it out of the sphere of mere youthful high spirits—

or low spirits. And the morning or the year or the decade after the excitements of rebellion have passed, it may be discovered that a valuable continuum in culture has been seriously injured—to the detriment of the very aims for which the action was taken.

I do not argue against change, including radical change. I do argue against nihilism as a necessary first step for progress. Besides, this film nihilism contains a bitter contradiction. It is often a manifestation in art of discontents elsewhere, of anger at older generations' betrayal of certain ideals. But the best art of the past—in all fields—is expression [425] of those ideals, often despite society's apathy toward them. In discarding that inheritance of art, the rebels discard much of the best work that the human race has done for the very ideals that galvanize this new rebellion.

There is a parallel between this devotion to the underground film in many of the Film Generation and an element in the "new left," the new political radicalism. Some of radical youth are engaged in genuinely creative action: antimilitarism, antidiscrimination, support of various economic programs. But many of them equate radicalism with personal gesture and style—revolt consummated by bizarre hair and dress, unconventional sexual behavior, flirtations with drugs. One who is aware of the valid basis for disaffection can still regret the introversions and futilities of these gestures. Likewise, one hopeful for the invigoration of the American film can doubt the pertinence of comparable gestures in this field: the exaltation of meaninglessness in film as a statement of meaninglessness in the world: the praise of juvenile irreverence—perennial in art—as a new formulation of myth; the approval of a social criticism that is devoid of intellectual foundation and political belief.

I dwell on the partiality to these experimental films not to counterbalance the happy fact of the Film Generation's existence but precisely because of its existence. Art has never been well created for long independently of an audience; in fact, history shows that audience response feeds great eras of art (painting in Renaissance Italy, the drama in Elizabethan England and neoclassic France, the sudden, ravenous worldwide appetite for silent-film comedy).

Speaking in the large, I believe that the Film Generation has the power to evoke the films that it wants, even though that generation is a minority and despite the harsh conditions of production and exhibition around the world. *All* films will not alter, nor should they, but if the dynamics of cultural history still obtains, an insistent group of art takers can—sooner or later, one way or another—have an effect on art makers. The effect is circular. The audience obviously cannot do it alone; there have to be talented artists. But talent is a relative constant in the human race; it is sparked by response and, even at its best, can be dampened by neglect. (Think of Herman Melville's twenty years in the Customs House.)

Thus, by a logical progression, we can see that the Film Generation has extraordinary powers. If it is true (as I have claimed) that [426] film is the most pertinent art at present; if it is true that the young generation is closer to the film than to other arts; if it is also true that audience appetite can evoke art; then, it follows that the Film Generation has the opportunity to help bring forth the best and most relevant art of our age. And it is the possible impediment to this opportunity that makes a devotion to culturally baseless, essentially sterile films seem wasteful.

I am aware that the above puts an almost ludicrously large burden on this Film Generation. In effect, it is almost to ask them to solve the problems of cultural transition, to define what culture will become. The problem is not to be solved in any one locus, even when the locus—film and its audience—has come into being quite naturally. It is never to be solved; it is only to be confronted continually, particularly in an age that is *not* an age, that is a rapid series of continually shifting points. But the size of the conclusion does not diminish the opportunity.

There is not much question among the thoughtful that we live in a time of the most profound cultural change, when the very purposes of art, as well as its content, are being transformed. The New American Cinema is one manifestation of that upheaval. In my view, most of its films that I have seen are of minuscule importance, but the implication in most of them is important: the implication that what's past is quite dead. The art of the future may be divorced from present concepts of humanism; it may find its pertinences in modes that, to most eyes, now look cold or abstract or even antihuman. But they will have been made by men who would not be what they are, whatever that may be, without the precedents of culture; and if that new art, whatever it may be, is to be held to its highest standards, the best of the past needs to be brought forward with us. The real *use* of our inheritance in the contemporary situation would throw a good deal of illumination on much of the new that is now adulated. The Kelmans tell us that an Antonioni is only seemingly free, that he is trapped by attempting to renovate the past. But, to take Antonioni as an example, it is precisely the effort to alter in an altered cosmos without returning Western culture to Year One that may keep a cultural future possible; may sustain us as we travel from a terrain that once was fruitful to one that has not yet been sighted. We don't want to starve en route.

As an important part of this process—this rescue operation, if you [427] like—the Film Generation can demand a new film from the serious film-maker that is more than a gesture of denial. Such a generation, joined with the past and therefore truly equipped to outgrow it, may eventually get in its films what the Kelmans have prematurely claimed: a new social cohesion, a new fertile and reassuring mythos. If these come, they will manifest their presence, not so much by the blown prose of rhapsodists as by an irony: middle-of-the-road art will imitate the new film. That film will certainly not be ignored, as the majority now ignore underground efforts. When the imitation begins, then authentically progressive artists and audiences will know that they have thus far succeeded, and will know it is again time to move forward.

So the Film Generation, flaws and all, represents both a circumstance and an opportunity. On the whole it is, I believe, the most cheering circumstance in contemporary American art. That generation can be a vital force, or it can twiddle its strength and chances away in irrelevant artistic nihilism, in engorged social petulance. One does not ask them to "save" film forever. In the long run, the history of the film will be the same as that of all arts: a few peaks, some plateaus, many chasms; but the present chance—a rare one—could save much time in the development of this young medium. The foreseeable future is all that, reasonably, we can have hopes or anxieties about in art. The Film Generation can help to make the foreseeable future of film interesting and important. Let us see. [428]

18. Learning from the Beatles
Richard Poirier

Has anyone been able completely to ignore *Sgt. Pepper's Lonely Hearts Club Band?* Probably not. But the very fact of its immense popularity with people of every age and persuasion is almost a guarantee of its not receiving the demanding critical attention that it calls for. It isn't enough to say that it is the latest and most remarkable of the thirteen albums composed and performed by the Beatles since 1964; some such claim could have been made for each album when it appeared. *Sgt. Pepper* isn't in the line of continuous development; rather, it is an eruption. It is an astounding accomplishment for which no one could have been wholly prepared, and it therefore substantially enlarges and modifies all the work that preceded it. It sends us back to the earlier Beatles not for confirmation of the fact that they have always been the best group of their kind. Rather, we listen for those gestations of genius that have now come to fruition. And the evidence is there: in each album which, while being unmistakably theirs, is nonetheless full of exploratory peculiarities not heard on the others; in the way the release even of a single can set off a new surge of energy in their many imitators; in a self-delighting inventiveness that has gradually exceeded the sheer physical capacities even of four such brilliant musicians. The consequent necessity for expanded orchestral and electronic support reached the point where the Sgt. Pepper album had to be wholly conceived in studio with as many as forty-eight instruments. Meanwhile, still in their mid-twenties they have made two movies, *A Hard Day's Night* and *Help!*,

SOURCE: Partisan Review 34, no. 4 (Fall 1967): 526–46. Copyright © 1967 by Partisan Review. Reprinted by permission.

which are in spots as good as the Marx brothers, and their most talented member, John Lennon, has written two books of Joycean verbal play that suggest why no one is ever in danger of reading too [526] much into the lyrics of their songs. The Beatles are now beyond patronization, and this is especially satisfying to those like myself who have wondered how much longer the literary academic adjudicators could claim to be taking the arts seriously by promoting a couple of distinguished novels every year, a few films, some poems, maybe a museum show and, if they're really lucky, a play.

Of course to delay a revolution there are ways and ways of finally paying considered attention to the lower orders. One way is to sociologize in the manner, McLuhan or pre-McLuhan, that forces the good and the bad in the popular arts to lie down in the same categories. There'll surely be a piece announcing, say, that the Beatles "represent"—a favorite word in the shelving process—not just the young but an aristocracy of the young. And of course they are aristocratic: in their carelessness, their assumption that they can enact anyone else's life just for the fun of it, their tolerance for the things they do make fun of, their delight in wildness along with a disdain for middle-class rectitudes, their easy expertness, their indifference to the wealth they are happy to have, their pleasures in costume and in a casual eccentricity of ordinary dress, their in-group language not meant, any more than is Bob Dylan's —another such aristocrat—to make ordinary sense. That kind of accommodation is familiar by now, and so is another, which is to admit them into the company of their "betters." You know, the way jazz is like Bach? Well, sometimes they are like Monteverdi and sometimes their songs are even better than Schumann's. But that won't work either. Liverpool boys of their sort have been let into Eton before, and not on the assumption that it would be the style of Eton that would change.

It won't be easy to accommodate the Beatles, and that's nowadays almost the precondition for exciting the pastoral concern of Responsible Critics. Literary and academic grown-ups will discover that their favorite captive audience, the young in school, really have listened to the Beatles' kind of music and won't buy the yarn of significance that ensnares most adult talk about the other arts. Any effort to account for what the Beatles are doing will be difficult, as I've learned from this not very extensive and inexpert try, but only to the extent that talking about the experience of any work of art is more difficult than talking about the theory of it, or the issues in it or the history around it. The results of any such effort by a number of people [527] would be of importance not just for popular music but for all the arts. Peope who listen to the Beatles love them—what about that? Why isn't there more talk about pleasure, about the excitement of witnessing a performance, about the excitement that goes into a performance of any kind? Such talk could set in motion a radical and acutely necessary amendment to the literary and academic club rules. Since the exalted arts (to which the novel, about a century ago, was the last genre to be admitted) have all but surrendered the provision of fun and entertainment to the popular arts, criticism must turn to film and song if it is to remind itself that the arts really do not need to be boring, no matter how much copy can be made from the elaboration of current theories of boredom.

Critical confrontations initiated in this spirit could give a new status to an increasingly unfashionable kind of criticism: to close-up, detailed concern for performance, for enactment and execution in a work of art. Film and song, the two activities in which young people are now especially interested, and about which they are learning to talk fairly well, may yield something to other kinds of scrutiny, but they yield much more to this kind. So does literature, on the very infrequent occasions when it is so treated. The need is for intense localization of interest and a consequent modesty of description, in the manner of Stark Young's dramatic criticism, or Bernard Haggin's writing about classical music and jazz or Edwin Denby and, more recently, Robert Garis on ballet. Imagining an audience for such criticism, the critic thinks not of a public with Issues and Topics at the ready, but rather of a small group of like-minded, quite private people who find pleasure in certain intensive acts of looking and listening. Looking and listening to something with such a group, imaginary or real, means checking out responses, pointing to particular features, asking detailed questions, sharing momentary excitements. People tend to listen to the Beatles the way families in the last century listened to readings of Dickens, and it might be remembered by literary snobs that the novel then, like the Beatles and even film now, was considered a popular form of entertainment generally beneath serious criticism, and most certainly beneath academic attention.

The Beatles' music is said to belong to the young, but if it does that's only because the young have the right motive for caring about it—they enjoy themselves. They also know what produces the fun [528] they have, by phrase and instrument, and they're very quick, as I've discovered, to shoot down inflated interpretations. They should indeed exercise proprietary rights. This is the first time that people of school age have been tuned in to sounds invented not by composers approved by adults but in to sounds invented by their own near contemporaries, sounds associated with lyrics, manners and dress that they also identify as their own. David Amram, the New York Philharmonic's first resident composer, is understandably optimistic that this kind of identification will develop an avidity of attention to music that could be the salvation of American musical composition and performance. Perhaps in some such way the popular arts can help restore all the arts to their status as entertainment. To help this process along it isn't necessary that literary and academic grown-ups go to school to their children. Rather, they must begin to ask some childlike and therefore some extremely difficult questions about particular works: Is this any fun? How and where is it any fun? And if it isn't why bother? While listening together to recordings of popular music, people of any age tend naturally to ask these questions, and I've heard them asked by young people with an eager precision which they almost never exhibit, for want of academic encouragement, when they talk about a poem or a story. Their writing about this music isn't as good as their talk, at least in the magazines I've been able to get hold of, like *Vibrations, The Broadside* and, perhaps the best, *Crawdaddy*. In written criticism they display some of the adult vices, including at times a nearly Germanic fondness for categorization: the Mersey beat, the raving style, trip songs, the San Francisco school, the love sound, folk-rock and the rock-folk-pop tradition are typical of the terms that get bandied about with desperate and charming hope. Reviews of popular music in the major newspapers and magazines are much worse, however, and before the Sgt. Pepper album practically no space even for an intelligent note was given the Beatles in any of them. Now that they've begun to appear, any adult easily victimized by a reputed generational gap need only read reviews of *Sgt. Pepper* in the *New York Times* and the *Village Voice* by Richard Goldstein to discover that youth is no guarantee of understanding. In his early twenties, he is already an ancient. Some of his questions—does the album have any real unity?—were not necessary even when originally asked [529] some two thousand years ago, while others are a bad dream of Brooks and Warren: the "lyrical technique" of "She's Leaving Home" is "uninspired narrative, with a dearth of poetic irony." The song is in fact one of *Sgt. Pepper's* satirically funniest cuts, though someone Goldstein's age mightn't as easily see this as someone older. Recognition of its special blend of period sentimentality and elegance of wit is conferred upon the listener not by his being chronologically young but by his having once lived with that especially English blend of tones from Beatrice Lillie or Noel Coward, and their wistful play about the genteel.

Nearly all the songs on the Sgt. Pepper album and the two singles released here since then—"All You Need Is Love" and "Baby You're a Rich Man"—are in fact quite broadly allusive: to the blues, to jazz hits of the thirties and forties, to classical music, early rock and roll, previous cuts by the Beatles themselves. Much of the comedy in these songs and much of their historical resonance, as in the stately Wagnerian episode in "A Day in the Life," is managed in this way. Mixing of styles and tones remind the listener that one kind of feeling about a subject isn't enough and that any single induced feeling must often exist within the context of seemingly contradictory alternatives. Most good groups offer something of this kind, like the Who, with the brilliant drummer Keith Moon. In songs like "Don't Look Away" and "So Sad about Us," Moon, working with the composer-guitarist Pete Townsend, calls forth a complicated response in a manner nicely described in *Crawdaddy* by Jon Landau, one of the best of the reviewers I've read: "Townsend scratches his chorus, muffles his strings, or lets the chord stand out full depending on what Moon is doing—the result being a perfectly unified guitar-drum sound that can't help but make you feel happy even while the lyrics tell you to feel sad." The Beatles have often in the past worked for similar mixtures, but they now offer an additional nuance: especially in later songs, one of the interwoven strands is likely to be an echo of some familiar, probably clichéd musical, verbal or dramatic formula. These echoes, like the soap-opera background music of "She's Leaving Home" or the jaunty music-hall tones of "When I'm Sixty-four," have the enriching effect that allusiveness can have in poetry: of expanding a situation toward the simultaneous condition of pathos, because the situation is seen as recurrent and therefore possibly insoluble, [530] and comic, because the recurrence has finally passed into cliché.

Any close listening to musical groups soon establishes the fact that as composers and performers the Beatles repay attention altogether more than does any other group, American or English. They offer something for nearly everyone and respond to almost any kind of interest. The Rolling Stones, the Left Banke and the Bee Gees are especially good, but in none of these is there an inventive productivity equal to that of Lennon, McCartney or their producer George Martin, whose contributions of electronic and orchestral notation really make him one of the group, particularly now that their performances are to be exclusively in studio. Only Dylan shows something equivalent to the Beatles in his combination of talents as composer, lyricist and performer. In performance the Beatles exhibit a nearly total theatrical power. It is a power so unencumbered and so freely diverse both for the group and for each of its members that it creates an element of suspense in whatever they do, an expectation that this time there really will be a failure of good taste—that attribute shared by only the greatest theatrical performers. They never wholly lose themselves in anyone else's styling, however, or in their own exuberance; they never succumb to the excitements they generate, much less those of their audience. It's unthinkable that they would lend themselves for the rock and wreck sequence of the Yardbirds in Antonioni's *Blow-up*. That particular performance, quite aside from what it contributed to a brilliant film, is a symptom of the infiltration even into popular music of the decadence by which entertainment is being displaced by a self-abasing enactment of what is implicit in the *form* of entertainment—in this instance, of group playing that gives way to animosities and a destructive retaliation against recalcitrant instrumental support. When the Beatles sound as if they are heading orchestrally into self-obliteratig noise, it is very often only that they may assert their presence vocally in quite the opposite direction: by contrasting choirboy cooing, by filigrees of voice-play coming from each of them, as in the reprise of "Sgt. Pepper," for instance, or, as in "Lovely Rita," the little choral oo's and gaspings—all of these suggesting, in their relation to solo, crosscurrents of feeling within an agreed area of play. Manners so instinctively free and yet so harmonious could not be guided from outside, either by an audience or even by directorial [531] guidance, however much the latter did help in rescuing them from the tawdry enslavement to Elvis Presley, an otherwise profitable influence, in their first, fortunately hard-to-find recording of 1961 made in Hamburg with Ringo's predecessor at the drums, Peter Best.

As is the taste of all great performers—in athletics, in politics, in any of the arts—the taste of the Beatles or of Dylan is an emanation of personality, of a self that is the generous master but never the creature of its audience. Taste in such instances is inseparable from a stubbornness of selfhood, and it doesn't matter that the self has been invented for the theater. Any self is invented as soon as any purpose is conceived. But the Beatles are a special case in not being a self at all. They are a group, and the unmistakeable group identity exists almost in spite of sharp individuation, each of them ,except the invisible Martin, known to be unique in some shaggy way. There are few other groups in which even one or two of the members are as publicly recognizable as any of the Beatles, and this can't be explained as a difference simply in public relations. It is precisely this unusual individuation which explains, I think, why the Beatles are so much stronger than any other group and why they don't need, like the Who, to play at animosities on stage. The pretense doesn't communicate the presence of individual Who but rather an anxiety at their not instinctively feeling like individuals when they are together. The Beatles, on the other hand, enhance the individuality of one another by the sheer elaborateness by which they arrive at a cohesive sound and by a musical awareness of one another that isn't distinguishable from the multiple directions allowed in the attainment of harmony. Like members of a great athletic team, like such partners in dance as Nureyev and Fonteyn or like some jazz combos, the Beatles in performance seem to draw their aspirations and their energy not from the audience but from one another. Their close, loyal and affectionate personal ties are of course not irrelevant. The incentive for what they accomplish seems to be sequestered among them, a tensed responsiveness that encourages from Harrison, as in "And Your Bird Can Sing," what sounds like the best guitar playing in the world and which provokes the immense productivity of Lennon and McCartney. The amount they have composed might be explained by commercial venture but not the daring and originality of each new single or album. Of course the promise of "new [532] sounds" is itself a commercial necessity in their business, as the anxieties of the second album of the Jefferson Airplane indicate, but the Beatles will soon release their fourteenth, and it's not merely "new sounds" that they produce, an easy enough matter with orchestral support, electronics and Asiatic importations. They produce different styles, different musical conceptions and revisions of sentiment that give an unprecedented variety to an artistic career that had its proper beginning a mere four or five years ago. The freshness of each effort is often so radically different from the one before, as any comparison among *Rubber Soul, Revolver* and *Sgt. Pepper* will indicate, as to constitute risk rather than financial ambition—especially three such albums, along with a collection of earlier songs, *Yesterday and Today,* in a period just over eighteen months. They are the ones who get tired of the sounds they have made, and the testings and teasings that produce each new album are self-inflicted. If they are careerist it is in the manner not of Judy Garland, reminding us in each concert of "Somewhere Over the Rainbow" and the pains of show biz, but of John Coltrane who, when he died in July at forty, was also about to give up performance in public altogether, even though his reputation as one of the most influential musicians in jazz and its greatest saxophonist guaranteed him an increasingly profitable concert career. His interest in music was a continually exploratory one, an effort to broaden the possibilities, as the Beatles do now in studio, of his music and his instruments. Like Harrison with his guitar, he managed with the soprano sax to produce a nearly oriental sound, and this discovery led him to an interest in Indian music much as Harrison was led to the study of the sitar. And again like the Beatles, Coltrane's experimentation was the more intense because he and his sidemen, Elvin Jones and McCoy Tyner, achieved a remarkable degree of liberating, energizing empathy. Almost all such champions are extraordinary and private men who work with an audience, as the phrase goes, only when that audience is composed of the few who can perform with them. Otherwise, the audience is what it ought to be: not participants but witnesses or only listeners to a performance. The audience that in the theme song of *Sgt. Pepper* is so "lovely" that "we'd like to take you home with us" is a wholly imaginary one, especially on a record contrived as an escape from public performance. [533]

Aloof from politics, their topicality is of music, the sentiments and the social predicaments traditional to folk songs, and ballads. Maybe the most important service of the Beatles and similar groups is the restoration to good standing of the simplicities that have frightened us into irony and the search for irony; they locate the beauty and pathos of commonplace feelings even while they work havoc with fashionable or tiresome expressions of those feelings. A particularly brilliant example is the record, released some weeks after the Sgt. Pepper album, with "Baby You're a Rich Man" on one side and "All You Need Is Love" on the other. "Baby You're a Rich Man" opens with an inquiry addressed by McCartney and Harrison to Lennon, who can be said to represent here a starry-eyed fan's version of the Beatles themselves: "How does it feel to be / One of the beautiful people?" This and subsequent questions are asked of the "rich man" in a reverentially high but devastatingly lilting voice, to the accompaniment of bursts of sitar music and the clip-clopping of Indian song. The sitar, an instrument Harrison studied in India for six weeks with the renowned Ravi Shankar ("George," he reported, "was truly humble") here suggests not the India of "Within You, Without You" evoked on the Sgt. Pepper album, the India of the Bhagavad Gita. It is rather another India, of fabulous riches, the India of the British and their Maharajahs, a place for exotic travel, but also for josh sticks and the otherworldliness of a "trip." All these possibilities are at work in the interplay of music and lyrics. Contributing to the merely social and satiric implications of the song, the Indian sounds operate in the manner of classical allusion in Pope: they expand to the ridiculous the cant of jet-set, international gossip columns—"one of the beautiful people" or "baby, you're a rich man now," or "how often have you been there?" But, as in Pope, the instrument of ridicule here, the sitar, is allowed in the very process to remain unsullied and eloquent. The social implications of the song carry more than a hint of self-parody since the comic mixtures of verbal and musical phrasing refer us to similar mixtures that are a result of the Beatles' fantastic fortune: Liverpool boys, still in their twenties, once relatively poor and now enormously rich, once socially nowhere and now internationally "there," once close to home both in fact and in their music but now implicated not only in the Mersey beat but in the Ganges sound, in travel to India and "trips" of a kind for which India set the precedent for centuries. [534]

Most remarkably, the song doesn't sort out its social satire from its implicitly positive treatment of drugs. Bob Dylan often puns with roughly the same intention, as in "Rainy Day Woman #12 & 35," a simple but effective example:

Well, they'll stone you when you're trying to be so good,
They'll stone you just like they said they would.
They'll stone you when you try to go home,
Then they'll stone you when you're there all alone.
But I would not feel so all alone:
Everybody must get stoned.

In the Beatles' song, the very same phrases that belong to the platitudes of the "beautiful people" belong also, with favorable connotations, to the drug scene. The question, "And have you travelled very far?" is answered by Lennon, the "beautiful" person, with what socially would be a comfortable cliché: "Far as the eye can see." But the phrase is really too outmoded for the jet age and thus sends us back to the original question and to the possibility that the "travel" can refer to a "trip" on LSD, the destination of which would indeed be "as far as the eye can see." Most of the lyrics operate in this double way, both as social satire and drug talk: "How often have you been there?/ Often enough to know," or "What did you see when you were there?/ Nothing that doesn't show" or "Some do it naturally" (presumably an acidhead by nature) to which the answer is "Happy to be that way." The song could pass simply as social satire, though to see that and that only is also to be the object of satire, of not knowing what implications are carried even by the language you make fun of for its imprecisions. The point, and it's one that I'll come back to, is that the argot of LSD isn't much different from the banalities of question and answer between a "beautiful" person and his bedazzled interviewer. The punning genius of Lennon is evident here perhaps more effectively than in his two books, *In My Own Write* and *A Spaniard in the Works,* with their affinities to Edward Lear as well as to the Joyce of *Finnegans Wake.*

The Beatles won't be stuck even within their most intricate contrivances, however, and they escape often by reminding us and themselves that they are singers and not pushers, performers and not propagandists. The moment occurs in "Baby You're a Rich Man," as it does in other songs, near the end, in the question "Now that you've found another key / What are you going to play?" Necessarily [535] the question refers us to their music while at the same time alluding to the promised results of drugs—a new "key" to personality, to a role as well as to the notes that one might "play." Similar uses of words that can allude both to the subject of the moment and to their constant subject, musical creation, occur in "All You Need Is Love" ("Nothing you can sing that can't be sung"), with implications we'll get to in a moment, and in the second song on the Sgt. Pepper album, "A

Little Help from My Friends." Sung by Ringo the "help" refers most simply to affection when there is no one around to love and it also means pot supplied by a friend. However, at the beginning of the song it explicitly means the assistance the others will give Ringo with his singing, while the phrases "out of tune" and "out of key" suggest, in the broadest sense, that the number, like the whole occasion, is in the mode not of the Beatles but of Sgt. Pepper's Lonely Hearts Club Band: "What would you think if I sang out of tune, / Would you stand up and walk out on me. / Lend me your ears and I'll sing you a song, / And I'll try not to sing out of key. / Oh, I get by with a little help from my friends, / Mmmm, I get high with a little help from my friends, / Mmmm, going to try with a little help from my friends, . . ."

One of the Beatles' most appealing qualities is their tendency more to self-parody than to parody of others. The two are of course very close for performers who empathize with all the characters in their songs and whose most conspicuous moments of self-parody occur when they're emulating someone whose style they'd like to master. At such moments their boyishness really does shine forth as a musical virtue: giving themselves almost wholly to an imitation of some performer they admire, their necessary exaggeration of his style makes fun of no one so much as themselves. It's a matter of trying on a style and then—as if embarrassed by their own riches, by a self-confident knowledge that no style, not even one of their own invention, is more than a temporary exercise of strength—of laughing themselves out of imitation. Listen to the extravagant rendering on *Beatles '65* of Chuck Berry in "Rock and Roll Music" or their many early emulations of Presley, whose importance to their development is everywhere apparent, or the mimicry of Western music in "Act Naturally" on one of their very best albums, *Yesterday and Today,* or the McCartney imitation of Little Richard singing "Long Tall Sally" [536] on the *Beatles Second Album.* It's all cowboys and Indians by people who have a lot of other games they want to play and who know very well where home is and when to go there. Parody and self-parody is frequent among the other groups in the form of persistent stylization, but its object is almost always some clichéd sentiment or situation. Parody from the Beatles tends usually, and increasingly, to be directed toward musical tradition and their own musical efforts. This is at least one reason why "All You Need Is Love," recorded on the reverse side of "Baby You're a Rich Man," is one of the most important they have ever done, an indication, along with the Sgt. Pepper album, of so sophisticated an awareness of their historical achievements in music as to make it seem unlikely that they can continue much longer without still further changes of direction even more radical than their decision not to perform henceforth for live audiences. "All You Need

Is Love" is decisive evidence that when the Beatles think about anything they think musically and that musical thinking dictates their response to other things: to "love," in this instance, to drugs and social manners in "Baby You're a Rich Man Now" and throughout the Sgt. Pepper album.

I doubt that any of these subjects would in itself prove a sufficient sustenance for their musical invention until first called forth and then kindled by some musical idea. At this point in their career it is impossible, given their and George Martin's musical knowledge and sophistication, that the title "All You Need Is Love" should mean what it would mean coming from any other group, namely hippie or flower love. Expectations of complications are satisfied from the outset: the repetition, three times and in a languorous tone, of the phrase "love, love, love" might remind us of the song of the aging Chaplin in *Limelight*, a song in which he keeps repeating the word throughout with a pitiable and insistent rapidity. Musical subterfuge of lyric simplicity occurs again when the title line, "all you need is love," picks up a musical trailer out of the thirties ballroom. The historical frequency of the "need" for love is thus proposed by the music, and it is as if this proposition emboldens the lyrics: "Nothing you can do that can't be done," "nothing you can sing that can't be sung," "nothing you can know that can't be known," "nothing you can see that can't be shown— it's easy"—this is a sample of equally ambiguous assertions that constitute the verbal substance of the song, [537] even while the word "love" is being stretched out in choral background. And like the ambiguous language of "Baby You're a Rich Man," the phrasing here sounds comfortably familiar—if you had love you could do anything. Except that isn't really what the lyrics imply. Rather, the suggestion is that doing, singing, knowing, seeing have in some sense already been done or at least that we needn't be in any particular sweat about them; they're accepted as already within the accustomed range of human possibility. What has not been demonstrated to anyone's satisfaction, what hasn't been tried, is "love." "Love" remains the great unfulfilled need, and the historical evidence for this is in endless musical compositions about it. Far from suggesting that "love" will solve everything, which would be the hippie reading of "all you need is love," the song allows most things to be solved without it. Such a nice bit of discrimination issues from the music and thence into the lyrics. Interestingly enough, the lyrics were meant to be simple in deference to the largely non-English-speaking audience for whom the song was especially written and performed on the BBC worldwide TV production of "Our World." "Normally," the Beatles' song publisher Richard James later observed, "the Beatles like to write sophisticated material, but they were glad to have the opportunity to write something with a very basic appeal." But so was Shakespeare at the Globe, and we know how unsophisticated he could be. The simplicity is entirely in the initial repetitions of title line and the word "love," a verbal simplicity first modified by the music and then turned into complications that have escaped even most English-speaking listeners.

Lennon and McCartney's recognition through music that the "need" for love is historical and recurrent is communicated to the listener by instrumental and vocal allusions to earlier material. The historical allusiveness is at the outset smart-alecky—the song opens with the French National Anthem—passes through the Chaplin echo, if that's what it is, to various echoes of the blues, and boogie-woogie, all of them in the mere shadings of background, until at the end the song itself seems to be swept up and dispersed within the musical history of which it is a part and of the electronics by which that history has been made available. The process begins by a recurrence of the "love, love, love" phrase, here repeated and doubled as on a stalled record. It then proceeds into a medley of sounds, fractured, [538] mingled musical phrases drifting into a blur which my friend Paul Bertram pointed out to me is like the sounds of a radio at night fading and drifting among the signals of different stations. We can make out fragments of old love songs condemned to wander through the airways for all time: "Green Sleeves," a burst of trumpet sound I can't identify, a hit of the thirties called "In the Mood," a ghostly "love you, yeah, yeah, yeah" of "She Loves You" from the *Beatles Second Album* of 1964 and, in the context of "All You Need Is Love," a pathetic "all together now . . . everybody!" of the old community sing. Far from being in any way satiric, the song gathers into itself the musical expression of the "need" for love as it has accumulated through decades of popular music.

The historical feeling for music, including their own musical creations, explains, I think, the Beatles' fascination with the invented aspects of everything around them, the participatory tenderness and joy with which they respond to styles and artifact, the maturity with which they have come to see the coloring of the human and social landscape of contemporary England. It's as if they naturally see the world in the form of *son et lumière:* as they say in a beautiful neighborhood song about Liverpool, "Penny Lane is in my ears and in my eyes." Not everyone their age is capable of seeing the odd wonder of a meter maid—after all, a meter maid's a meter maid; fewer still would be moved to a song of praise like "Lovely Rita" ("When it gets dark I tow your heart away"); and only a Beatle could be expected, when seeing her with a bag across her shoulder, to have the historically enlivened vision that "made her look a little like a military man." Now of course English boys out of Liverpool can be expected, it says here, to be more intimate than American boys from San Francisco with the residual social and cultural evidences from World War II and even from the First World War. In response to these and other traces of the past, however, the Beatles display an absolutely unique kind of involvement. It isn't simply that they have an instinctive nostalgia for period styles, as in "She's Leaving Home" or "When I'm Sixty-four," or that they absorb the past through the media of the popular arts, through music, cinema, theatrical conventions, bands like Sgt. Pepper's or music-hall performers. Everyone to some extent apprehends the world in the shapes given it by the popular arts and its media; we all see even the things that are new [539] to us through that gridiron of style that Harold Rosenberg imagines as a debilitating shield in front of the British Redcoats even as they first entered the American terrain. No, the Beatles have the distinction in their work both of *knowing* that this is how they see and feel things and of enjoying the knowledge. It could be said that they know what Beckett and Borges know but without any loss of simple enthusiasm or innocent expectation, and without any patronization of those who do not know. In the loving phrases of "Penny Lane," "A pretty nurse is selling poppies from a tray / And tho' she feels as if she's in a play, / She is anyway."

It isn't surprising that drugs have become important to their music, that they are leading an effort in England for the legalization of marijuana, partly as a result of the conviction and sentencing on drug charges of two of the Rolling Stones, and that in response to questions, Lennon, McCartney and Harrison have let it be known that they've taken LSD. At least four of the songs on the Sgt. Pepper album are concerned with taking a "trip" or "turning on": "A Little Help from My Friends," "Lucy in the Sky with Diamonds," "Fixing a Hole" and "A Day in the Life," with a good chance of a fifth in "Getting Better." Throughout the album, the consciousness of the *dramatis personae* in the songs is directed more or less by inventions of media or of the popular arts, and drugs are proposed as one kind of personal escape into the freedom of some further invention all on one's own. Inventing the world out of the mind with drugs is more physically risky than doing it by writing songs, films or wearing costumes, but danger isn't what the songs offer for consideration, and it's in any case up to the Beatles alone to decide what they want for their minds and bodies. Instead, the songs propose, quite delightfully and reasonably, that the vision of the world while on a "trip" or under the influence of a drug isn't necessarily wilder than a vision of the world through which we travel under the influence of the arts or the news media. Thus, the third song on the album, "Lucy in the Sky with Diamonds," proposes that the listener can "picture" a "trip" scene without taking such a "trip" himself. Here, as in "Baby You're a Rich Man," the experience of a "trip" is wittily superimposed on the experience of ordinary travel: "Picture yourself on a train in a station, / With plasticine porters with looking glass ties, / Suddenly someone is there at the turnstile, / The girl with kaleidoscope [540] eyes." Of course the images could come as easily from Edward Lear as from the experience of drugs, and Lennon has claimed that the title of the song is not an anagram for LSD but was taken from a drawing his son did at school. Lennon, the author of two books of Joycean punning, knows to the point of hilarity that one meaning denies the presence of another, which it has hidden inside, only to all strangers and the police. Still his reticence is obviously a form of the truth. The Beatles won't be reduced to drugs when they mean, intend and enact so much more. "Acid," Harrison told the Los Angeles *Free Press* in August, "is not the answer, definitely not the answer. It's enabled people to see a little bit more, but when you really get hip, you don't need it." Later, to Hunter Davies of the *London Sunday Times,* McCartney announced that they'd given up drugs. "It was an experience we went through and now it's over we don't need it any more. We think we're finding other ways of getting there." In this effort they're apparently being helped by Maharishi Mahesh Yogi, the Indian founder of the International Meditation Society, though even on the way to their initiation in Bangor, North Wales, Lennon wondered if the experience wasn't simply going to be another version of what they already knew: "You know, like some are EMI and some Decca, but it's really still records."

The notion that we "picture" ourselves much of the time anyway without even willing it, that we see ourselves and the world in exotic images usually invented by someone else, is suggested throughout the Sgt. Pepper album, even on the cover, with its clustered photographs of world-shaping "stars" of all kinds. In "A Day in the Life," the last song and a work of great power and historical grasp, the hapless man whose role is sung by McCartney wants to "turn on" himself and his lover—maybe us too—as a relief from the multiple controls exerted over life and the imagination by various and competing media. The sad little "oh boy" interjected by McCartney's sweet, vulnerable voice into orchestral movements of intimidating, sometimes portentous momentum, expresses wonderfully how the victim is further confounded by the fact that these controls often impose themselves under the guise of entertainment:

> I read the news today oh boy
> About a lucky man who made the grade
> And though the news was rather sad [541]

> Well I just had to laugh
> I saw the photograph.
> He blew his mind out in a car
> He didn't notice that the lights had changed
> A crowd of people stood and stared
> They'd seen his face before
> Nobody was really sure
> If he was from the House of Lords.
> I saw a film today oh boy
> The English Army had just won the war
> A crowd of people turned away
> But I just had to look
> Having read the book.
> I'd love to turn you on. . . .

The news in the paper is "rather sad" but the photograph is funny, so how does one respond to the suicide; suicide is a violent repudiation of the self but it mightn't have happened if the man had followed the orders of the traffic lights; the victim isn't so much a man anyway as a face people have seen someplace in the news, in photographs or possibly even on film; and while a film of the English army winning the war is too dated for most people to look at, and maybe they don't believe in the victory anyway, the man in the song has to look at it (oh boy—a film) because he has read a book about it and therefore it does have some reality for him. "Turning on" is at least a way of escaping submission to the media designed to turn on the mind from the outside—quite appropriately the song was banned on the BBC—and loving to turn "you" on, either a lover or you, the listener, is an effort to escape the horror of loneliness projected by the final images of the song:

> I read the news today oh boy
> Four thousand holes in Blackburn
> Lancashire
> And though the holes were rather small
> They had to count them all
> Now they know how many holes it takes
> To fill the Albert Hall.
> I'd love to turn you on.

The audience in Albert Hall—the same as the "lovely audience" in the first song that the Beatles would like to "take home" with them?—are only so many holes: unfilled and therefore unfertile holes, of the earth and therefore holes of decomposition, gathered together but [542] separate and therefore countable, utterly and inarticulately alone. Is this merely a bit of visionary ghoulishness, something seen on a "trip"? No, good citizens can find it, like everything else in the song, in the daily news—of how Scotland Yard searched for buried bodies on a moor by making holes in the earth with poles and then waiting for the stench of decomposing flesh.

Lennon and McCartney in their songs seem as vulnerable as the man in "A Day in the Life" to the sights and sounds by which different media shape and then reshape reality, but their response isn't in any way as intimidated, and "turning on" isn't their only recourse. They can also tune in and play the game, sometimes to show, as in "A Day in the Life," how one shaped view of reality can be mocked out of existence by crossing it with another. They mix their media the way they mix musical sounds or cross lyrics of one tone with music of quite another—with a vengeance. It's unwise ever to assume that they're doing only one thing or expressing themselves in only one style. "She's Leaving Home" does have a persistent cello background to evoke genteel melodrama of an earlier decade, and "When I'm Sixty-four" is intentionally clichéd throughout both in its ragtime rhythm and in its lyrics. The result is a satiric heightening of the love-nest sentimentality of old popular songs in the mode of "He'll build a little home / Just meant for two / From which I'll never roam / Who would, would you?" The home in "When I'm Sixty-four" is slightly larger to accommodate children, but that's the only important difference: "Every summer we can rent a cottage / In the Isle of Wight, if it's not too dear / We shall scrimp and save / Grandchildren on your knee / Vera Chuck & Dave." But the Beatles aren't satisfied merely with having written a brilliant spoof, with scoring, on their own authority, off death-dealing clichés. Instead, they quite suddenly at the end transform one cliché (of sentimental domesticity) into another (of a lonely-hearts newspaper advertisement) thereby proposing a vulgar contemporary medium suitable to the cheap and public sentiments that once passed for nice, private and decent: "Send me a postcard, drop me a line, / Stating point of view / Indicate precisely what you mean to say / Yours sincerely, wasting away / Give me your answer, fill in a form / Mine for evermore / Will you still need me, will you still feed me. / When I'm sixty-four." [543]

The Sgt. Pepper album and the singles released here just before and after it—"Penny Lane," "Strawberry Fields Forever," "All You Need Is Love" and "Baby You're a Rich Man"—constitute the Beatles' most audacious musical effort so far, works of such achieved ambitiousness as to give an entirely new retrospective shape to their whole career. Nothing less is being claimed by these songs than that the Beatles now exist not merely as a phenomenon of entertainment but as a force of historical consequence. They have placed themselves within

18. Learning from the Beatles

a musical, social and historical environment more monumental in its surroundings and more significantly populated than was the environment of any of their early songs. Listening to the Sgt. Pepper album one thinks not simply of the history of popular music but of the history of this century. It doesn't matter that some of the songs were composed before it occurred to the Beatles to use the motif of Sgt. Pepper, with its historical overtones; the songs emanated from some inwardly felt coherence that awaited a merely explicit design, and they would ask to be heard together even without the design.

Under the aegis of an old-time concert given by the type of music-hall band with which Lennon's father, Alfred, claims to have been associated, the songs, directly or by chance images, offer something like a review of contemporary English life, saved from folksong generality by having each song resemble a dramatic monologue. The review begins with the Sgt. Pepper theme song, followed immediately by "A Little Help from My Friends": Ringo, helped by the other Beatles, will, as I've already mentioned, try not to sing out of "key," try, that is, to fit into a style still heard in England but very much out of date. Between this and the reprise of Sgt. Pepper, which would be the natural end of the album, are ten songs, and while some are period pieces, about hangovers from the past, as is the band itself, no effort is made at any sort of historical chronology. Their arrangement is apparently haphazard, suggesting how the hippie and the historically pretentious, the genteel and the mod, the impoverished and the exotic, the Indian influence and the influence of technology are inextricably entangled into what is England. As I probably shouldn't say again, the Beatles never for long wholly submerge themselves in any form or style, so that at the end of the Indian, meditative sonorities of "Within You, Without You" the burst of laughter can be taken to mean—look, we have come through, an assurance [544] from the Beatles (if it *is* their laughter and not the response of technicians left in as an example of how "straights" might react) that they are still Beatles, Liverpool boys still there on the far side of a demanding foreign experience. This characteristic release of themselves from history and back to their own proper time and place occurs with respect to the design of the whole album in a most poignant way. Right after the reprise of the Sgt. Pepper song, with no interval and picking up the beat of the Sgt. Pepper theme, an "extra" song, perhaps the most brilliant ever written by Lennon and McCartney, breaks out of the theatrical frame and enters "a day in the life," into the way we live now. It projects a degree of loneliness not to be managed within the conventions of Sgt. Pepper's Lonely Hearts Club Band. Released from the controls of Sgt. Pepper, the song exposes the horrors of more contemporary and less benign controls, and it is from these that the song proposes the necessity of still further release. It does so in musical sounds meant to convey a "trip" out, sounds of ascending-airplane velocity and crescendo that occur right after the first "I'd love to turn you on," at midpoint in the song, and after the final, plaintive repetition of the line at the end, when the airplane sounds give way to a sustained orchestral chord that drifts softly and slowly toward infinity and silence. It is, as I've suggested, a song of wasteland, and the concluding "I'd love to turn you on" has as much propriety to the fragmented life that precedes it in the song and in the whole work as does the "Shantih, Shantih, Shantih" to the fragments of Eliot's poem. Eliot can be remembered here for still other reasons: not only because he pays conspicuous respect to the music hall but because his poems, like the Beatles' songs, work for a kaleidoscopic effect, for fragmented patterns of sound that can bring historic masses into juxtaposition only to let them be fractured by other emerging and equally evocative fragments.

Eliot is not among the sixty-two faces and figures, all unnamed and in some cases probably quite obscure, gathered round the Beatles on the cover, a pictorial extension of the collage effect which is so significant to the music. In making the selection, the Beatles were understandably drawn to figures who promote the idea of other possible worlds or who offer literary and cinematic trips to exotic places: Poe, Oscar Wilde, H. G. Wells, along with Marx, Jung, Lawrence of Arabia and Johnny Weismuller. They are also partial to the kind of theatrical person whose full being is the theatrical self, like W. C. Fields, Tom Mix, Brando and Mae West, who has delightfully adapted such Beatle songs as "Day Tripper" to her own style. Above all, the cover is a celebration of the Beatles themselves who can now be placed (and Bob Dylan, too) within a group who have, aside from everything else, infused the imagination of the living with the possibilities of other ways of living, of extraordinary existences, of something beyond "a day in the life." So it is indeed like a funeral for the Beatles, except that they'd be no more "dead" than anyone else in attendance. There they are in the center, mustachioed and in the brassed and tassled silk of the old-time bands, and, with brilliant, quite funny implications, they are also represented in the collage as wax figures by Madame Tussaud, clothed in business suits. Live Beatles in costumes from the past and effigies of the Beatles in the garb of the present, with the name of the Beatles in flowers planted before the whole group—this bit of slyness is of a piece with not sorting out past and present and promised future in the order of the songs, or the mixed allusiveness to period styles, including earlier Beatles' styles or the mixing and confoundings of media in songs like "When I'm Sixty-four" or "A Day in the Life." The cover suggests that the Beatles to some extent live the past in the present, live in the shadows of their own as well as of other people's past accomplishments, and that among the imaginative creations that fascinate them most, the figures closest at hand on the cover, are their own past selves. "And the time will come," it is promised in one of their songs, "when you will see we're all one, and life flows on within you and without you." As an apprehension of artistic, and perhaps of any other kind of placement within living endeavor, this idea is allowable only to the very great. [546]

19. This Place of Entertainment Has No Fire Exit: The Underground Press and How It Went
Jesse Kornbluth

Being hip in America has become big business. To make it these days, you have to do your thing reasonably well, but it's more important to be interesting and quotable—in fact, it helps to sound even freakier than you are. And after all the hustle, after you've finally had your big moment in the national media orgy, you'd better remember to avoid any sentiment that might seem human; if you're uncool too often, the fans withdraw your tenure. [91]

This means, quite simply, that the groovy psychedelic underground we've talked so much about these last few years is now just another pillar of the society it claims to reject. The hip ghettos have their own version of the stock market, with reputations dependent on the quality of your grass, the cut of your clothes, the size of your record collection. Like all recent advances, the drug-music-media explosion of two years ago has become a scene, and as in other scenes, a cultural *mafioso* determines what's going to happen next. Last year, all the underground media were breathless over Janis Joplin and the Big Brother Band, and though their album was so marginal that its producer refused to let his name appear on the cover, it went to number one and stayed there for weeks. This year, someone seems to have decided that the scene is blues, and Columbia Records has signed a Texas albino named Johnny Winter for $300,000, a sum that would buy a dozen black guitarists of equal heaviness.

Do you dig it when they burn you? Or as the winters seem colder, as

Source: *Antioch Review* 29, no. 1 (Spring 1969): 91–99. Reprinted by permission of the publisher.

your circle of friends tightens around your throat, do you pretend that it's still getting better all the time, that an underground persistently lives only to love you?

In the 18th century, it was thought that whatever is, is right. This gave added significance to the lives of the "important" people; they became celebrities. Whatever the Biggies decided would happen generally happened. The Press watched the Biggies, and reported their activities as History, with a few "human interest" stories thrown in for variety. And that is the way the authorized popular history of the last two centuries reads.

The lives of the unimportant people were left to novelists, poets, and the other unacknowledged social workers of the world. But with the media explosion and the bountiful economy of the last few decades, the little folk have rapidly become more important. Not important enough to have much control of their lives, of course, but just powerful enough to enable them to see how really crippled they are by modern society. And now, the dichotomy between Things As They Are and Things As They Might Be is so severe that we're all starting to freak out.

Any fool can buy a gun and change the shape of history, as the bigtime pundits phrase it.

A microbiologist writes in *Unless Peace Comes:* "The most disturbing aspect of biological warfare is the possibility it might give to small groups of individuals to upset the strategic balance."

Any kid can drop a tab of LSD and get the goodGodword.

"Magic is afoot," says Leonard Cohen.

So it's harder to fool kids these days, at least in the old, *New York Times*-y ways. The television freaks don't bother to read at all if they can help it—the latest rage in California is the stoned comic book—[92] and those who do read tend to read very closely. They read Jung and Nietzsche, the *I Ching* and R. D. Laing, Marcuse and Canetti, Vonnegut and Richard Brautigan. They're wide awake, or try to be, and they're not very interested in the Biggies, except to wonder where the next area of repression will be. They know, as Canetti writes in *Crowds and Power,* that "for every great name in history, a hundred others might have been substituted. There is never any dearth of men who are both talented and wicked."

Eldridge Cleaver has suggested that the most important battleground of the future isn't between the races—it is the war between white kids and their parents. The underground press, rock music, drugs and the New Left are only the initial weapons in that assault; unfortunately, they have become so successful that they, too, have been incorporated into the swinging style of modern, switched-on America. And this leads us straight into a series of desperate paradoxes.

The interesting thing about the phenomenon we've come to call the underground press is that it seems quite dead these days. Most of the papers are printing the same ritualized reports of drug busts, leftist paranoia, and catch-all astrology, badly designed and graphically artless. It's winter everywhere, especially in our heads, and the universe seems to have slid into sludge—no one has anything to say that urgently requires saying. The underground press was at best a reflection of the lives of its creators; now that those lives have been maimed by the experience of the last two years, the papers are cynical, exclusive, and cater to an increasingly ingrown audience.

It's not made easier, of course, by the peculiarly macabre proclivity of midcult to "discover" a trend as it's starting to fade; the mass media serves simultaneously as executioner and alchemist. So the underground press that's finally beginning to Make It isn't the underground press I loved, the underground press that suffered and fought just to exist, but always kept a sense of humor about the war—no, of those original 125 members of the Underground Press Syndicate, about half have folded and most of the rest have been completely transformed.

So while the underground press is moribund, the underground press business is booming, and even the Mafia wants to get into the act. Johnny Carson wears a Nehru jacket. The copy-boys at Time-Life are said to make $500 a week dealing grass to their editors. Paste-on moustaches have made it into the mainstream of the American fantasy. In a land where everyone (except the poor and the black) is hip, no one is hip, and words exist only to be emptied of meaning. Thus:
- Andy Warhol does television commercials for an "Underground Sundae."
- A new quiz show pits parents against their children. Predictably, it's called "Generation Gap."
- "If it's not in the *New York Times* Index, maybe it didn't happen." [93]

In spite of MassHip, there are still 125 "underground" papers, with a circulation of one to three million. The oldest of the underground magazines, *The Realist,* now distributes 100,000 copies of each issue. The *East Village Other* (EVO) prints between 60 to 80,000 and has gone national, and the *Los Angeles Free Press* is doing at least as well. The *Village Voice,* the grandfather of the hip newspapers, has a circulation of 125,000, and has gracefully retired from the fray to print more advertising than news.

But when you sell 100,000 copies of anything, when you have a fulltime advertising staff (and the L.A. *Free Press* is said to have installed a time clock so the employees can punch in), it's less than ingenuous to accept "underground" status. So the concept has been quietly redefined to mean, simply, that We haven't quite won yet. It's a small point, I know, and perhaps overly prissy of me in these "revolutionary" times, but I think this redefinition is indicative of the depressing change that's affected so many of these papers in the last two years.

Once upon a time, about a generation ago—that is, back in 1967—a feeling flashed through America. For the first time, a lot of young people had the same sense of life. And the same message came to many: It's beautiful. You can do more to enjoy it. And free yourselves, because the Crazies control the planet.

At that time, on the flip side, LBJ was dominating the straight media with his Vietnam freakout and his daily announcement that the Emperor had clothes, and someone was twisting the arms of the communications Biggies (or do they twist their own arms?) to get them to say that the Emperor's suit never looked better. That's when we first saw how very Zen this country can be; why, when they call it "the communications industry," they mean exactly that. So the first priority was to get our own news networks and broadcast our version of The Truth. And the message was poster-simple then: LOVE.

Considered as a movement in itself, the high point of the underground press was Winter-Summer of 1967. Simultaneously, the advances in studio rock music and the availability of marijuana at absurdly low prices were making a national though disorganized "youth movement" possible. We broke through our private fears, and for the first time in anyone's memory, people came together for reasons that had nothing to do with politics.

It was a wonderful and amazing circus. Everyone had access to everyone else, and people went out of their way not to judge each other. It didn't even matter if you had a crewcut and worked for IBM as long as you had the lovelight in your eyes and were willing to lay back and groove. If you had something to say, if you were doing something you wanted to show the world, you just walked into your local underground paper, and more [94] frequently than not your message was circulated. In San Francisco, the Communications Company went so far as to distribute daily street broadsides; if something was happening, the community knew about it. And because we young freaks *were* news, we were cool enough to avoid role-playing and ego-tripping.

The papers were printed with varying degrees of care. *Avatar* and the *San Francisco Oracle* were the products of thousands of man-hours and the attention of dedicated artists; the more typical papers were paste-up montages of someone's misreading of McLuhan. But it didn't really matter what was said; the point was that these toys were our own, and everything worked. There was so much to enjoy at one time—Sgt. Pepper, stoned sex, Country Joe and the Fish, the Love-Ins and the beautiful newspapers—that we were overstimulated, living in a stunned and prolonged ecstasy. A friend of mine spent a blissful day that summer computing the Great Progression: If every dedicated pot-smoker turned on just two of his friends, by 1975 the entire world would be stoned.

It's difficult to say what destroyed this spirit. It's fashionable to argue that too much acid, too many undisciplined kids, and too much publicity made the underground press so self-conscious that it began to devour itself. Or perhaps it was that the love we felt was too generalized to last—when you love everyone, when you can spend hours appreciating a drawing in something as impermanent as a newspaper, you can't continue to function efficiently in the straight world. And you can't go on repeating the loveword indefinitely if you want to sell papers.

What happened, I think, is that too many papers started taking themselves too seriously. For $200, almost anyone could start a paper, and almost anyone did—this flooded the hip media scene until the local underground paper became as institutionalized as the head shop. Underground editors became mini-celebrities. It meant something to put out a paper, and the informal symposia conducted in the *Look* and *Time* articles on the hippies elevated the papers to the position of spokesmen for a movement.

The record companies, at about this same time, found in these papers an inexpensive and effective advertising outlet; their ads sustained many papers that would otherwise have certainly folded after the summer. And when the sexploitation companies saw that these papers would print just about anything, they flooded them with ads.

So an over-extended medium became unwittingly professional, and papers in search of a direction found one of the Two Answers: Politics and Religion. The Boston *Avatar* had Mel Lyman, a banjo player who had once stunned the Newport Folk Festival by playing "Rock of Ages" for 20 minutes, and who now claimed to be God. The *Oracle* plunged into the occult. And the student-oriented urban papers embraced the New Left.

People who thought it a good tactic to call all cops "pigs" began writing for the papers, and the originals either left or were forced out. Soon most of the underground press read as one paper, and could easily be considered as such; you couldn't tell *The Rat* from the *Guard-*

ian from the San [95] *Francisco Express-Times*. Amidst the furor against the war, readership was increasing, and the militants wrongly took this new support for a sign to go even further. So we were awash on a wave of inanity:

- *The Berkeley Barb* printed an article calling for 1,000 young men to undertake an armed *kamikaze* attack on the Pentagon.
- New York's *Rat* reported, in an article about the Nixon inauguration: "Very young kids were militant and brave in the street-fighting. The less time you've spent being molded into a sitting position in a classroom, the more freely you move through inhibitory brain patterns and throw the rock."
- Even *Rolling Stone,* which replaced *Crawdaddy!* as the Bible of rock criticism, romanticized the "revolutionary" sound of the MC-5, a group that has finally made a commercial success out of pure alienation.

Those who opposed the militants became the revisionist enemies of the Revolution. As early as 1966, Ken Kesey had put the radicals down ("There's only one thing that's gonna do any good at all . . . and that's everybody just look at it, look at the war, and turn your backs and say . . . Fuck it . . ."), but the high-school kids wanted their own scene, distinct from that of the older hippies. And because high-school students are more "oppressed" than college kids, the underground papers they started created a disciplinary controversy that had nothing to do with the papers' contents. With only a little coaching from the college radicals, however, the high schools had their own underground press service (HIPS), and a rhetoric straight from the latest SDS convention.

The original underground papers suddenly seemed dull. The Liberation News Service, founded in 1967 by Marshall Bloom and Ray Mungo, had tried to disseminate more than straight political propaganda to its 400 members, but there too the radicals were increasingly coming to power. By August of 1968, Bloom and Mungo couldn't counteract the leftist staffers, and they retired to the New England countryside, where they periodically publish a softer, more personal newsletter.

The *Oracle* folded. EVO moved into funk-a-delic cartoons, Yippie politics, and six to eight pages of "personal" ads a week ("SEEKING GROOVY COUPLES, ac/dc male, attractive, tall, well-hung, desires meaningful relationships with males, females, or couples who can groove"). Only *Avatar* didn't change its purpose: "We're not foolin' but we'll not be dismal either. We have nowhere else to go, we have nothing to lose, we want only to talk with you in the best form we know."

But consistency of vision created other problems, and *Avatar* found itself isolated from the informal fraternity of underground papers. The Fort Hill community, which produced the paper as the history of their

New Age lifestyle, became increasingly self-involved; the urgency of Mel's message in its turn frightened the local police force, and because it was an election year in Cambridge, and the Fort Hill folk looked like hippies (no matter what they said), and because *Avatar* was now up to 40,000 circulation and was expanding to New York, the City of Cambridge began a [96] program of harassment which resulted in the arrest of thirty-seven street salesmen. It was a nice civil-liberties issue, but it took two weeks in court out of these lives—and because the salesmen were also the editors, the missionary zeal again became political.

The first arrests are always like warm-up pitches—the police throw hard, just to see if the batter ducks away. To the surprise of the Cambridge City Fathers, the *Avatar* declared war on them, mocking their hypocrisy, lampooning "obscene" literature, finally publishing an issue entirely written by the Fort Hill children. (The street salesmen were arrested for this, too.) Through it all, the community was having a goofy sort of fun.

But the economics of publishing an underground paper don't allow for this much fun. *Avatar's* circulation was halved by the bad publicity, the Fort Hill people became disenchanted with the newspaper medium, and worst of all, Mel Lyman announced that he wasn't going to write any more. The New York branch was still interested, but the Boston staff closed its office. "We have set before you all that we can say," Wayne Hansen wrote. "The rest becomes a dull repetition. I can no longer write. I can't do favors. I can't help anyone, I can't hurt anyone. It's the end of the tether. Remember me. . . ."

Avatar was the last of the original papers to suspend publication; the others moved further into sexploitation and acquired a new audience. *The Realist* and *Other Scenes*, a monthly anthology of hip news edited by John Wilcock, are now featuring stories about the Plaster Casters, two Chicago groupies who specialize in phallic art. *The Rat* puts you on with tabloid headlines: "INTIMATE LOVE SCENES . . . SCANDALS THAT SHAMED EVEN HOLLYWOOD." The *L.A. Free Press* balances "SPIDERS IN NIXON'S CABINET" with "WHIPS CHAINS & LEATHERS."

So sexual promiscuity is this year's Revolution. There are occasional efforts to recreate the old spirit, but they are plagued by police pressure even more than are the political journals; Atlanta's *Great Speckled Bird*, a beautiful paper in the tradition of *Avatar* and the *Oracle*, has been declared obscene by the police there. Sporadic efforts are made to resurrect *Avatar;* predictably, political types took it over last summer, until the Fort Hill people kicked them out and began a new cycle of *American Avatar*, a *Life*-sized, paperback-priced ($1 a copy) magazine with impeccable graphics by Eben Given and writing by Mel Lyman.

19. The Underground Press and How It Went 235

But the coffin isn't sealed on the underground press scene. The high school papers are the new standard bearers of journalistic freedom, and the urge to write is seeping into the junior high schools too. *Fortune* claims that 40% of the college students sympathize with the radical cause, so a campus-based network of papers clearly will continue to publish. And the Hip Establishment—*EVO*, the *Berkeley Barb*, the *L.A. Free Press*, and a few others—will ride with the trends as long as it's economically possible. [97]

The survival of the underground press as it now exists doesn't strike me as central to the experience of many young people I know. Most of the papers still publishing could disappear tomorrow, and the only true mourners would be the editors and advertisers. This isn't because the Youth Movement has been routed, or because it doesn't have anything to say any more—I think it's the end of one assault and the beginning of the next, and because the young are so plugged into media games, it seems similar to the situation in rock music, where the scene overextended itself and one good musician often carried an entire group. Now the best musicians from the various groups are playing together as superbands; soon, it is rumored, the self-acknowledged elite of the underground press will publish a supermag. No reliable information comes from California, but it is thought on the East Coast that the magazine would be published from the country, perhaps from the Liberation farm in Massachusetts. The editors would be the cream of the underground editors—among them are Marshall Bloom, Ray Mungo and Steve Diamond of LNS, Carl Nagin, Brian Keating and Wayne Hansen of *Avatar*, Steve Lerner of *The Village Voice*, the *Avatar* artist-in-residence, Eben Given and its designer, John Wilton.

In the world of the Restons and the Buchwalds, these are not names that stick in the mind. To appreciate their work requires patience, a great deal of empathy, and a taste for whimsy. Still, to get these people at work on one journal, free from the pretensions of the "underground," might just be the only way to start the old cycle going.

The greatest fear in America is the fear of death, and second, I think, is the fear of having too much fun, the fear of pleasure without pain, pleasure you don't have to pay for. Out of all the despair which most underground papers articulate to the exclusion of all else, we enter a period of great hope. We've been down so long that any movement will bring us up, and the long-overdue retreat to the country will probably provide the spark the original hippie papers provided in 1967. I know it's fashionable to speak darkly of the Nixon years, and in some circles the present period is thought to be a return to the 1950's, but I think we're going to witness a revival of the happiness of 1967.

This time, we'll really be hip—we'll support only those people who seem to be valuable to our head. We won't be suckered by sympathetic exploitation reporters from the Biggies. And we won't waste our energy in aimless debate with people who will never understand what we're about. Now that all of our projects to save the world have failed, we have only ourselves to save, and the papers we print will be the record of that attempt.

"Free yourselves," *The Rat* editorializes, and *Open City* has begun a series of accounts by people who have renounced American society; their current issue contains information about communal farms and life in the woods. [98]

In New York, ten-year-olds recently demonstrated against an organization which conducts military drills for children. When an elderly man told one of the young protesters that he saw nothing wrong with a boy learning the proper use of guns, the answer was unequivocal: "Then, sir, I don't think we have anything more to say."

As Marcuse explains, freedom and tolerance in America are often repressive; if everyone can say anything, words are devalued, because all situations become relative. The underground press never understood this, and its papers punched the Establishment as if it were made of bricks instead of marshmallows. This time perhaps we'll know enough to avoid exhaustion through shadow-punching. This time perhaps we'll reach a purer form of journalism, with free minds reaching out for other free minds. This time perhaps we'll brighten a future that otherwise seems very bleak. And if we succeed at this, if a supermag gets enough money to rejoin the fun, or even if the local papers once again get interested in real communication, we may even make ourselves happy. And if we make ourselves happy—and in an imaginary interview with Jerry Rubin, Eldridge Cleaver is supposed to have yelled, "Happiness at any cost!"—why, it's possible that the new underground will drive the crusty old Establishment right into business, where it belongs. [99]

20. Truth and Consequence: Some Notes on Changing Times and the Muckrakers
Louis Filler

Living in the midst of revolution, it behooves us to seek insight into the processes which rule us. I am constantly awed by our assumptions and confusions. We "communicate," constantly using such words as liberal, reactionary, romantic, realistic, utopian, inevitable, and others. But stop the action; ask what any one of these words mean, and watch the "dialogue" slow down and perhaps break up. How could it be otherwise, with catastrophe waiting for us around every corner, and with friends not infrequently looking much like mortal enemies?

Dialogues can be an evasion of differences. Our unspoken agreements can keep us from discovering our real feelings and desires. Progressivism and its by-products—and, notably, the muckrakers—have, to some extent, settled into clichés. I propose a somewhat broader view of their content. It could help us to probe our memories, and, possibly, to revise our estimate of them.

The muckrakers survive as an idea, and as a historical reality. As an idea they suggest possible comparisons with the present; perhaps they can tell us something about our own journalistic expectations. I suspect this way of looking at the muckrakers varies from [27] person to person. Muckraking as an idea seems to us uncertain: sometimes admirable, sometimes less so. Sometimes it seems to us irrelevant. There are those who believe they get more than enough news, and that they can do without sensationalism or aggressive journalese. Others among us

Source: Antioch Review 28, no. 1 (Spring 1968): 27–41. Reprinted by permission of the publisher.

think news is hard to come by, or that it is manipulated for partisan purposes. The "credibility gap" worries us more than does the credulity gap.

But few of us can readily see the uniqueness of muckraking. We recall that we have had journalists in modern times who died trying to report intimate details of our several wars, and presently oversee not only the Vietnam War but its attendant scandals. We observe that each year has its quota of lurid sensations, and that they get amply reported. We are aware of Drew Pearson and other sophisticated behind-the-scene correspondents. In general, "muckraking" popularly means irresponsibility and straining for effect.

Historically, muckraking is better regarded. It suggests great journalistic achievements. Ida M. Tarbell, Lincoln Steffens, and Ray Stannard Baker are mentioned over and over again, in textbooks, for instance, as having made real and significant studies of the public affairs of their time. To be sure, their work is probably better respected than the overall movement of which they were part. Charles Edward Russell is scarcely remembered at all—can you mention one of his books or accomplishments? David Graham Phillips's *The Treason of the Senate* is not usually cited as great or memorable. One recent study of the Senate chides it, or him, for failing to realize the Senate's virtues. Thomas W. Lawson's *Frenzied Finance* probably sounds on the face of it as more florid than informative.

Still it is curious that Steffens's *The Shame of the Cities* has not caught on as relevant to our painful urban problems. Why not? The reason may be, in part, that we are willing to admit the cities are in bad shape, but can't see how Steffens's work of half a century ago can bear upon the matter. Besides, he says nothing about the Negroes. . . .

So muckraking as sensation seems passé; we have plenty of sensations. And muckraking as a guide seems out of date; what can it tell us about our current great clichés, Vietnam and civil rights? Let me hasten to say that I sympathize to some degree [28] with this feeling of frustration and negativism I have been trying to describe. There are good grounds for it. Only, I doubt that we can afford to indulge our feelings of self-pity and bafflement. We have to understand where we are; and that means, one way or another, measuring the present by the past. So let us look at some of the legends of muckraking and see if they tell us anything about ourselves.

The Muckrakers and Their Public:

Those who think well of Tarbell, Steffens, and some others of their generation note their moral concern for good citizenship, and also their

20. Some Notes on Changing Times and the Muckrakers 239

practical achievements: pure food and drug legislation, modernized insurance laws, anti-trust actions, and so on. In general, these are seen as well-intentioned pioneer efforts which fell short of the mark. The muckrakers admittedly did *something*. But Woodrow Wilson did more, didn't he?—and the New Deal still more. The muckrakers roused the public, but were inefficient in leading it very far. One recent study even, invidiously, sees the muckrakers as essentially conservative and appealing to conservative wants.

What is missing here is a look *at the public itself,* to determine its intentions and capacity. A straight look at it takes us forward to our own day, as well as back to the muckrakers.

Their books and articles ranged the whole gamut of social interests, including such questions as democracy, health, religion, and the plight of the Negroes. But, eagerly following up actual reader-response, they emphasized the most publicly-arresting issues, of course. These most immediately, and materially, affected the overall public: food and drugs, tenements, insurance, and the more obviously brutal aspects of city government.

Some students of these events find this disappointing. But how well have they weighed the stakes involved? For example, they assume the virtue of the reform cause. Yet it was resisted; and resisted by partisans who thought they were defending something more important than reform, namely, free enterprise. They argued that once you began regulating private affairs, there would be no end to the authority bureaucrats could wield over plain people. This seemed to reformers (and may seem, at first glance, to you) [29] callous in a time which saw, for example, harmful and fraudulent patent medicines on the market. But obviously, there were—and are—in a free society some circumstances which could not—and cannot—be easily pinpointed as right or wrong.

For instance, take advertising. What is an honest advertisement? What have you the right to assert in behalf of your product? Righteous indignation suggests there can be no end to probing the accuracy of an advertising claim. *But will it result in anybody buying the product?* What does the public want? Does it always prefer "honest" products to glamorous—or what we would today call status—products?

Clearly, we have not only to weigh the advertiser in the balance, but the public itself. If it in effect *forces* the advertiser to trump up fantastic claims for his merchandise, in order to compete, then the public—the public itself—shares responsibility for the result. It is getting what it wants, or at least what it deserves. Several years ago, a manufacturing company in the doldrums was quickly taken out of them by the single solution of its new and quick-stepping president. He raised the price of his product. That was all.

I pass by other problems creating truth in advertising, fair measure, reasonable prices, and all the rest. You have as much right to believe your soap, or shoes, or whatever, the best in the world as I have to root for my local team. Americans admire winners and are willing to pay accordingly. Also, we *do,* apparently, buy the box, sometimes, at least as much as the contents. We do *not* necessarily want products which will last indefinitely. In short, we are very human, and as such have to consider whether the muckrakers were realistic or romantic in imagining that their readers truly wanted thievery exposed and a reign of perpetual goodness and justice begun. Of course, no movement can get under way without breeding excessive hopes and demands. The muckrakers spawned their quota of idealists who clearly anticipated eternal peace and happiness for all.

But before we ask what the ultimate judgment on muckraking could be—how it compares with other movements we recognize and admire— let me refer to the more basic, more mysterious problem of the workings of our democracy. Take the pure food fight: almost classical in its script of heroes and villains. On one side we have the furtive and conspiratorial heavies, plotting to coin profits at the expense of public health. And on the other, the clean-cut crusaders, demanding truth and social justice. Upton Sinclair, you recall, wrote *The Jungle* as a tract favoring socialism. His readers soon made it clear that they wanted none of that. So-called "condemned meat," on the other hand, hit them harder. It hit them in the stomach. There was a public outcry against contaminated meats, and also against worthless and harmful pseudo-medicines. So once again there is a happy American ending. In 1906, the Pure Food and Drug Administration is set up to protect our health, and some crusaders and most of the public rest from their labors.

Time passes. Pure Food and Drug employees go on working at undramatic details of their assignments. They also ponder improvements in the law, and without marked assistance from journalists and reformers, who have turned to other concerns. The public is busy with many things, including the soaking up of bootleg hooch in the 1920's, the problem of getting enough to eat in the 1930's, and the problem of overeating thereafter.

And now, in the 1950's comes truly sensational news. Cigarettes may be harmful. Recall our human tendency to become panicky over mere rumors concerning epidemics and disease. And these are no mere rumors. The authority of the Surgeon-General's Office stands behind these new warnings. There is a brief wave of interest and alarm—very brief. A brief dip in the purchase of cigarettes. A kind of revolution takes place in the tobacco industry. Then cigarettes rise to new heights of popularity, accompanied by advertising, premiums, songs, and whatnot

20. Some Notes on Changing Times and the Muckrakers 241

which raise questions about the fundamental sanity of the reading and TV-viewing public. As I write, the popularity of cigarettes is still rising.[1]

[31]
There are other questions associated with this tobacco phenomenon: fascinating economic and even technical questions. For example, how much does tobacco cost, as compared to filters? And what, think you, is the effect of either on the price of cigarettes? But more crucial may be the psychological factor. What does the public *really* want—want at the bottom of its unconscious inner life? Is it interested in reform? Or is it, perhaps, more interested in anti-reform? It tolerates not merely cigarettes, but marijuana, and not merely marijuana but its after-effects. It swallows pills of every description, on little or no evidence of their possible malignity. Whatever else muckraking may or may not tell us in this connection, it can, at least, give us a point of reference with respect to our past behavior.

In assaying any developments, we need to avoid emotional readings. Conditions are not always what they seem. We can set down any random series of clichés—Abraham Lincoln freed the slaves; Theodore Roosevelt busted the trusts; Franklin D. Roosevelt ended the depression—and have fun and profit picking them to pieces. I like to recall John Adams's realism in refusing in 1798 to lead his Federalist Party into an all-out war with revolutionary France. President Adams saw, as his more hysterical associates did not, that what was going on in France, despite excesses, was not a barbaric orgy. The French were simply enduring a difficult social change-over, from feudalism to capitalism and its democratic trappings. We could negotiate with France. This stand cost Adams his political head, but we generally honor him for preventing our unofficial war with France from turning into a drawn-out and disreputable one.

There have been many other occasions when our choice was not necessarily between honor and dishonor, or between a stupid public and a high-minded one. Our business has been, rather, to understand the kind of *social process* we were passing through, and the kind of language we employed to help us do so. A public is a complicated mechanism. Walter Lippmann would later opine that there was not one public but many publics. Let us consider what the American people may have

---

[1] In this year of grace, it seems worthwhile to mark our progress in the field. According to our Department of Agriculture—tobacco is grown by the good earth—we have consumed a record number of cigarettes—552 *billion* in 1967—and are likely to beat that record in 1968. Affluence and military demands are credited with this giant boost to industry: 11 *billion* more cigarettes than were "consumed" in 1966. The implication would almost seem to be that the "poor" do not smoke cigarettes, or, at least, not enough to influence the tally sheet.

been trying to say during the "muckraking era," and how effectively they said it. [32]

Techniques for Change: American Need and American Methods:
Orators in the 1890's kept the air blue defending, on one side, American free enterprise, and, on the other, the rights and practices of big business. Populism and the trust became symbols of freedom and centralization. But note that *both* Populism and the trust spoke for a capitalist America. In 1903, the Elkins Act outlawed secret railroad rebates and other discriminations which worked hardships on farmers and small businessmen along the line. Elkins was a wealthy industrialist and railroad man, and his Act is not usually considered a reform measure, even though rebates had upset anti-trust spokesmen for thirty or more years.

Why was the Elkins Act not a victory for reform? Because American railroads had become so unified by 1903 that rebates no longer aided consolidation. They were a nuisance to the railroad titans and an unnecessary aggravation to Americans fearful of trust power. What the "man in the street" wanted was legislation which could *regulate and control* railroads in some definable public interest, rather than *destroy* them. And it was the Hepburn Act of 1906, not the Elkins Act, which began modern regulation. Senator Elkins opposed the Hepburn Act.

I give the above as a sample of the workings of the public mind. Some of its radical spokesmen wanted government ownership of railroads. Most Americans who read muckraking exposes couldn't bring themselves to go that far. They have never been able to. Regulation, yes—after a long and exploratory fight. Socialism—no. Americans are all temporarily inconvenienced millionaires, unwilling to give up entirely their dream of somehow, sometime finding and winning the unbelievable, undeserved, undedicated, unpurposeful Big Bonanza, complete with fame, women, and a Sense of Tragedy.

The United States in 1900 suffered acute needs. We had built cities with little foresight. (I say "we"; if you want our money, you must accept our history.) We had assimilated hordes of new-type immigrants, but with little preparation and no program for advancing or controlling them. We had sprawled across the continent, and loaded Congress with old and picturesque representatives from a dozen new western states.

As a result, there was suffering and unrest in the cities and in the rural sections. There is suffering and unrest today, and the key [33] question is whether we have anything to learn from the older troubles. True, children eked out their lives in mines and mills. Women were rudely accommodated to industry. Usurers and brutal foremen kept workingmen in line. So what? Children are strong enough today to

20. Some Notes on Changing Times and the Muckrakers 243

make up an economic force. The Beatles have been all but knighted. The aggressive American female is famous the world over. And we know the power of unionism. As for our much-discussed dissatisfaction and unhappiness, you can't have everything.

I will leave you to ponder the details of Reform Era predicaments, and their meaning, if any, to us. What may strike you as important is the fact that then as now, local and sectional differences were extreme, so that basic knowledge of them, which might enable reformers to deal with them, was lacking. New York and San Francisco, Atlanta and Madison, Wisconsin, were worlds apart. What they acutely required was a movement toward *communication* which would give them a common interest and enable them to help one another.

Does this sound idealistic, romantic? Consider the case of Joseph W. Folk in St. Louis: a young, religious lawyer, elected by the city bosses to be a do-nothing circuit attorney. Lincoln Steffens's *Autobiography* tells this tale with his usual zest and penetration: how the young man undertook a campaign against corrupt councilmen, how he found witnesses to defy threats, and evidence to confound the local Democratic political machine.

Note that Folk embarrassed the politicians, but could not shake their power. He stood soon to be unseated and forgotten, when Steffens visited St. Louis. Steffens cooperated with local journalists and reformers and published in *McClure's* his famous article, "Tweed Days in St. Louis," one of the first of the muckraking articles.

What did he accomplish? He threw a *national* spotlight on what had previously seemed to people involved no more than a *local* situation. Readers everywhere understood that what was happening in St. Louis was happening at home. Steffens's article took the affair out of the hands of the local big-shots, who could have controlled it, and gave it over to more widely disseminated authority which could now judge St. Louis in larger terms and dispose of its problems. [34]

As a result, Folk was elected governor of Missouri when he could not have been re-elected circuit attorney. Moreover, the St. Louis story was repeated many times, with variations, elsewhere. The muckrakers did more than "expose" St. Louis politics. They taught *method* for coping with them to reformers everywhere.

True reform is a painful process. It means not tearing up the cities, but tearing up old habits of thought and disavowing old associations. It means, not exactly curbing self-interest, but directing it into more useful channels. It means getting antagonistic and unfamiliar social elements to work together. It means education; I suppose I should add true education.

It is possible to achieve a kind of reform while by-passing its more difficult and cooperative aspects. Our own recent efforts to end poverty and inequality by law would rank with such efforts. But we seem to be more aware that such "victories" can be superficial, and merely serviceable to a few scattered individuals and pushers. It can help our perspective to contrast our own civic efforts and achievements with those of earlier do-somethingers.

The muckraking journalist involved himself in every aspect of reform. Like Reginald Wright Kauffman, he lived in settlements and wrote about them. Like George Creel, he exposed conditions in such a city as Denver, and participated in its partial reconstruction. Like Charles Edward Russell, he moved actively from Populism to Progressivism to Socialism, while writing outstandingly on a score of civic problems and investigating the possibilities of social democracy at home and abroad.

Like Brand Whitlock he was writer, reformer, and administrator. Most reformers carried ingredients of all these roles. Individually, however, they ranged from La Follette, who is better known for his practical activities than for *La Follette's Magazine,* to David Graham Phillips—I am not sure what he is best remembered for, but he did stir the imaginations of readers in his time.

The muckrakers did not *transform* the country. But they distinctly helped *modernize* it. They created a working vocabulary for further social change. Coast to coast we were ready to move on to further controversy, further experimentation as a result of their labors and those of their supportive readers.

I deem it important to emphasize the old-fashioned nature of the muckraker's crusade. I don't deplore this. Everything ultimately becomes old-fashioned. The burden of proof is on us to be able to draw living fragments from it, and to use them wisely in newer times. For example, how much power ought the President of the United States to wield? How does T.R. compare with L.B.J. in this respect? Or corporate strength: can you put J. P. Morgan and General Motors in one perspective? And how would your estimates compare with those of Gustavus Myers, and others of the older movement?

Or take the more basic tenet of popular psychology and morals. Theodore Roosevelt made the "square deal" immortal and the "square man" admirable. You know what "square" has come to mean, and your opinion is at least as important as that of the Hippies.

It would be remarkable if you had not something to add or qualify to what the muckrakers said. We have been through two world wars, a major depression, world-shaking revolutions, and literally world-shaking technological revelations. We would be inept, indeed, if we could not raise questions the old reformers didn't.

And yet their failures are not theirs alone. This is not the place to

20. Some Notes on Changing Times and the Muckrakers 245

compare their record with that of the so-called Youth Generation which followed theirs, or the Yes, We Have No Bananas crusaders, or of others down to ourselves. But it is obvious that we would be smart not to judge too cruelly, lest we be judged. We have a need to learn how to be useful to one another, rather than to tear down.

I see two questions drawing out of the muckraking experience. How do we create an effective common denominator of social purposes—what we have lately been calling a national purpose? And how do we get to communicate those purposes to one another?

The muckrakers managed to answer these questions for their own time. Their responses were weak in the foreign affairs sector—their public was simply not concerned for foreign affairs. Blame, if you will, the muckrakers for the fiasco of a war to make the world "safe for democracy"; it no more than helps define what they did do. And, incidentally, have we developed a more adequate perspective on World War I—with fifty years in which to do so? What have we added to understanding beside Snoopy's fantasies? Our own failures in the field should soften our attitudes toward [36] the earlier generation of reporters and scribes. They were part of a tragedy, not a conspiracy.

There were other fields in which the muckrakers targeted for limited objectives. Most notable at this time would be the problem of the Negroes. It merits notice that my story of the muckrakers was a pioneer in "integrating" the Negroes with other circumstances in American life. Earlier treatments did not perceive Negroes as a factor in Progressivism, but as a social problem separated from it. Were the muckrakers inadequate in their response to Negro agitation? Should they have followed W.E.B. Du Bois's view of America?—or Martin Luther King's, if he has one?—or Rap Brown's? Would one of these, or all of them together have made for a truer portrait of the Negro situation, as compared with that of other ethnic groups and sectional or economic interests?

If you think in such terms, then there is still more—more and more and more—that wants doing with respect to the muckrakers. For example, what did they think or do about the Indians? And about the Mexican-Americans? What about the Poles in Chicago? Did they (and do they) receive economic justice? And what about the aged and infirm of any racial or ethnic group?

It happens that the muckrakers did not view the problem of democracy from such a perspective. They were concerned for manifest legal injustice and brutal displays of strength. They despised charity and the indiscriminate and corrupt equality of the big city machines. But what needs to be grasped is that they lived in a world of family, friendships, and loyalty which was in some ways radically different from ours. I say "in some ways," because I am not persuaded that our world can, in the long run, do without those social quantities, or that welfare and mass entertainment can substitute for them to any degree. Certainly, there have been shifts in values and relationships. But only a fool—I say only a fool—will imagine that he has manufactured substitute values for living because of our big-city mass production developments. And only a fool will believe him.

Efficiency Is Not Enough:

I have already noted that Americans are ambivalent toward reform. On the one hand, they were alarmed by the power and activities of the large corporations. On the other hand, they were [37] and are unwilling to be deprived of the benefits of mass production. They gave a certain amount of sympathy to the Little Man, and made Louis D. Brandeis famous as a watchdog of his rights. Much of the sympathy, however, was mere lip-service, as is ours, so far as our Small Business Administration is concerned. More and more, Americans were receptive to the expert. The Reform Era is the era of Taylorization—of time-study experiments, of scientific management ideas. Efficiency became the rage. Our modern equivalent is the worship of the computer.

What does this tell us about efficiency or the computer? To answer this question, focus on 1912. It is a key date. Its tendencies and fulfillments light up our own era, with all its crises and self-appreciation. Suddenly, the muckrakers are gone. The public has withdrawn its support from them. It thinks it can do without self-assertive journalists and free enquirers. It feels more and more secure, having such strong candidates as Theodore Roosevelt and Woodrow Wilson vying for its attention and suffrage. I note that today we also seem to have our choice of would-be Public Servants, eager to help.

Woodrow Wilson's first administration was once famous for the sweeping nature of its reforms. Some of them no longer look impressive: an Underwood free trade tariff which did not bring free trade; a Clayton anti-trust act which did not curb trusts; a Federal Trade Commission which did not prevent unfair methods of competition in or out of interstate commerce; a Federal Reserve System which could not prevent 1929. What can you do to revive excitement about such milestones?

Not much. But we can try at least to discern what that generation was striving for: *an efficiency movement, rather than a reform movement; reforms administered from above, rather than welling up from below.* And let this be said for them with their *New Republic* and for us with our equally enigmatic *Ramparts:* it is evident that whatever mistakes they made, whatever weaknesses they were subject to, they were right in principle. We cannot do without an elite. Our lives are too complicated for us to go individually soap-boxing with any effectiveness. But, also, we cannot do without the older verities. We cannot do without character, and hope, and aspiration, and the language and experiences which enable us to tell the fraud from the real. I [38] am not sure how important it is whether people smoke cigarettes or not, but I am very sure that we cannot live with our present cities. And without valid individuals and organizations we will not regain our control of them.

We need to reach "the people," but we need also to reach each other, before we can hope to build up promising social complexes and configurations. How to do so is a practical question, but, I underscore and insist, it is also and urgently a cultural question. We cannot afford specialists who know all about machinery and statistics, and nothing about human nature. We cannot afford persons like the Air Force cadet who was enthusiastic about his Service's brand-new plant near Colorado Springs, and who cheerfully explained to a journalist that it had everything except tradition, and who needs tradition? This was shortly before a substantial number of his mates attempted to institute a tradition of cheating at the Academy.

Practical questions are also cultural questions. And the public needs poets and storytellers to help articulate a pattern of its valid and fructifying desires. I look at our present literary shambles, and assert that it can learn from the muckrakers in both respects. The best of the muckrakers had imagination. They lived with the questions they discussed. They sought ways to present them so that they could be appreciated by anyone who had decent instincts and understanding. They helped create places in which people could meet and work out solutions.

Strategic to such undertakings in their generation was the settlement house. Here was a private agency which attracted intellectuals, workers, immigrants, public officials—almost every species of citizen—to help define the social needs of the city. I do not mean that we today need new settlement houses. We have them already, and conscientious men and women running them. But, somehow, they are no longer strategic.

But what would be more strategic? We know that money by itself will not buy effective anti-poverty agencies. We know that trying to ape the New Deal will not give us a Newer Deal. Times have changed, not only since the 1900's, but since the 1920's and 1930's. Conditions are different. Our distraught younger generation [39] is keen on appreciating this fact, but as weak as its elders in providing solutions for today.

We could use a public debate capable of clarifying the interests and strengths of our various publics. But I suggest that it will be a futile debate if it lacks the third dimension of experience, presented and analyzed without impudence, and in what we call depth.

We need the competence of city planners and social workers. But we need as much, perhaps more, the competence of writers who can understand them and challenge them, if necessary, and bring professionals and concerned citizens together for what we call "a meeting of minds." How we create clichés as a substitute for the tangibles we lack! How many conferences and "dialogues" have you attended to no purpose?

Yet, we need such writers and other humanists more than the technicians, because the latter can always be evoked by money and status incentives, Humanists of the proper stripe cannot. They can only be a product of the public will. And we have lost much we would have to regain before we can hope to meet again on real levels of sophistication. We have lost much of our sense of history as experience. We have lost almost all of our poetry. I have even heard the concept of "the whole man" ridiculed by a sociologist proud of his asinine "specialty," without any spontaneous retorts of indignation from his large audience.

As a result of such dulled and blinded social understanding, we get caught in fantastic traps, and are not even dismayed by being shown up in all our public bankruptcy. How did we come to produce what one writer called The Red Decade, and then go on to what is almost universally called The McCarthy Era? How did we come to produce, at great public expense, such a dreary fiasco as our U-2 adventure and its bizarre pilot, Gary Powers? Our Bay of Pigs catastrophe is classic in its utter, unpardonable ineptness. It can be said plainly that there were hundreds of experts who knew, not conjecturally but absolutely, what the realities were in Cuba. But, from the University of Florida to the University of Southern California, they were not asked, they were not consulted.

Worse, our subsequent journalism was largely a study in rationalization, rather than in soul-searching analysis. The fault, I emphasize, is the public's as well as the journalist's. But there is no gain in second-guessing or in upbraiding. Our problem is always to make the future more promising than the past. And I therefore suggest:

We need to be more sophisticated. Henry Miller and Jack Kerouac, Mort Sahl and Lenny Bruce represent ignorance and naïveté. Ralph Nader is not enough. He thinks Americans want safer cars, whereas we have seen that it is not yet clear what Americans want. We need to mull over our modern crises and determine what they mean to us. Hence, there is no question at all of admiring muckraking for muckraking's sake, let alone of hoping to apply "the lessons of the past" mechanically to the present. It is rather a question of studying our social psychology and learning to deal with it, as one citizen to another. The muckraking experience can help us do so. Fresh, energetic reading of its particular missions and techniques must give enlightening results in the present—it can't help doing so. [41]

21. Five Myths of Consumership
Dallas Smythe

Andrew Fletcher said in 1704, "I believe if a man were permitted to write all the ballads, he need not care who should make the laws of the nation." Our culture includes not only traditional forms of "high" culture such as painting and literature but also "popular culture"—the radio and TV, the screen and theatre, pocket books, phonograph records, popular songs, pornography, both "hard" and "soft," etc. Indeed the borderline between popular culture and all consumption goods has been obliterated by Madison Avenue. For at least a generation now we in North America have become accustomed to endowing our automobiles with virility, our refrigerators with sensual pleasure, our breakfast cereals with athletic prowess, our shaving cream with the taste of lemon/lime. I argue that our popular culture is dominated today by an economic system that regards life, people and things primarily as aspects of consumption. The basic myth of our culture is that consumption is the goal of life.

Twenty years ago Harold Innis said that the purpose of institutions is to help us make the right decisions at the right time. He went on from there to say that the application of mass production to the communications industry (referring then just to print media and radio) had atomized previous institutions—the family, the church, the labor union—over the preceding eighty years. We must now recognize that the constituencies of these institutions are substantially under the control of the private government which is our privately owned economic system. This is not

Source: *The Nation*, January 20, 1969, pp. 82–84. Reprinted by permission of the publisher.

21. Five Myths of Consumership 251

to say that evil men run the economic system, or that a conspiracy has betrayed our nonbusiness institutions or taken them over. But it is to say that, pursuing its rational self-interest, the business community *as a whole* has created a situation whereby we subordinate our lives to its values. We live according to the consumption myth. How does it work?

A society, looking at North America as a unit, is like a voluntary organization—a club, or a neighborhood improvement association—in that it works from an agenda that is agreed to either explicitly or implicitly. What is left off the agenda does not get considered attention. And popular culture, by filling our time with commercial actions and values, sets an agenda which gives consumption the top priority. I recall a recent advertisement in the *New York Times* which filled a full page with the message: "Buy Something." The popular culture's imperative—"Buy Something"—is the most important educational influence in North America today.

Just as a society lives by the agenda set by its popular culture, the popular culture rests on the agenda established by mass communication. The top priority for the mass media is consumption. Mass communications market mass-produced consumer goods. Without the marketing services of the communications media, the consumer goods industries—food, automobiles, drugs, etc.—could not dispose of their mass-produced products.

The mass media perform this marketing function by educating the population to be dutiful consumers. The [82] educational process starts early. Before they can read, almost before they can talk, children are exposed to the bombardment of advertising messages on TV and radio. Skillfully engineered "point of sale" displays reinforce the educational experience when a mother shops the supermarket, with her child perched on the shopping cart, monitoring the whole operation. In this way, the child learns the importance of products. Lessons so learned are reinforced daily throughout our lives.

The explicit commercial message is thus the prime item on the commercial mass medium agenda. Commercial announcements on TV cost much more per minute than do the entertainment programs they frame. They are engineered with great care and much experimentation by the most sophisticated techniques.

This raises an interesting question. Is the broadcast program material the product which the commercial broadcasting industry produces? The program material cannot be the chief product because it brings in no revenue from the audience to the broadcasting station. In fact, in economic terms, the program material broadcast commercially is a giveaway

—an inducement to the population to become viewers or listeners. The chief product of the commercial broadcasters is the audience itself. Viewers and listeners are counted by market surveys, evaluated in terms of income level, age and sex, packaged and sold to advertisers.

In saying that the program material is a giveaway, I do not mean to overlook its importance. It is in fact carefully engineered. Take *The Monkees,* for example, which was engineered as any consumer commodity is engineered. The market was researched. Other entertainers, and particularly the Beatles, were analyzed to determine what characteristics in a program would "deliver" a young audience to the advertiser. A formula was developed, and the agency or network set out to recruit the elements that would fill it. The young men who came to comprise the Monkees did not even know one another until this process was near completion. From among hundreds at auditions, each was selected because he best embodied some appeals, some myths, which would "draw" and "hold" the audience. But this was only the beginning. The Monkees had to be publicized, advertised. Crowds had to be created and manipulated to produce pushing and fighting for autographs. The public had to be taught to resonate when the myth which is *The Monkees* was mentioned. At that point the broadcasters were ready to produce *the audiences* for *The Monkees* which could be sold to the advertisers.

Finally, on this point, national advertisers tell their writers just what sort of entertainment they wish to broadcast. One major advertiser of breakfast food in the United States and Canada not long ago was instructing its writers:

> In general, the moral code of the characters in our dramas will be more or less synonymous with the moral code of the bulk of the American middle class, as it is commonly understood. There will be no material that may give offense, either directly or by inference, to any organized minority group, lodge or other organizations, institutions, residents of any state or section of the country, or a commercial organization of any sort. This will be taken to include political organizations, fraternal organizations, college and school groups, labor groups, industrial, business and professional organizations, religious orders, civic clubs, memorial and patriotic societies (Anti-Tobacco League, for example), athletic organizations, women's groups, etc., which are in good standing.
>
> We will treat mention of the Civil War carefully, mindful of the sensitiveness of the South on this subject. No written material may be used that might give offense to our Canadian neighbors. . . . There will be no material for or against sharply drawn national or regional controversial issues. . . . Where it seems fitting, the characters should reflect recog-

nition and acceptance of the world situation in their thoughts and actions, although in dealing with war, our writers should minimize the "horror" aspects. . . . Men in uniform shall not be cast as heavy villains or portrayed as engaging in any criminal activity. There will be no material on any of our programs which could in any way further the concept of business as cold, ruthless and lacking all sentiment or spiritual motivation.

Similar instructions go out to writers from many national advertisers. If such a process took place in schools or universities we should call it indoctrination and brainwashing. It is no less brainwashing when it takes place on the instruction of private business. Commercial indoctrination educates us in the myth that consumption is a sufficient goal, a sufficient substance for life. This is the basic myth.

A second, correlative myth cultivated systematically by mass media and the private enterprise system, is that the consumer is king; that he rules the system; can always turn off the switch, is in fact free to choose among products. If there were any substance to this myth, the Madison Avenue myth makers and their platoons of consumer preference engineers would not have done their job and not earned their salaries. Unfortunately, they have done their jobs and earned their salaries, large though they may be.

A third myth grows directly out of the pivotal importance of the commercial mass media to the marketing of goods. This is that some special magic resides in "communication." When an institution, be it the family, the church, a government agency, a business organization faces any kind of internal problem, the up-to-date "sophisticated" reaction is to call the difficulty one of communication. The aura that attends the doctor, or for that matter [83] the medicine man, now surrounds those who call themselves experts in communications. Possibly no single person has contributed more to this mystification than Marshall McLuhan, whose brilliant but unsystematic essays serve to confuse people and thus create the mystery which requires the services of a medicine man for practical application. The hearty welcome which McLuhan's theme, "The medium is the message," receives from advertisers, their agencies and broadcasters is not surprising. If the content of the mass media is not important, if the medium *is* the message, then criticism of program policy is irrelevant. "The medium is the message," whatever McLuhan means by it, translates only too easily into the proposition that the act of consumership is the sufficient object of the exercise.

The fourth myth connected with the consumer system is designed to obscure the fact that the huge corporations which dominate North American economic life have preempted large chunks of the roles formerly played by other institutions. In the United States, where this myth originated, it centered on the assumption that the corporation is a legal entity and hence similar to an individual. Thurman Arnold put it this way in *The Folklore of Capitalism:*

> Since individuals are supposed to do better if left alone, this symbolism freed industrial enterprise from regulation in the interest of furthering any current morality. The laissez-faire religion, based on a conception of a society composed of competing individuals, was transferred automatically to industrial organizations with nationwide power and dictatorial forms of government.
>
> This mythology gave the Government in Washington only a minor part to play in social organization. . . . Government in Washington was supposed to act so as to instil "confidence" in great business organizations.

One way of exposing this myth is to define government. It is any organization the final decisions of which are subject to no immediate appeal. In North America, then, there are parallel systems of government; the private and the public. And in essential matters the former has the last word. President Kennedy came off second best when he tried to overrule the steel companies a few years ago and his successor learned the lesson.

The fifth myth arises out of the fourth. It is that if the public government makes decisions in matters of communications policy application, this is censorship and automatically bad, but if private government makes such decisions, all will be well. A relatively small number of such decisions, made in the operation of the mass media of communications, involves the mass production of enormous amounts of content. I suggest that the myth that public government is malevolent while private government is benevolent is insupportable, especially in the absence of democratic process in the private government's decision making.

If this analysis of the myth-making picture of our consumption-tied economy is valid, what could, what should, be done about it? This is a question which the young people who so disturb many of us have been wrestling with for some time. While there is no single explanation for the increasingly urgent protests being made by beatniks, hippies, the New Left and the Yippies, one evident basis for their behavior is that they reject the consumer-tied system as inhuman, immoral and indecent. Their studied defiance of convention in matters of dress, hair styling and domestic arrangements is a protest against the irrelevance of the pursuit of consumption on a continent and in a world where other goals should prevail.

They tell us what these problems are: stubborn pockets of poverty where the delights of consumption are bitter illusions; neglect of the right of minority groups to a cultural identity of their own; abuse of the environment by the pollution of air and water which an unplanned economic system forces on us; irrational military adventures; imperial exploitation of underdeveloped by developed nations, and so on.

The young people's protests overlap those of the blacks whose concern for "soul" is also a defiance of consumership values. By their irritating, even infuriating, tactics, the young people are trying to force our attention upon these problems. Before cracking down on them from positions of power in the North American institutional structure, we should listen carefully to what they—the young and the blacks—are protesting.

If these protest movements do not manage to get the agenda of problems sorted out more sensibly—if the consumer society manages to absorb these rebellious people into safe, Establishment niches, then we shall be in trouble even deeper than we are today. We shall have proved ourselves so indoctrinated to the consumption-based life that we no longer care enough to take over our own institutions and make them serve our human needs.

Do I have a panacea—any easy solution to the problems arising from our slavery to what Erich Fromm calls the *"homo consumens"* myth? Of course not. I do feel that an essential first step toward that solution is to confront the facts honestly and, as Freud said, to face our guilt squarely. Assuming that that was done, I would say the next step was to rub the brainwash off some traditional notions. For example, the notion of planning. Faced with the necessity of planning for survival, the people of this continent have never shrunk from it. And I mean by planning simply policy making, followed by action, regardless of whose toes are stepped on.

We face a seamless web of persuasion and power based on the consumption drive of North American private industry. If the people are to be masters of their own fate they must plan for cultural survival. Planning does not mean breaking the machines or denying ourselves the benefits of modern technology. The Scandinavian countries, Holland and Switzerland, have disposed of that bugaboo. Planning does mean that public decisions must be accepted even when they tell private enterprise when and where and how to invest its capital. That is the nub of the planning issue and it must be squarely faced. If we do not accept planning on those terms, we have no real proposal for putting man first and consumption second. If we do plan on those terms, the mass media and the popular culture will be obliged to cultivate myths more compatible with human dignity and human values than the cluster of myths surrounding the consumption which now guide our lives. [84]

22. After Smokey the Bear, What?
Howard Luck Gossage

The word "image" is very popular in advertising, though not with me. I prefer the word "identity," what one *really* is; whereas "image" only means how one appears to other people. "Image" also has a somewhat fraudulent sound, as though you are trying to put something over which isn't entirely true. There's another, practical, reason for preferring "identity" over "image": it requires much less upkeep. Identity is like the sun, it radiates energy from a solid mass. Image, on the other hand, is like a balloon, all surface, and spends far too much of its time avoiding pin pricks.

Advertising as an industry has always been morbidly preoccupied with its own image; largely, I think, because it has little notion of its real identity. So it is not surprising that many of us have grave reservations about the system generally, even though we may find satisfaction in our own work.

I didn't realize how widespread these reservations were until a few years ago when advertising was having one of its recurring attacks of chronic imagitis; which is like Madison Avenue flu except that you only lose face, not the account. I can't recall exactly what [1] brought on this particular attack. Either the Feds had caught some of the boys trying to make a piece of non-sandpaper look better groomed through better shaving, or the Food and Drug folks had taken exception to frosting an angel food cake on TV with brushless lather.

At any rate, *Time* decided to do a round-up story on how advertising

Source: A speech before the Western Association of Advertising Agencies, January 27, 1969. Reprinted by permission of Mrs. Gossage.

men felt about advertising morals. Eventually they got down to me and a *Time* reporter came by and interviewed me for 45 minutes, during which time, knowing me, I probably didn't shut my mouth once; thousands and thousands of golden words. The next week *Time* sent by a photographer *and* a reporter who wanted to clear up a few points from my earlier filibuster. He was wonderfully attentive and respectful as I blatted out my brains for another 45 minutes.

A couple of weeks after that the story appeared and, with feverish fingers, I opened to the business section of the magazine, wondering how many pages they had devoted to my world-shaking opinions. My picture was there, all right, but out of 90 minutes of talk, just one sentence, a direct quotation; it was this: "I don't know a first-class brain in the business who has any respect for it." That was it in its entirety: "I don't know a first-class brain in the business who has any respect for it." [2]

Well, I almost fainted. I'm an outspoken man, and I'm sure I said it, but that's a pretty blunt statement to see in print with nothing to soften it or qualify it. And I had no wish to overly offend all the people I know in advertising. And I was certain that I'd get a lot of telephone calls and letters from people who were offended. A day passed, a week passed, a month passed, and not one call or letter attacking me. I didn't broach the subject myself, of course. Then one day, I was riding in a plane from New York with one of our industry's most eminent spokesmen, also quoted in the *Time* article, and I asked him if he'd noticed my published comment. He said, of course he had. I told him I hadn't gotten one beef from it and I wondered why. He said, "Well, Howard, I guess it's true, isn't it?"

Is it true? If it is, I can think of several reasons why. They aren't secrets; they are perfectly evident to anyone inside the business. The first to come to mind is the general level of ethical hypocrisy. The 4As and, I imagine, your own association, have rules condemning speculative presentations—which is advertisingese for stealing—at least, not from one another, and yet, I wonder whether there is an agency man in this room who hasn't at some time been party to stealing an account from somebody else in this room. I don't know what the answer to this is except [3] to repeal the rules. Of course you could resign from the association, but that would be even worse. It's nice to be able to keep your eye on a lot of your competitors at one time, even though it's only once a month at dinner.

Another thing which is likely to breed a certain amount of disrespect for advertising among its practitioners is the triviality that constitutes most of big advertising. I mean just that: the big money in advertising is not in important items and commodities, but in products that are economic pipsqueaks: deodorants, cosmetics, beverages, soaps, toothpaste, hair preparations, patent medicines, tobacco, breakfast foods, and so on. These constitute most of the dollar volume of national advertising; over 80 percent of television, for example. Well, there is nothing wrong with advertising these products except that (if you're the type that thinks about such matters) it may dawn on you that if they didn't advertise at all it wouldn't make very much difference to anybody —or to the economy. Oh, it would affect the client's economy and our economy, but that would be the end of it. The world would just be a little quieter as everybody switched over to private labels.

This realization is liable to give you a sense of futility, especially as you get older in the business. Mr. James Webb Young, perhaps the dean of American copywriters, had an interesting thing to say on this subject a few years ago. I asked him how he happened to retire [4] from the advertising business, and he said: "One morning I woke up and I didn't give a hoot whether they sold more Quaker Oats than I sold Cream of Wheat."

A third factor that is apt to affect our regard for the business we are in are the abuses of public trust and public taste. These will range from incidents smacking of downright fraud accompanied by action from the FTC to simple bad taste and a disregard for the decent opinion of mankind. The industry tries to pretend that these incidents are few and far between and that, when they do occur, they are committed by fringe or fly-by-night operators. It just isn't true; they happen all the time, and the bulk of intelligence-insulting, banal, tasteless advertising is done by the biggest agencies for the biggest clients. If you doubt this, just watch television objectively, especially during the day or late at night. That a great many of these abuses can be laid at the door of the media makes little difference, for it is advertising and its system that bears the blame and is, in fact, ultimately responsible.

Well, you may say, most of the defects I have mentioned are present in any business or profession in some form or another. That may be so, but there is an important difference: advertising is the single most powerful propaganda medium the world has ever seen. Moreover, it directly or indirectly controls all of our mass media. [5] I can be more specific. The fact is that advertising will tend to shape all the contents of any communications medium that it dominates economically, and in our society that is very nearly the lot. Commercial broadcasting has always been entirely dependent on advertising for its existence, and publications have given over more and more of their financial control to advertising's absentee landlordism over the years. With economic control automatically goes control over content; not by intent, but through the simple ability of advertising to bestow or withhold its favors.

If a TV station, for example, is not getting its share of advertising it will change its programming pretty damn quick, and generally so that it is exactly like other programming which advertising already cottons to. If you have wondered at the dreary sameness of broadcasting, this is the reason. If you are looking for a culprit to blame, it is the economic process which permits it. This same process has knocked off, or materially changed, most national magazines during your lifetime; and over half of our metropolitan newspapers have died, not because their readers didn't want them but because advertisers didn't. No hard feelings, of course; nor any other kind, as we shall see.

That advertising is the possessor of this awesome, if unsought, power over our freedom of the press is, I think, unarguable. That it doesn't want it and shouldn't have it is immaterial. The truth is that advertising [6] has got it *and* the responsibility implicit in such enormous power.

In the face of all this, it seems positively girlish for big advertising, as personified by the 4As, to be so absorbed by concern for its own image as to sponsor a recent book which, as far as I can see, consists of but one question from first to last: "What do you think of me?" This book, titled *Advertising in America: The Consumer View,* is jointly sponsored by the American Association for Advertising Agencies and the Harvard Business School. After years of research and collating of results, it came out last summer in a rosy glow of self-congratulations somewhat reminiscent of those old newspaper editorial cartoons of Capital and Labor shaking hands.

At first I was a little puzzled by this strange mating although I could see why the advertising boys were pleased at posing with the Harvards: respectability at last! But I couldn't see why it should work the other way around, until I remembered how far down the academic totem pole a business school is at any university. At Harvard it must rank with, but after, Phys Ed. And the advertising department must rate considerably below that. [7] (This is more than just a guess on my part. A few years ago I taught for a term at an Eastern university and, shortly after I arrived, the president gave a reception for all the "Distinguished Visiting Professors," as they called us. I was introduced to one of my new colleagues, a European, the Dean of the Faculty of Arts and Letters at the University of Brussels. The president of the university said, "Mr. Gossage here is from San Francisco; he is one of our distinguished visiting professors this year." The Belgian said, "Oh really? Of what?" And the president said, "Advertising." Well, fellows, you should have seen his face; it was as though somebody had hit him over the head with a two-by-four. He stared at me speechless for maybe fifteen seconds before he was led away like a stunned ox.)

Back to our book, as it explains in the lengthy foreword, it concerns itself with only two things: (1) How much do consumers like or dislike particular ads or categories of ads? and (2) What do consumers think of advertising generally? Not to keep you on tenterhooks, the answer to the first question is: they like some ads, they don't like others. The answer to the second is less clear-cut: 41 percent of Americans think of themselves as favorable toward advertising; 14 percent unfavorable, 34 percent have mixed opinions, and 8 percent are indifferent. Now this may not seem like much of a vote of confidence, and the pickings may seem pretty pallid after all that research. But what else can you expect when you ask questions like that? [8] And what is wrong with questions like that? They remind me of that story about the reporter who interviewed Abraham Lincoln's widow as she was leaving Ford's Theatre. He asked her: "Aside from that, Mrs. Lincoln, how did you like the show?" In other words, such aesthetic questions—and their answers—have no real significance when isolated from the process that causes them. What I mean is this: whether a given ad—or every ad—which appears in a medium pleases or displeases is beside the point. Advertising, through its economic domination, tends to control the entire medium, programming, editorial matter, and all. It is a total environment. So to ask consumers how they like the ads alone is like asking a galley slave what he thinks of the job calisthenicswise. It utterly disregards advertising's encompassing role in our mass media and its implied higher public obligation.

Before proceeding, I see no evidence that the advertising industry is in the slightest aware that this higher obligation exists. Indeed, this joint 4As-Harvard effort will probably be hailed in some quarters as the high watermark of advertising's public responsibility. In confirmation of this, the book quotes the Chairman of the 4As' Committee on Improving Advertising as saying: "For what may be the first time in American business history, as important industry has not only agreed to live in a fishbowl, but has exhibited the glass bowl itself and invited the world to look in." [9] Now, this is a perfectly sincere statement, I'm sure. Unfortunately, an industry which, inadvertently or not, controls our mass communications is not a fishbowl, but a vast ocean. And all 200 million of us are in it together.

If advertising is only dimly aware of its own identity, it may be because it has no very profound sense of public responsibility. The late Nicholas Samstag, himself an advertising man, once said: "To explain to the advertising industry that public responsibility goes beyond Smokey the Bear is like trying to convince a ten-year-old that making love is more fun than a chocolate ice cream cone."

Advertising's industry-wide efforts in the public weal have, over the years, been consistent and well-meaning, though not enough to offend anybody. Of the resulting ads, I can't think of one that was in the slightest debatable, unless you are against safe driving or for cancer. In fairness, the industry *did* take a firm, fearless stand some years ago. During World War II, it came out four-square against Hitler and for buying Series E Bonds. Lately, the effort seems to have settled down to warnings about throwing garbage out of moving cars and the inadvisability of being really poor. And of course there is always "Keep California Green." I've often wondered how you'd go about doing that; do you take a bucket of water from home and slosh it on the yellow hills during the dry season? [10]

Nor must we forget Smokey the Bear. I am sorry to relate that Smokey, far and away advertising's most successful public service campaign, is viewed as a pure horror by many noted conservationists and ecologists. It seems that in the natural course of events, any given stretch of forest will have a localized ground fire that burns off the accumulating underbrush about once every six years. Smokey, however, as you know, absolutely forbids *any* fires at any time. Therefore, the brush piles up and piles up so that once every twenty years, when lightning strikes or spontaneous combustion—which I have never really understood—occurs, you get a real monster of a fire that wipes out everything.

I don't know why this news about Smokey being a flop cheers me up, but it does. I think it must be because every time I see one of those posters with him staring right at me with those mournful eyes I am sure that he thinks I, personally, set the last forest fire with my own two hands.

Now, I can understand why these industry public service campaigns are so innocuous. I imagine that the possible subjects all go through committees, and you know how committees are. But the one thing that advertising could undebatably do—reformation and improving of our communications media—is never tackled at all. [11] This, despite the fact that advertising is the one force, because of its economic power, that could improve things. Do things need improving? I think so. More and more magazines and newspapers fold every year. It seems to me that advertising would wish to remedy that if only because you can't run magazine and newspaper ads if you don't have magazines and newspapers. I have often wondered why, when a city's newspapers are strike-bound, the advertising industry does not step in and offer to intermodiate, if not out of public spirit, then out of self-interest. The mediocre mess that characterizes television and radio broadcasting certainly could stand some cleaning up, and advertising alone has enough economic heft to insist on it. As it stands, greedy practices on the part of station operators make broadcasting a worse and worse buy every day; not to mention the fact that the citizenry, to whom broadcasting legally belongs, deserve a good deal better than they are getting. We, as individuals, deserve better too; I'd like to be able to turn on the TV set without turning it off immediately.

Could advertising as an industry really do something about our media? I don't think there's any doubt about it. You know the riddle that goes: "What do you get when you cross a budgy and a tiger? I don't know, but when it speaks, I listen." There's no threat like an economic threat. [12] Thus far I have spoken of advertising responsibility only in industry-wide terms. The media reforms I have suggested are beyond the scope of a single agency, no matter how large. I should imagine, however, that if an association such as yours should devote one tenth of the time and effort that went into the 4As-Harvard effort we might see some really worthwhile results. I can tell you that if advertising doesn't do it, that somehow, sometime—possibly sooner than you think—there will be one hell of a shakeup and legislation will remove the matter from our hands entirely.

It's the sort of thing that has happened to the automobile industry already. And it will probably happen to the communications industry in the same way: a Ralph Nader will come along and amplify on just what I have been talking about tonight. And there it will be, the biggest, messiest scandal in the history of our country: buying and selling of free public franchises for private gain, corruption in high places and all. It may be much noisier and smellier than the Nader affair, because, nice as it is to have safe cars, it is not one of our constitutional guarantees, and freedom of the press is.

I think that reformatory legislation is inevitable—starting with the putting of teeth into the Federal Communications Commission. I think it would be splendid and wise if the advertising industry, as its first worthwhile act in the public interest, led the parade [13] instead of being dragged along behind it. However, my guess, judging on past performance, is that it will be dragged along, screaming bloody murder every inch of the way.

Interestingly enough, the advertising industry's timidity and mediocrity at dealing with the hard facts of our time is not necessarily true of individual agencies. Some very fine and effective campaigns have been instigated by agencies acting on their own, and the number of these campaigns increases all the time. A couple that come to mind are Young and Rubicam's "Give a Damn" ghetto improvement campaign and Carl Ally's continuing Clean Air project. Los Angeles agencies have seemed to me unusually active in public causes; I am particularly aware of Carson/Roberts' efforts over the years.

I have a notion that these projects, which are now regarded as extracurricular activities, will more and more become the chief work of advertising agencies, corresponding more or less to the editorial or

22. After Smokey the Bear, What? 263

program material in a medium; whereas product advertising will be occupying the same relative positioning as it does in a magazine or newspaper—essential but in balance. An advertising agency is in fact a medium and ought to regard itself so. Perhaps this is the answer to advertising's search for identity. [14]

There are a couple of reasons for thinking this may come to pass, or is already becoming so. In the first place, there is evidence that advertising is obsolescent as a marketing tool but is relatively unexplored as a propaganda medium. I use propaganda in the original sense of propagation. I personally believe that advertising's future is in the propagation and cultivation of ideas, and not necessarily on a free, public service basis. Our agency specializes in propagational advertising, and we do it for money. I think that the market will increase dramatically in the near future as business finds it more and more desirable, and necessary, to speak to people—not consumers—about the real problems of our world and our society—and to do it interestingly and engagingly. It is beginning to dawn on even the most obtuse corporate minds that we are in the midst of a real revolution on every level of our existence and that profits, sweet though they may be, may have little meaning if there is no world left to spend them in.

Actually, I think that enlightened business thinking is considerably ahead of advertising in this respect. And I also think that advertising had better tool up as rapidly as it can so that it is able to anticipate and express this thinking. The chief reason for advertising's existence is to give tongue to the needs of business. In the past, this has consisted mostly of selling the product. But the product itself is changing from an item, or even a range of items, to an idea, an involving process. [15]

I think the time is rapidly passing when either advertising or the business it serves can afford to squander so much talent and thought and wealth on merely selling things. The world is moving very fast and there is a great deal to do. I think we had better do what we can while there is still time to do anything at all. [16]

23. The Press at Bay, 1970
Elie Abel

A word, to begin with, concerning the theme of these remarks. I have chosen to discuss "The Press at Bay" and you have every right to ask that I define my subject matter precisely. At bay, the dictionary tells us, means: "The state or position of one obliged to face an antagonist, or a difficulty, when escape is impossible."

Fair enough. Clearly the American press today faces antagonists and difficulties as never before in my lifetime. It is my contention that the press—by which I mean not only our daily newspapers, weekly magazines and other periodicals, but also broadcast news whether on radio or television—is under suspicion and to a degree on trial. It finds itself seriously challenged by elements in government and by loud voices emerging from that great gray mass of readers and viewers whom, in less parlous times, H. L. Mencken was fond of dismissing as the Booboisie. Mencken also coined the aphorism that no publisher ever lost money by underestimating the intelligence of the American people, not a view that any newspaperman would dare to utter in our day even if he believed it were still true.

I can remember when newspapers, together with their editors and publishers, enjoyed a kind of immunity or, if you prefer, a kind of benign neglect on the part of the public or, for that matter, the government. How the press organized itself, who owned it, what party line it

Source: Annual Memorial Lecture sponsored by the Twin Cities Local, American Newspaper Guild, AFL-CIO, and the School of Journalism and Mass Communication, University of Minnesota, Minneapolis, October 15, 1970. Reprinted by permission of the author.

followed, how faithfully or unfaithfully it reported the news—all this was a matter of supreme indifference to the average reader. If he happened to live in a sizeable city, say 30 or 40 years ago, he might have a choice of newspapers competing in the same marketplace. He could take the one that most nearly reflected his own tastes and attitudes or the one that he found the least objectionable. But our reader of the Thirties left it to a handful of specialists to ponder such questions as how newspapers were put together and by whom controlled, or how the men they employed were recruited or trained, or whether they came from the Southwest or the Northeast. [3]

Newspapermen as members of an honorable craft—and I, for one, will not quarrel with anyone who contends that we are at best craftsmen, striving to become professionals—could be pretty nosy about how the public business was conducted. The nosier, in fact, the better the newsman. So newsmen have no right to complain if the public pokes its nose into their business today. In the United States—somewhat less so in the United Kingdom—newsmen have demanded the right to peer into the inner workings of government at all levels and, if they were nosy enough, frequently succeeded. All this in the name of the people's right to know, not (heaven help us) in the name of their proprietor, whose primary qualification to publish a newspaper most often could be related to the wisdom he had shown in choosing his father or grandfather. No, it was always in the name of the people that the press demanded to know how public money was being spent. To the point where a private business, conducted for profit, came to regard itself as a species of public institution—at the very least, a common scold, at best a kind of ombudsman.

Leave aside for the moment, the proprieties of such an arrangement, the individual owner's sense of responsibility or lack of responsibility toward his community or his readers. Never mind whether he was brave or cowardly, progressive or reactionary, unselfish or greedy, worthy or unworthy of trust. We'll get to that later.

The fact of the matter is that you can trace back the role of the press as ombudsman a very long way. In 1774, for example, the first Continental Congress, meeting in Philadelphia, addressed a letter to the inhabitants of Quebec, outlining the rights to which all citizens of British North America were or, ought to be, entitled, and listing among these rights, the freedom of the press. It was perhaps a notion that needed some explaining 200 years ago. The importance of press freedom, in the words of that letter, amounted to this:

> . . . besides the advancement of truth, science, morality and arts in general in its diffusion of liberal sentiments on the administration of govern-

ment, its ready communication of thoughts between subjects and its consequential promotion of union among them, whereby oppressive officers are shamed or intimidated into more honorable and just modes of conducting affairs.

The press as the instrument, mark you, of shaming oppressive officers into more honorable and just conduct; quite apart from looking to it as the means of advancing the arts, sciences, morality and truth; what a burden of responsibility fell upon the poor printers of that day with their battered cabinet of type and their primitive hand-cranked press. Publishers could still be poor in those days; few of them, I am sure, were welcome in the best homes or clubs. That came later. Yet so overpowering was the late 18th-century belief in the word that these half-starved printers, ink-stained [4] wretches, were somehow expected to serve as teacher, preacher, ombudsman and guardian of truth, all at once.

Not a bad prospectus, that, for a newspaper or television program in 1970. But where is the contemporary editor or producer who would dare to aim so high? Where the contemporary public official or educator who would accept such a division of labor in the community?

If the aims of the press today are less exalted than those suggested by the Continental Congress, its performance long ago outstripped those pamphleteering forebears, many of them so wildly partisan that they disallowed even a pretense of fairness. Go back, as I have done, and look at some of the journals which chronicled, for example, the American Revolution. To the Boston Gazette and the Newport Mercury in 1776, the men who painted their faces black to dump those celebrated cases of tea in Boston Harbor were patriots, of course, patriots, heroes, rebels with a just cause. But the Tory press of the time, concerned with maintaining British colonial rule, denounced them as: "Truly amoral men . . . religious hypocrites . . . treacherous and seditious . . . of morose and sour tempers." In short, the very notion of objectivity or fairness, of presenting more than one side of any public issue so the citizens could make up their own minds, was undreamed of. One wonders what Spiro Agnew would have made of that kind of reporting.

It seems to me a mighty irony that the press should be losing credibility with the public at a time when its standards are higher than ever before. Consider, for example, the recent testimony of Attorney General Mitchell by way of justifying subpoenas designed to extract from reporters information that they have gained through confidential relationships with such news sources as, for example, Black Panthers.

It is the very strength of the press today—both editorial and economic—(Mitchell says) which has helped to bring on this controversy over the subpoena power.

Editorially, more and more news organizations are giving coverage to the type of controversial events which tend to come under government scrutiny. And their news coverage of these developments has become more intense and more sophisticated. Because of their healthy economic conditions, news organizations today are willing to detach a reporter for weeks, or even months, to study one issue.

Now you might have thought that a Federal official so concerned for the public welfare might follow this glowing tribute to a free and independent press with a solemn commitment to avoid any action that might undercut that independence, intimidate honest reporters and rob the people of the truth they need to live by. If so you would have misjudged John Mitchell. For he goes on to say:

The result is that the American people are not only told about [5] the surface news event, which may itself entail a violation of the law, but the public is also told about the planning of the event, the personalities of the major players, and the alleged motives of the group involved. . . . ALL FACTORS, the attorney general adds, somewhat ominously, OF SOME CONSEQUENCE IN AN INVESTIGATION.

There are times, Mr. Mitchell says, when reporters and photographers have more information about a case under investigation than the government itself . . . information that the government, in his words, "finds difficult, if not impossible, to obtain through its investigatory agencies."

In short, the press often does a better job of investigating than the FBI. And it follows as night follows day that the press must, when called upon, make up for the shortcomings of the FBI by surrendering its own information, photographs, tapes or films to the law enforcers. So much for the Mitchell Doctrine, in its latest, most refined form. What does it tell us about the future? First, quite directly, that the more thorough and penetrating the performance of the press, the more frequently will it be called upon to assist the government in prosecutions. The other side of the coin, not stated explicitly, presumably reads that if the press will lay off the big, tough, investigative stories, the government will leave the newsmen alone. It's not a bargain that appeals to me or, I would think, to most working reporters and editors.

There is, it seems to me, no blinking the central issue: any editor or publisher who submits to this kind of pressure from on high is turning his own reporters into informers, more specifically, unpaid agents of the prosecuting branch of government. He may in so doing buy good will in certain powerful quarters. But he is at the same time, I would contend, driving a coach and horses through the First Amendment and forever forfeiting any moral claim to its protection.

I would add that in this terrible, turbulent time, when the press is so widely viewed with suspicion, it is more important than ever before that responsible reporters should have access to the dissidents and the radicals in our midst. Without accurate information, democracy is blind; and in its blindness can easily stumble, doing irreparable damage to itself and to all of us as citizens.

The heart of the argument against compelling journalists to testify as to their sources or other confidential matters is this—that the very act of handing over notes or tapes or film to the prosecution has the effect of drying up those sources. This can scarcely be regarded as a new or radical doctrine. The Supreme Court, in a variety of contexts and cases over many decades, has repeatedly emphasized the value of anonymity in the collection or dissemination of information. The Court also has recognized that the effect of identifying those sources of information has been to stifle First Amendment freedoms out of fear of retaliation or punishment. [6]

You may well ask how it is that the free flow of news has not long since dried up. The answer is that until recently, prosecutors, government officials and others in a position to compel testimony have, for the most part, recognized at least *de facto* the privilege commonly asserted by newsmen. And in those rare instances where an interrogator sought to breach the privilege, the newsman has, almost uniformly, gone to jail or paid his fine rather than disclose his sources.

What has changed today is the climate of opinion: when so much of the populace is worried, unhappy, or frightened, federal prosecutors (taking their cue from Attorney General Mitchell) have tended to operate on the assumption that the celebrated silent majority is bound to approve any step taken in the name of law and order—even if someone else's Constitutional liberties are overriden in the process.

It is a battle that is never finally won or lost, I suppose. Each generation must fight its own battle against those who would suppress or tamper with the free flow of information. We are in the thick of just such a battle now. And not all the would-be suppressors are to be found in the Department of Justice. Consider, for example, the Vice President of the United States. Just a few months ago, I heard a distinguished lady journalist emeritus—I hope that does not sound too unchivalrous a description—reproach press people for behaving like sensitive plants whenever they are attacked or criticized. She was talking about the press response to Vice President Agnew's richly alliterative, and in my view intellectually impoverished, broadsides against us effete snobs. Her advice was to ignore Agnew, or laugh him off and get on with the job.

It is possible, I suppose, to laugh off some of the more simple minded things the Vice President has said. He argues, for example, that decisions about what news to ignore and what to play up are made by a handful of men who live in the Sodom and Gomorrah of our time, Washington and New York; they bask, he says, in their own provincialism (unlike, say, the wordly wise citizens of Towson, Maryland); moreover, they read the same newspapers and, horror of horrors, they talk constantly to one another. That makes them very special, you understand. Garagemen, undertakers and computer programmers, presumably, talk to themselves, not to one another. That's why they belong to the silent majority.

But there is another, more fundamental aspect of Agnewism that I, for one, do not find even faintly comic. It is the plain threat to impose upon the media a new Federal standard of what is news and how it should be reported, a threat that has already had its effect on some television broadcasters, enforcing further timidity upon the timid. They have a great deal to be timid about, you understand, because their licenses to do business at a spectacular profit come up for renewal by the FCC every three years.

Some accuse the press of showing an exaggerated alertness toward even the faintest trace of oppression or suppression on the part of higher authority; [7] a deeply American trait. That shrewd observer, Edmund Burke, in his second speech on conciliation with America back in 1775, described the educated people of the colonies as stubborn and litigious.

In other countries, Burke said: "The people, more simple, and of a less mercurial cast, judge of an ill principle in government only by an actual grievance; here they anticipate the evil and judge of the pressure of the grievance by the badness of the principle. They augur misgovernment at a distance, and sniff the approach of tyranny in every tainted breeze."

May I suggest that the process so acutely discerned by Burke almost 200 years ago is at work in our society today. I grant you, for example, that it may be premature to speak of a great wave of repression rolling across the land, a favorite theme with certain young radicals today. It hasn't happened yet; and it need not happen if we remain alert and courageous. But I cannot find fault with any reporter, editor or publisher—or for that matter *any concerned citizen* in this Age of Concern—who seeks to anticipate the evil that appears to loom up just over the horizon; to sniff the approach of tyranny, as Burke said, in every tainted breeze. Surely if we wait for tyranny to establish itself before raising the alarm it will then be too late.

The woods are full of media critics these days and some of the things they have to say are contradictory. For example, a national commission on violence criticizes broadcasters and the press for not giving more access to militant minority groups. The Vice President of the United States blasts the media for giving *too much* voice to militants and not enough to the Silent Majority. Obviously the critics can't have it both ways. My good friend Wes Gallagher, general manager of the Associated Press, has done some thinking on these matters and has come up with what he calls two immutable laws governing criticism of the media: First, criticism by the Government rises in direct proportion to the amount of news printed or broadcast which reflects unfavorably on the Government and its policies. Second, criticism by the public rises in direct proportion to the amount of news read or heard or seen that does not fit the reader's or the listener's preconceived ideas of what the news should be.

I would go a step further than Mr. Gallagher. I would argue that the public, to the extent that it has risen up in its wrath to smite the media today, is less concerned over how the news is reported than with the often grim, sometimes terrifying reality that is being reported. News today more and more is, and must necessarily be, concerned with the shortcomings of our society and of mankind in general. One can speak of the quality of life in America's great cities today only with heavy irony. The President orders American troops into Cambodia without Congressional sanction and in the certain knowledge that he is sharpening the alienation of young America from its elders. It has almost become a tiresome commonplace to talk about the poisoned air we breathe, the polluted waters that we drink or bathe in. The swift march of modern technology is creating problems faster than they [8] are being solved. More than 100 years after the Civil War a great many Black Americans are still waiting for deliverance. In the world at large there are today 136 accredited nations instead of the 66 that existed at the end of World War II. A great many of them are quarrelling with one another or actually warring with one another. And any effort to report the news of all these happenings is bound to discomfit, shake, even terrify many viewers. Not one of these unpleasant realities will go away by being ignored. Not one will dissolve if the press, in order to accommodate those readers and viewers who would like good news, were to report upon them in an optimistic and thus an inherently false way. That is the state of the world we live in. And if I had to fault the performance of the press and the broadcast media it would be that they treat some of these very major problems in too superficial a manner.

Perhaps it's not worth the effort to demolish Vice President Agnew's rather ramshackle argument. But the thought has occurred to some of us that applying the standards he and his claque would like to see in force must necessarily lead to the suppression of reality, that is to say, of truth. I, for one, cannot believe that the safety of the Republic depends upon a conspiracy to keep the people in ignorance. On the contrary, I can see graver dangers to American safety and survival arising from a stubborn refusal to look unpleasant facts in the face.

The men who wrote the Bill of Rights could never have accepted such a doctrine. They believed that a confrontation between the government and the press would benefit the people and assure them against arbitrary rule.

Admittedly, at the time the First Amendment was written this was a different country: small, weak, isolated from the embroilments of Europe. The press in those days was also small, weak and constantly on the edge of bankruptcy, needing perhaps more protection than it does today. But the adversary relationship between press and government is not obsolete, except as journalists make it so by being too fat, lazy and comfortable. We need it more than ever today, when government has become so enormous and impersonal that the citizen, alone and even in the mass, cannot seem to deflect it from its programmed course.

It is, I am sorry to say, an unequal contest. And I for one have no doubt that the proper role of the press, the Constitutional role, moreover, is to illuminate the faults and failings of our society where it finds them so that the people may know and demand their just redress. I wonder and worry whether most journalists are equal to the task: bold enough to attack the powerful; compassionate enough to defend the defenseless; tough enough to keep the heat on even when the kitchen gets very hot indeed; honest enough to admit their own errors on the front page, rather than back among the want ads.

I would be the first to agree that too many newspapers, broadcast stations and networks have not measured up to these high demands. With little [9] or no prompting, I could talk for hours about things that, in my view, the press does badly. But all of you have your own ideas on that score; in any case I would rather talk about some of the things that might be done to make it better and more responsible than to dwell on past failings.

I would submit that the time for letting things slide is past; that we are in something like a crisis of confidence, affecting all media, whether print or broadcast; and in my judgment we cannot much longer postpone a united effort to examine the shortcomings of the press—most broadly defined—to deal with that crisis by the most rigorous self-scrutiny.

It is my sober—and sobering—opinion that if we do not make the effort to police our own ranks, to label and expose malpractice where we know it exists, to raise and then maintain ethical standards, to deal honestly with the most vulnerable elements in the community, then others, less qualified and less kindly disposed, will move in and do the job for us.

Now I for one would have the gravest doubts about the kind of licensing for journalists recently proposed by Dr. Menninger, least of all any arrangement by which a government agency—be it state or federal—would have the power to decide who is—and who is not—qualified to work as a journalist.

But there are other remedies in our own hands if we have the wisdom and the strength to act. A number of ideas have been kicked around in recent months: Press Councils on the British model, for example; grievance machinery within the American Society of Newspaper Editors; a national institute or center or academy for continued study and appraisal of the communications media; even a new Hutchins Commission. I have no fixed preference in the matter. I am not wedded to any particular form or procedure, so long as two essential points are kept in mind: First, the job must be done by journalists sitting in judgment on their peers, not by outsiders; second, when fault is to be found it must be specific, naming names, so the public at large may know what is happening.

This nation is so vast and so various that a national press council would have what seems to me an impossible job just keeping track of the print and broadcast output. The task, in my judgment, can only be done on a local or regional basis. And I have a modest proposal to put before you tonight. It is that these Twin Cities, Minneapolis and St. Paul, might show the way for the rest of us by setting up a Twin Cities Press Council right here. You already have a Twin Cities Newspaper Guild. Your great symphony and your ball club now transcend city limits. Why not try, for the purpose of elevating standards in the craft as a whole, to use this broad community as a testing ground? The Press Council idea has not, till now, had a trial run in any metropolitan area of the United States. The Twin Cities strike me as perhaps the best place to determine whether it is an idea of value for the rest of the country.

You have many advantages here: strong newspapers, enlightened management, [10] broadcasters who are many of them genuinely concerned for the public interest; this great university and the many other excellent colleges and universities close at hand; a vital tradition of free inquiry.

This need not be a vastly expensive undertaking; not if your major publishers and broadcasters pledge their cooperation and support. And if the experiment is successful, it would (I suspect) transform the attitudes of many in the community, building trust and confidence in those standards of accuracy, responsibility and true professionalism that we claim for ourselves.

The press today, like the stag at bay, finds itself hounded by antagonists; escape may no longer be possible. In my judgment it must turn and confront the attacker, fighting as if its life were at stake. But it must at the same time look to its own shortcomings. A cowardly press or one so complacent that it does not see the need for self-improvement in a hurry, will get no better than it deserves. [11]

Bibliography

In addition to the works cited previously in this volume, the following books are relevant to the study of the mass media in the United States.

Bagdikian, Ben. *The Information Machines: Their Impact on Men and the Media.* New York: Harper & Row, 1971.

Barton, Roger. *Media in Advertising.* New York: McGraw-Hill, 1964.

Berlo, David K. *The Process of Communication: An Introduction to Theory and Practice.* New York: Holt, Rinehart & Winston, 1960.

Bogart, Leo. *The Age of Television.* New York: Frederick Ungar, 1956.

Boorstin, Daniel. *The Image; Or, What Happened to the American Dream.* New York: Atheneum, 1962.

Budd, Richard W., and Brent D. Ruben, eds. *Approaches to Human Communication.* New York: Spartan, 1972.

———, Robert K. Thorp, and Lewis Donohew. *Content Analysis of Communication.* New York: Macmillan, 1967.

Catledge, Turner. *My Life and the Times.* New York: Harper & Row, 1971.

Cohen, Bernard D. *The Press and Foreign Policy.* Princeton, N.J.: Princeton University Press, 1963.

Dizard, Wilson P. *Television: A World View.* Syracuse, N.Y.: Syracuse University Press, 1966.

Duncan, Hugh. *Communication and Social Order.* New York: Oxford University Press, 1962.

Ellul, Jacques. *The Technological Society.* New York: Knopf, 1964.

Emery, Edwin. *The Press and America: An Interpretative History of Journalism.* Englewood Cliffs, N.J.: Prentice-Hall, 1962.

Friedrich, Otto. *The Decline and Fall of the Saturday Evening Post.* New York: Harper & Row, 1970.

Friendly, Fred W. *Due to Circumstances Beyond Our Control.* New York: Random House, 1967.

Gerald, J. Edward. *The Social Responsibility of the Press.* Minneapolis, Minn.: University of Minnesota Press, 1963.

Glessing, Robert J. *The Underground Press in America.* Bloomington, Ind.: Indiana University Press, 1970.

Guback, Thomas. *The International Film Industry: Western Europe and America Since 1945.* Bloomington, Ind.: Indiana University Press, 1969.

Hixson, Richard F. *Isaac Collins: A Quaker Printer in 18th Century America.* New Brunswick, N.J.: Rutgers University Press, 1968.

Hunt, Todd. *Reviewing for the Mass Media.* Philadelphia: Chilton, 1972.

Jacobs, Norman, ed. *Culture for the Millions? Mass Media in Modern Society.* Boston: Beacon Press, 1965.

Johnson, Nicholas. *How to Talk Back to Your Television Set.* Boston: Little, Brown, 1970.

Kael, Pauline, *I Lost It at the Movies.* Boston: Little, Brown, 1965.

Key, V. O., Jr. *Public Opinion and American Democracy.* New York: Knopf, 1961.

Klapper, Joseph T. *The Effects of Mass Communication.* New York: Macmillan, 1962.

Lacy, Dan. *Freedom and Communication.* Urbana, Ill.: University of Illinois Press, 1965.

Larsen, Otto N., ed. *Violence and the Mass Media.* New York: Harper & Row, 1968.

Liebling, A. J. *The Press.* New York: Ballantine, 1964.

Lofton, John. *Justice and the Press.* Boston: Beacon Press, 1966.

Lyle, Jack, ed. *The Black American and the Press.* Los Angeles: Ward Ritchie Press, 1968.

MacDougall, Curtis D. *The Press and Its Problems.* Dubuque, Iowa: William C. Brown, 1964.

Machlup, Fritz. *Production and Distribution of Knowledge in the United States.* Princeton, N.J.: Princeton University Press, 1962.

Meier, R. L. *A Communications Theory of Urban Growth.* Cambridge, Mass.: M.I.T. Press, 1962.

Minor, Dale. *The Information War.* New York: Hawthorn, 1970.

Peterson, Theodore. *Magazines in the Twentieth Century.* Urbana, Ill.: University of Illinois Press, 1964.

Poirier, Richard. *The Performing Self.* New York: Oxford University Press, 1971.

Ramsaye, Terry. *A Million and One Nights: A History of the Motion Picture.* New York: Simon and Schuster, 1964.

Reston, James. *The Artillery of the Press: Its Influence on American Foreign Policy.* New York: Harper & Row, 1967.

Rivers, William L. *The Opinionmakers.* Boston: Beacon Press, 1965.

―――, et al. *Backtalk: Press Councils in America.* San Francisco: Canfield, 1972.

―――, Theodore Peterson, and Jay Jensen. *The Mass Media and Modern Society.* San Francisco: Rinehart Press, 1971.

Rosenthal, Raymond, ed. *McLuhan: Pro & Con.* New York: Funk and Wagnalls, 1968.

Schickel, Richard. *Movies: The History of an Art and an Industry.* New York: Basic Books, 1966.

Seldes, Gilbert. *The New Mass Media: Challenge to a Free Society.* Washington, D.C.: Public Affairs Press, 1968.

Smith, Alfred G., ed. *Communication and Culture.* New York: Holt, Rinehart & Winston, 1966.

Steiner, Gary A. *The People Look at Television: A Study of Audience Attitudes.* New York: Knopf, 1963.

Talese, Gay. *The Kingdom and the Power.* New York: World, 1966.

Tebbel, John. *Compact History of the American Newspaper.* New York: Hawthorn, 1963.

Thayer, Lee. *Communication and Communication Systems.* Homewood, Ill.: Irwin, 1968.

Yu, Frederick T. C., ed. *Behavioral Science and the Mass Media.* New York: Russell Sage Foundation, 1968.

Research and Discussion Topics

Use the following comments from the articles in this book for further contemplation and research on the mass media:
1. "If there are going to be any revolutions in the communications business, they will come about because of change in technology, not conscience."
2. "How's one to be defended against the overwhelming crash of reality?"
3. "The form of print is single-leveled."
4. "Social reorganization must precede technological reformation."
5. "Reporting is not democratic to the point that everything posing as fact has equal status."
6. "Trying to report a war without irony is a bit like trying to keep sex out of a discussion of the relations between men and women."
7. "Taste is a matter of instances, not precept."
8. "Perhaps the popular arts can help restore all the arts to their status as entertainment."
9. "The top priority for the mass media is consumption."
10. "In the circumference of a circle beginning and end coincide."

Other issues for further consideration:
1. Prepare a proposal to repeal and/or rewrite the First Amendment and articulate your rationale.
2. Compare and contrast film and song as the process and the means of human communication.

3. The impact of ownership upon the content of mass media.
4. Truth. Objectivity. Value-free. Neutrality.
5. Preparation of journalists for war reporting.
6. Politicians' use and/or misuse of mass media during election campaigns.
7. Dynamism of everyday life as reflected in television, newspapers, novels, poetry.
8. Occasions when and if government, as representative of the people, has the right to call upon the discretion of the press.
9. A code of ethics for dissemination of information about crime and court proceedings.
10. Fantasy as a basic human need.
11. Hero-worshiping as a psychological phenomenon.
12. The Protestant Ethic, capitalism, and the media.
13. Role of ethnic press in the history of the United States.
14. Press councils as a way of community control of media.
15. The mass media in the year 2000.
16. The mass media as representative of those who hold power.
17. Medium is the message.
18. Communications technology and the quality of human life.

The Contributors

Joseph P. Lyford, journalist and sociologist, is professor of journalism at the University of California at Berkeley and consultant to the Center for the Study of Democratic Institutions at Santa Barbara. He is the author of numerous articles and books, including *The Talk in Vandalia* and the *Airtight Cage*. In 1967 he received the Sidney Hillman Foundation Award in Literature.

Marshall McLuhan, the Canadian communications theorist, is best known for his ideas about the ways the media and technology shape society and perceive of themselves. In 1963 the University of Toronto appointed him head of its Center for Culture and Technology. He also held the Albert Schweitzer Chair in Humanities at Fordham University in New York. Among his many publications are *The Mechanical Bride, The Gutenberg Galaxy,* and *Understanding Media*.

Patrick D. Hazard is professor of English at Beaver College, Glenside, Pa. In 1961–62 he was director of the Institute of American Studies, East-West Center, University of Hawaii. He is a contributor to several journals and is a film consultant to Time Life Inc. As a scholar of American culture, he is interested in major themes in literature alienation, war, depression, the rise of the welfare state, and the problems of the artist in mass culture.

Theodore Peterson, a student of press performance, is dean of the College of Journalism and Communications, University of Illinois. He maintains that the press of any nation takes on the form and structure of the society in which it operates. He is author and coauthor of several articles and books, the best known of which are *Magazines in the Twen-*

tieth Century, Four Theories of the Press, and Mass Media and Modern Society.

Herbert I. Schiller, professor of communications at the University of California at San Diego, is principally concerned with questions of cultural invasion and communications and national development. In addition to Mass Communications and American Empire, his recent books include Superstate: Readings in the Military-Industrial Complex and Mind Management in the United States. Articles by him have appeared in TRANS-action, Society, and Psychology Today.

Royal D. Colle, associate professor in the Department of Communication Arts at Cornell University, is currently interested in the problems of communicating with special groups, such as rural, low-income people, using modern communication technology. He is the author of many publications and serves as consultant to the World Bank on family planning and population communication. In 1970–71 he helped the Ford Foundation establish a communication center at the Uttar Pradesh Agricultural University in India.

James D. Williams, former editor of several black newspapers, has served as director of the Office of Information and Publications, U.S. Commission on Civil Rights. He is at present director of communications for the National Urban League.

Andrew Kopkind has been a reporter for the Washington Post and Time and an editor of the New Republic. He was founder and editor of Mayday and Hard Times, weekly newspapers. He has served as Washington correspondent for the New Statesman and Le Nouvel Observateur. His books include America: The Mixed Curse. He was president of the New Weekly Project Inc., 1968–70.

J. Anthony Lukas, who won a Pulitzer Prize in 1968 while a reporter for the New York Times, is now a freelance writer. His journalistic assignments have included the Congo and India. He was a Nieman Fellow at Harvard in 1968–69 and his articles regularly appear in Harper's, Esquire, the New York Times Sunday Magazine, and Reader's Digest. Recently Lukas helped to establish [More], a periodical devoted to evaluation of New York news media. His books are Barnyard Epithet and Other Obscenities: Notes on the Chicago Conspiracy Trial and Don't Shoot—We Are Your Children.

Otto Friedrich, an editor at Time, has been a journalist for more than twenty years. He was managing editor of the Saturday Evening Post from 1965 until the magazine's suspension in 1969, an experience that enabled him to write Decline and Fall, an account of the Post's last years that won the George Polk Award as 1970's best book on the press. He has also published two novels, *The Poor in Spirit* and *The Loner*, a collection of essays, *The Rose Garden*, and, in collaboration with his wife, Priscilla, several children's books. His most recent book is *Before the Deluge: A Portrait of Berlin in the 1920's*.

Victor Bernstein has worked for newspapers in Providence, Rhode Island, San Francisco, New York, and Berlin. He was a staff writer for *PM* and managing editor of the *Nation* for eleven years. He is a member of the Foreign Policy Association and a contributor to *Redbook*. His publications include *Final Judgment: The Story of Nuremberg*. He is currently a freelance writer living in Connecticut.

Jesse Gordon, editorial consultant to the *Nation*, served for a time during 1961–62 as the only American correspondent in Cuba. In addition to the *Nation*, he has worked for the North American Newspaper Alliance and the Associated Press. His articles have appeared in the *Southwest Review*, the *Churchman*, the *Toronto Telegram*, and the York, Pa., *Gazette and Daily*. He is also a guest lecturer in journalism at New York University.

William L. Rivers, professor of communications at Stanford, is the author of *The Opinionmakers* and *The Adversaries*, which deal with the journalistic coverage of political and governmental affairs in Washington. He writes a column, "Monitoring Media," for *The Progressive* magazine. His scholarly concern is with the social responsibility of American mass media, and he recently completed several experiments in press councils. *Backtalk: Press Councils in America* reports the findings.

Nathan B. Blumberg, a former Rhodes scholar and now professor of journalism at the University of Montana, is author of *One-Party Press?* and coeditor of *A Century of Montana Journalism*. He has worked for the Associated Press, the *Denver Post*, and the *Washington Post*. In addition to Montana, where he has been a dean and teacher since 1956, he has served as a visiting professor at Pennsylvania State University, Northwestern University, and the University of California at Berkeley.

Michael J. Arlen, a general assignment reporter and former television columnist for the *New Yorker*, has been a *Life* reporter and juror for the Alfred DuPont–Columbia Survey of Broadcast Journalism. His books are *Living-Room War* and *Exiles*, the latter a family portrait. His father was the successful and celebrated writer of the 1920's, Michael Arlen.

Nicholas Johnson, son of the famous semanticist Wendell Johnson, is author of numerous articles and the book, *How to Talk Back to Your*

Television Set. When appointed to the Federal Communications Commission by President Johnson he was the youngest man ever to serve that body and soon became its most controversial member.

Stanley Kauffmann, the noted film and theater critic, recently issued his second volume of film criticism, *Figures of Light.* He is also co-editor of the anthology *American Film Criticism: From the Beginnings to "Citizen Kane."* His other books include *The Hidden Hero, The Tightrope, A Change of Climate, Man of the World,* and *A World on Film.* He is film and theater critic for *The New Republic* and a visiting professor of drama at Yale University. He is currently preparing a series on landmark films for *Horizon* and is a regular book reviewer for *World.*

Richard Poirier, a leading American literary critic, is chairman of English at Rutgers University. His most recent books are *Norman Mailer, The Performing Self* and *A World Elsewhere: The Place of Style in American Literature.* His work appears regularly in *Harper's, Atlantic,* the *New York Times Book Review, Saturday Review,* and *Partisan Review,* on whose staff he served for many years.

Jesse Kornbluth is a 1968 graduate of Harvard, where he was managing editor of the *Advocate* and worked summers as a staff assistant at *Look.* He is editor of *Notes from the New Underground* and was jailed for selling Boston's *Avatar,* an underground newspaper, in Harvard Square. Recently he was a student at Harvard's Graduate School of Education.

Louis Filler is professor of American civilization at Antioch College. His studies in American culture and reform have included revaluations of concepts and movements in the light of contemporary events. A new paperback edition of his classic study *Crusaders for American Liberalism* appeared in 1968.

Dallas Smythe, an economist who teaches in the graduate communications program at the University of Saskatchewan, served for several years as chief economist for the Federal Communications Commission. The author of many articles and books, his most recent activities and interests center on the meaning of technology, particularly communications technology, in relation to national development. In 1971–72 he conducted communications studies in China, Chile, Japan, Hungary, Yugoslavia, and the United Kingdom.

Howard Luck Gossage, one of the nation's leading advertising men before his death in 1969, is often called the man who "discovered" McLuhan. His ad campaigns included Beethoven sweatshirts, the International Paper Airplane Contest, and the Irish whiskey ads in the *New Yorker*. At his death he was chairman of the board of a new company, Scanlan's Literary House, publishers of an iconoclastic literary magazine. He also aided *Ramparts* in its early days.

Elie Abel, dean of the Columbia Graduate School of Journalism, has been a foreign correspondent for the North American Newspaper Alliance, United Nations correspondent for the Overseas News Agency, foreign correspondent for the *New York Times*, Washington bureau chief for the *Detroit News*, and diplomatic correspondent for NBC. He is the author of *The Missile Crisis* and, with Marvin Kalb, *Roots of Involvement*.